How To Transform Words Into Stories

A comprehensive guide to write, promote & sell your book.

Published by Heartspace Publications
PO Box 1190, Bakery Hill, Victoria, 3350, Australia
Tel +61 450260348
www.heartspacebooks.com
mailto:pat@heartspacebooks.com

All rights reserved under international copyright conventions. No part of this book may be reproduced, stored in a retrieval system, or transmitted in any form or by any means electronic, mechanical, photocopying, recorded or otherwise without written permission from Heartspace Publications.

Whilst every care has been taken to check the accuracy of the information in this book, the publisher cannot be held responsible for any errors, omissions or originality.
© Pat Grayson 2024
ISBN 978-1-7635657-0-8
Published in Melbourne, Australia, February 2025
Originally published as How to Write – Right!
Version one – First published in 2010,
Copyright © 2010 Pat Grayson
Version two Copyright © 2022 Pat Grayson
Published in Melbourne
Edited by Julio Menochelli (Brazil)
Julio is a highly experienced ELT publishing professional with extensive background in English Language Teaching and Training
Qualifications:
BA in Language & Literature
BA in Law
Specialisation Degree in "The Business of Books"
Accredited memberships:
Royal Society of Arts

The London Chamber of Commerce and Industry
Association of Language Testers of Europe

Dedication

To you, new or experienced authors, as indeed you are a unique set of individuals. My hope is that this work makes your writing dream come true.

Contents:

PART ONE – ABOUT WRITING 15

- THE EARLY DAYS IN YOU WRITING CAREER 16
- ARE YOU READY TO BE AN AUTHOR? 17
- SPONTANEOUS WRITING 21
- WHY DO WE WRITE? 22
- CREATIVITY, AND THAT MYSTERIOUS CONNECTION! 42
- HOW DO I START? 53
- WRITING AND PLANNING 57
- PLOT 60
- MIND MAPS 64
- THE OPENING PAGES 67
- HOOKING THE READER 69
- STRUCTURING YOUR WORK 72
- WRITER'S BLOCK 75

PART TWO – CREATIVE WRITING 93

- WHAT IS CREATIVITY? 94
- IMAGINATION AND CREATIVITY 99
- CREATIVE VISUALISATION 110
- TIGHT WRITING 112
- SHOW, DON'T TELL 115
- USE AN OBSERVER IN SHOWING 120
- METAPHOR 121
- FLOW – THE RHYTHM OF SENTENCES 123
- FLOW-STOPPERS: 124
- SENSORY WRITING FOR CREATING IMAGES (REPRESENTATIONAL SYSTEMS) 132
- WRITING EMOTION 135
- INVENTING EXPERIENCE 141
- TENSION 142
- CHARACTERISATION 144
- NARRATION FOR FICTION WRITING 163
- DIALOGUE 167
- PLACE 172
- DETAIL 176

- Humour and fun 178
- Comic Relief 181
- Storytelling 183

PART THREE – GENRE 195

- Self-Help books 197
- Romance novels 198
- Science Fiction (Sci-Fi) 202
- Christian novels 206
- Literary writing 208
- Coffee table books 208
- Young Adults 209
- Historical Fiction 210
- Script 212
- Suspense/Thriller/ Mystery Novels/Crime Fiction 216
- Short Stories and Novellas 222
- Writing for children 226
- Trends 230
- Poetry 230
- Illustrations 238
- Magazine and newspaper writing 239
- Report Writing 248
- OTHER WRITING AND MISCELLANEOUS TIPS 253

PART FOUR – EDITING AND REVISION 261

- Style Manual 270
- American or UK English? 275
- Clichés 279
- Editing checklist to use when you edit 279
- Two book critiques 288

PART FIVE – TO HAVE PUBLISHED OR TO SELF-PUBLISH, THAT IS THE QUESTION 297

- Self publishing - the good and the bad 300
- Traditional publishing 302
- Preparation of the manuscript 303

VANITY PUBLISHING	306

PART SIX – MARKETING AND PROMOTION 315

MARKET RESEARCH	316
MARKETING AND PROMOTION	317
BUILDING THE BRAND	318
YOUR OWN WEBSITE	321
SEARCH ENGINE OPTIMISATION	322
KEYWORDS	325
METADATA	328
NIELSEN BOOKDATA OR BOOKSCAN	329
BACKLINKS	331
DOMAIN AUTHORITY (DA) AND PAGE AUTHORITY (PA)	331
BLOGS, FACEBOOK, TWITTER AND THE LIKE	333
YOUR NEWSLETTER	334
WHAT FOLLOWS ARE A FEW POINTERS:	335
AMAZON MARKETING	336
GOODREADS	338
TRADE MAGAZINE ADVERTISING	342
MEDIA KIT	342
BOOK REVIEWS	344
RETAIL OUTLETS	346
LIBRARIES	349
INTERNATIONAL BOOK RIGHTS	351

PART SEVEN – APPENDICES 353

APPENDIX ONE – THE RISE OF ARTIFICIAL INTELLIGENCE IN WRITING	354
APPENDIX TWO – MISCELLANEOUS	360
APPENDIX THREE – BOOK PRODUCTION	368
APPENDIX FOUR – RESOURCES	385
APPENDIX FIVE – INDEXES	390

Introduction

Transforming your Words into Stories is a book-creation journey that goes beyond mere writing advice, although there is oodles of that – it is a hands-on workbook designed to empower aspiring authors to delve into the realms of modern publishing, marketing, and the intersection of literature with artificial intelligence.

I am in the unique position of being a writer, an editor, and a publisher, and at seventy-two years of age I have been doing this for many years. At this phase in my life, it is more about giving. I give you my vast experience, and dare I say, my wisdom of all things to do with writing a book with the end-result of it being published. Within these covers you will read some of the greatest lines ever written as I borrow from great authors (past and current) and writing coaches from the distant and recent past, to help with explanations and advice (see for an online Bibliography as there are too many to list).

Some of the topics covered in this book:

- You want to write a book. Where do you start?
- How to advance from a novice to a first-rate writer?
- About storytelling.
- Do you need to learn grammar before you can write?
- Should you self-publish your book?
- Why most manuscripts do not work?
- Creativity – can you develop it?
- How do you develop writing ideas?
- How do you write what you mean to say?
- Why you need to make yourself a brand?
- Where is the book-publishing industry heading?
- Artificial Intelligence and authorship.
- Electronic books (ePubs)
- Editing, and literally hundreds of ideas, all designed to support you as a writer. And much more.

There are seven parts to How to Transform Words into Stories:

- About Writing. How to go about writing your book, skills, writing drills, and more.
- Creative Writing. Explores the skills to be a competent writer.
- Genre. Lists and explanations.
- Editing. Why attention to editing separates the serious from the not so serious writer.
- Publishing. The pros and cons of traditional versus self-publishing.
- Marketing and Promotion. How to promote and market your book.
- Appendix.
    a) Writing and Technology. Writing and AI.
    b) Book production
    c) Resources.

Lastly, I cannot teach you to be a creative writer, but you can, over time, teach yourself and create your own voice. All I can do is put you on the path, give you the vision, a pat on the back, and send you on your happy way. It is a lovely journey – enjoy it.

> Celebrated American author, Ray Bradbury, first wrote in libraries because he had nowhere else to write. He also used a hired typewriter, which he paid for by the hour.
>
> Pat Grayson

How to Transform Words into Stories — a review

I have read many 'how to' books on writing, but none of them quite like this one. Pat Grayson is a seasoned writer and publisher looking to give back to the writing community by presenting a life's worth of insight for the coming generations of scribes. All writers, and especially those relatively new to the industry, will find actionable and supportive advice among the book's 377 pages.

This work is a compendium of sorts and is chock full of varied topics for writers to dip in and out of. In fact, Grayson provides an index for this very purpose. Most books focus on the craft of writing or aspects of self-publishing and the publishing industry, but here, Grayson offers a guide to both. Those new to writing can hone their creative writing skills, before learning about genres and the editing process. If you are a more seasoned writer looking for advice on publishing, marketing and promotion, the chapters towards the end of the book will prove useful. The detailed sections on the publishing industry and book marketing will save new authors countless tough lessons and will help them speed towards successful launches.

Grayson includes so many rich and detailed quotes from other master scribes, this may well be the only book on writing you ever need to read. Rather than presenting a dogmatic view of what writing should and shouldn't be, Grayson uses advice from a host of experts to back up his points and demonstrate the variety of approaches. Readers can take heed of the advice that resonates best and suits their needs. Of course, all writers are different.

Another aspect I enjoyed is the 'workbook' approach, which uses practical tasks and exercises to help writers apply the approaches mentioned in each chapter. Writers with more time to hone their craft can implement techniques and learnings as they go.

As an author and writing coach myself, I highly recommend this book for writers. I wish it was available when I was beginning my career.

Philip Charter, is the author of four books of short fiction and works as a coach for multilingual writers.

The formatting of this workbook

This workbook is colour-coded to make navigation easier (different sections different colours).

Here follows, are symbols you will see throughout and their purpose:

> This box will contain an excerpt from a work by a famous writer that will help you understand humour, dialogue, and much more.
>
> This example is from Louis de Bernier's Captain Corelli's Mandolin, when Mandras has returned from the war:
>
> "With his clothes removed, Mandras shivered no more than he had done with them on. He was so pathetically reduced that Pelagia felt no shame in remaining with him even when he was naked, and she did not have to resort to delivering instructions from the far side of the door. His muscles gone, and his skin hung about his bones in flaccid sheets. His stomach bulged, either from starvation or parasites, and his ribs protruded sharply as did the bones of his spine. The shoulders and back seem to have bent and crumpled, and the thighs and calves had shrunk so disproportionately that the knees seemed hugely swollen. The worst of it was that when they peeled off the encrusted bandages upon his feet…"

 This symbol indicates a writing exercise you are to do.

As this is a writing and book-publishing course, I encourage you to work through the various exercises, sample writings and journaling. All are designed to assist you emerge at the other end of the workbook a competent writer.

• • •

 *This icon indicates a tip or writer's suggestions, such as: According to Para Publishing (American publishing company), 81% of people want to write a book sometime in their life.*

What you need to gain the most from this book/course:

- An A4 notebook with lines. In this book you will write your exercises and journaling. The front of your book will be for the writing of notes and comments, the back for exercises and miscellaneous writing.
- A thesaurus.
- A dictionary.
- A good grammar book.
- A quiet and comfortable writing space that you can call 'your own'.
- Willingness, enthusiasm, a desire to be a good writer, and about three hours per week.

The citations of authors used in this book are too numerous to use here. To view them please go to:

https://heartspacepublications.com/product-category/educational/

Part One – About Writing

As it says in *The Book Thief*, "Make the words yours … If your eyes could speak, what would they say?".

In this section important points will be covered:

- The early days in you writing career
- Are you ready to be an author?
- Spontaneous writing drills
- Creativity and that mysterious connection.
- Six mistakes novice authors make.
- Where do I start?
- Writing and planning.
- Plot.
- Mind maps.
- The opening pages.
- Hooking the reader.
- Structuring your work.
- Writer's block.

1

The early days in you writing career

Canadian poet and Pulitzer Prize winner Mark Strand starts this section for us, "I was never much good with language as a child. Believe me, the idea that I would someday become a poet would have come as a complete shock to everyone in my family."

> Continuing Captain Corelli's Mandolin:
> "She did not feel very much like a healer when she saw those feet, however; they were unrecognisable as such. They were a necrotic, multi-hued. A shell of puss and scab lay upon the inner winding of the abandoned bandages, and yellow maggots writhed and squirmed in flesh that was all but dead. "Gerasimos!" Exclaimed Drosoula, clutching her son's weathered shoulders for support as she tried not to faint away. The stench was inconceivably stupefying, and at last Pelagia felt herself flood with the sacred compassion whose absence has previously so appalled her."

When talking about his writing career, Australian author Christos Tsiolkas, said: "Failing to not earn money from your writing, or not winning awards or recognition, is not failing. You only fail when you tell yourself you have failed."

Part One – About Writing

Are you ready to be an author?

By answering the following twenty questions, you can measure if you are ready to be a writer and how determined you are to write a book.

Answer the following questions YES or NO.

- Do you tell your friends that you write? Yes/No………
- Do you spend adequate time editing you work? Yes/No………
- Do you get lost in your writing and lose all sense of time? Yes/No………
- Are you prepared to put many hours of slog into your writing? Perhaps as many as someone doing a Ph.D. degree? Yes/No………
- Are you willing to learn writing skills? Yes/No………
- Are you prepared to rewrite a manuscript if it has been rejected Yes/No………
- Will you do (almost) anything to be a writer? Yes/No………
- Do you allow your imagination to invent stories? Yes/No………
- Have you felt that you wanted to be a writer for longer than a year? Yes/No………
- Are you prepared to write even if you fail to bepublished? Yes/No………
- Do you yearn to be a published author? Yes/No………
- Do you read many books, of many genres ? Yes/No………
- Do you have favourite authors? Yes/No………
- Do you need the support of a partner to write? Yes/No………
- Do you know what subjects/genre you want to write? Yes/No………
- Are you prepared to have a lot of wasted material in your learning period? Yes/No………
- Are you still prepared to write, even if your spelling and grammar is poor? Yes/No………
- Do you like writing? Yes/No………

- Do you think you can research well for any book you may write? Yes/No.........
- Have you written anything in the last month? Yes/No.........
- Are you prepared to receive criticism from writing coaches? Yes/NO

Results:

- Count up all the YES answers.
- If you had ten or less YES answers – you lack (for now) sufficient motivation to be an author. But that can change with determination.
- If you had ten to fifteen YES answers – you are close but need more motivation. Perhaps set some personal writing goals. Look at the NO answers and consider what you can do to make them a YES.
- If you had fifteen or more YES answers – you are ready. It might be of benefit to revisit your NO answers and see if you can turn them around. By doing so you increase your odds.

Knowing your results, you should have a better idea of your willingness to become an author.

Return to this quiz once you have finished this workbook and do it again.

> Write down when you first thought you wanted to write. Try and remember what it felt like, how it excited you.

Part One – About Writing

From this time onwards consider yourself a writer as you only become a writer when you say you are a writer, not when the book is published, or recognition comes your way. For instance: eight-year-old Stevie loves football. He doesn't kick the ball very well – and has not yet learnt to head the ball – but he is a football player. He and his mother do not wait until he plays for Liverpool to call him a football player. He is a football player irrespective of his level of skill, after all, he will acquire these with practice. The same for you. You may not yet have the writing skill or ability but you will get there with determination.

> Using your new notebook (from now on I shall refer to it as your journal) write an outline of how you plan grow towards all the 'yes' questions of above.

To be a competent writer, you must read widely and analyse as you read. Reading is writing practice, no different from Stevie kicking the football against a wall. It will give you a wider understanding as to how other writers approach skills, such as metaphor or dialogue. The more you consciously analyse these the more you will be able to call on them in your writing. Being even more blunt: if

1

you do not read widely you will never make it as a competent writer!

HELPFUL TIPS

An interesting anecdote – in one of the writing circles I ran, there was a lady, Isabella, who was a skilful writer. Yet she did not consider herself a writer because she had not been published. Then one day she had an article published in a magazine. This did not satisfy her internal acceptance system and felt it was a fluke, so continued living the unachievable dream.

Your first writing drill. Write in no less than ten lines what your aspirations as a writer are. Give this a bold heading as we will return to this later.

To be successful as a writer: you must:
Develop your skills and abilities.
   Work hard, for without hard work no critical mass will be achieve. Luck: there is no doubt that luck plays an important role in success –
   being seen or not being seen, being at the right place at the right time. But the hard work, with its increased exposure will improve the odds.

Part One – About Writing

I am, by calling, a dealer in words; and words are, of course, the most powerful drug used by mankind – Rudyard Kipling.
And this piece from "The Writing Life" by Annie Dillard (1989): "When you write, you lay out a line of words. The line of words is a miner's pick, a woodcarver's gouge, a surgeon's probe. You wield it, and it digs a path you follow. Soon you find yourself deep in new territory. Is it a dead end, or have you located the real subject? You will know tomorrow, or this time next year."

Spontaneous writing

Spontaneous writing is a drill that teaches you many things about writing.
    You write for a set period (in your journal), usually around ten minutes, on a topic chosen at random. You start writing and do not lift your pen off the page for the selected time period. Do not worry about grammar, spelling or punctuation – do not slow the creative process. The only thing you need to worry about is getting your ideas down cohesively.
    With these writing drills, the subject matter is not important as you do not want to become too attached to the result.

When you write focus on the process, not the outcome.

Benefits of spontaneous writing:
- You learn to write quickly and with flow.

- It teaches you to start writing without procrastinating. You will be surprised at how easy it gets after a time. A good writer can write about anything any time. You need to be able to write under any circumstances, especially if you are away from your favourite desk – perhaps on a bus, in a noisy environment like a café, without preamble, fidgeting, or other delaying tactics.
- It will teach you how to write clearly.
- You will gain confidence.

Over the years I have seen amazing improvement in students, writing because of spontaneous writing exercises. If you are serious about writing, you should incorporate these into your daily life. I know of top-class writers who have done these drills all their lives.

British author Pat Barker (Silence of the girl), spoke about self-doubt when writing. To mitigate this, she first does all her research, and thinks deeply about what she's going to write about. When she is ready, she starts by writing as quickly as she can to 'outdistance' the voice within. She claims this method works for her. There are similarities between the spontaneous writing exercise and Barker's method.

Why do we write?

- Writing is cathartic.
- It is a great way to understand yourself.
  This statement will become obvious as the course progresses.

> Part One – About Writing

- Enables self-reflection. Putting your thoughts on paper can help to balance negativity.
- Writing stimulates, it can be a form of meditation and is informative.
- Consolidates understanding.
- Teaches, while entertaining.
- Provides a medium for sharing ideas.
- Helps widen your horizons.
- Allows you to remember things.
- And best of all – you experience the enjoyment of being lost in a creative task.

The writer's job, says British essayist Pico Lyer, is to watch his moods and thoughts, as captivating yet passing as the seasons, and decide which are worth sharing. Or in a cathartic way, understanding.

Do I need to learn grammar before I can write?

No, you do not, but it is important. Do not let poor grammar hold you back. I have known grammar aficionados who write terrible prose. I have also known people who have no skill with grammar write great stories, stories that are direct from the heart. Here is one such writing

> My people... all dead We only got a few left... that's all, not many. We getting too old. Young people... I don't know if they can hang on to this story... might be you can hang on to this story... to this earth... You got children... grandson. Might be your grandson will get this story... keep going... Hang on like I done My spirit has gone back to my country... my mother.

by Bill Neidjie, an Australian Aboriginal elder, from his work *Kakadu Man*:

What more could the above say? Better grammar would not improve the power of the piece; even without grammar it is clear and easy to follow.

Do not let your lack of education or understanding of grammar stop you. I have taught creative writing to people from disadvantaged communities and have had people say to me, that because those kids will not have any grammar it will be a waste of effort. I disagreed as the most important thing for a writer is to 'feel' the work. The grammar can be improved later.

If your grammar is suspect, apply the following:

Make sure that the full grammar settings in your word processing software are on (checked). Usually, the default settings only make use of about a quarter of the options. There are programmes that can help your grammar edit, such as Grammarly www.grammarly.com/ but I have found them to be too slow and clumsy for professional use.

When you spell-check, take your time, and make sure you take heed of all those prompts.

Part One – About Writing

Cathartic Writing – Writing as therapy

Deep within lurk emotions that *you* wish not to see. Writing brings to the conscious mind clarity of those emotions.

For cathartic writing, you can write 'dark' or write 'light'; it all comes from the same place, and it is all good writing practice.

Writing dark is an exploration of within, about things that you do not usually let out. It is better to bring the dark into the light, rather than to keep it buried – let your shadow side emerge.

One shadow-side text I wrote caused my brother to comment, "Patrick, you are not a well man". His comments did not matter, as I was in a frame of expansion.

That rare writer who comes alive on a page does it by giving of himself, by writing of meanings, and not just of fact or of things that have happened to him.

The deeper you navigate the more will emerge. This writing can be likened to the 'dark night of the soul' for creative people.

For this writing do not write with the conscious mind, write from the infinite self. When you compose from your authentic self you pass through dreams of your own making.

Many find their way to the world of writing through self-reflection with a pen in hand. This introspective journey is not only pivotal for personal development but also serves as fundamental training for honing one's writing skills. However, once the well of introspection is seemingly tapped (if such a point exists), a natural shift occurs, prompting scribers to direct their focus outward and delve into more external subjects.

1

The initial phase of introspection typically caters to personal interest, although the insights gained from this process can occasionally benefit others. On the other hand, the subsequent stage of writing involves an external focus, where the author's words have the potential to not only captivate but also aid, amuse, and entertain an audience.

Amor Towles, American novelist challenges the conventional notion of 'entertainment' in this context, advocating for a more profound connection with readers through the term 'engagement.' According to Towles, "The objective is not merely to amuse but to deeply involve and connect with the reader on a meaningful level."

> 'Who are you?' crooned the caterpillar.
> Alice replied rather shyly, "I……I hardly know. I know who I was when I got up this morning, but I think I must have changed several times since then."
> Lewis Carroll's Alice in Wonderland

Part One – About Writing

My Brother John

It was only years later that I ascribed my daydreaming to the German who locked me in the dunny for hours on end.

Dunny is a lovely Australian word, meaning an outside toilet. This dunny, like all dunnies of the period, was a tiny-box room, invariably made with wooden slats and a tin roof. All seemed to have rickety doors and spider webs in the corners. Dunnies were far enough away from the house so that an incoming breeze would not spoil meals. Yet not so far that it was a 'trek' – who wants to wake up in the middle of winter and traipse way up the garden?

Yes, after Mom absconded, Dad left my brother and me in the not too good care of a countryman of his. I call him the German because as I was only three at the time, I cannot remember his name. We stayed with him and his family on their farm, out back of Sydney.

The German did not like me and seemed to take delight in demonstrating this. One of his favourite pastimes was to lock me in the dunny whenever he went out. Whilst incarcerated, my brother John was given strict instructions not to let me out, otherwise he would regret it. Knowing the German, John was too petrified to buck the command.

I remember one such time; perhaps it was not just one time but all the times that a small child roll into one. I must have sat in that box all day. To start with, slithers of sunlight shone through the slats from behind me. Many daydreams later they were in my face, with dust particles dancing in the shafts of light.

I sat on the closed seat, otherwise, being just a little thing I would have fallen in. The wood became hard after a while and hurt my bum. Of course, there was no food, no water. I don't recall what went through my mind as the hours passed. I do however remember my brother – not once would he leave my side, or rather the side of the dunny. If I was about three, he would have been five. We did not talk, as he was the silent type. But, if suddenly I would ask, 'John, are yer there?

' there would always be the reassuring answer, 'Yeah.' His support was my solace.

Two hours later: 'John, ya there?'

'Yeah mate, I are'. He never wandered away or faltered in his vigilance to support his little brother. How my five-year-old brother took on this duty I'll never know, but I'll always be grateful.

An example of cathartic writing:

Analyse the above piece. Did it grab and hold your interest? Why did it, or why not? Did you notice the dialogue, that of young, rural Australian children?

But what about the cathartic aspect? Do you think the writer managed to express his emotions?

HELPFUL TIPS

"The inner child is the carrier of our personal stories"
advises therapist Jeremiah Abrams.
Some may describe their life with the aid of a pen, others
see their life because of
what their pen has told them!

Part One – About Writing

Excerpt from Bird by Bird: Some Instructions on Writing and Life by Anne Lamott (1994): "Good writing is about telling the truth. We are a species that needs and wants to understand who we are. Sheep lice do not seem to share this longing, which is one reason they write so very little. But we do. We have so much we want to say and figure out."

Tips for cathartic writing:

- Try writing as if your soul holds the pen.
- Your inner self wants to reveal itself, give it the space to do so.
- Your pen knows what to write – don't interfere.
- Remember, the first thing that you write about is the thing that you most want to express.
- Write as if you have nothing to lose – you have much to gain.
- Cathartic writing can be painful. Try to identify resistance, like feeling silly.
- Remember, it is all about discovery.
- Writing will clear and clarify.
- When writing about yourself, scan how you feel and put this down on the page.
- Cathartic writing forces us to be present and pay attention to the happenings in our own little world.

Casey Gerald, the author of There Will Be No Miracles Here, said, "The book industry is about the only industry that will pay you to investigate your own problems."

1

> For many, this next assignment will be one of your hardest. Write a minimum of one and a half pages on the major events in your life that have shaped you. This is a deep topic, one that needs honesty and clarity. Take your time, but complete the project, even if it takes a week. It must be clear and concise, and well edited, as I am sure that you will review it from time to time. You could write it like a novel where you are the main character, in first or third person.

Julia Cameron, author of the evergreen best seller *The Artists Way*, shows how writing a daily journal is healing and opens our creativity.

Friend and author, Dorian Haarhoff says, "*Our healing lies in telling our story.*"

The great novelist Stephen King said, "Writing is not life, it is a door back to life."

Thoughts on writing

Open your journal and write the heading, *Man in the snow*.

> Look at this image and tell me who is the man in the snow, where is he going, what is going through his mind?
> Once you finish, know that we will return to this story further on in the workbook.
> Write for four minutes without stopping.
> While writing, do not edit or look back at what you have written.
> Start now…

Part One – About Writing

Other than the first thirty seconds, I am sure it was easier than you thought it would be. As you continue practicing this method, even more complex topics will be easier to write.

Thinking I have been blessed to have read over a thousand books of many genres. From these I have gleaned that there is one attribute that separates mediocre writers from good and great writers. It is beyond writing and story telling ability – it is thinking. Not just thinking about the novel, but thinking about life, people, events, and politics. They are in tune with current events, as well as how those current events do and will affect humanity. They are able to place their

profound thoughts and insights almost seamlessly and metaphorically on the page. Good writers are therefore thought leaders. Another trait they mostly have is that they are not afraid to be bold and confront big topics. Alas, we cannot all be thought leaders, but we can still write, give enjoyment, support, make people happy, entertain, contribute to human culture, whilst entertaining ourselves and others.

Stephen King wrote in his book *On Writing*, "I believe large numbers of people have at least some talent as writers and storytellers, and that those talents can be strengthened and sharpened."

The best way to be a competent writer is to write. And, as celebrated and bestselling Scottish crime writer Val McDermidsaid, a good writer "perpetually tries to improve her writing skill. To keep it fresh, it does not get easier with each new book." She does feel that her writing is improving all the time.

What makes a good writer?

The difficulty is not to write, but to write what you mean; not to affect your reader, but to affect him precisely as you wish.
Robert Louis Stevenson.

Part One – About Writing

In your journal, write down what you think makes a good writer.
Now, write down which of the following characteristics you think you already have, and which you lack. I believe that to be a good writer you must:

Be organised.
Be or become creative.
Believe in your ability to entertain readers.
Have pride in your work.
Be or become a storyteller.
Have something to say.
Have views on the most important issues of the day.
Enjoy writing.
Have the time to write.
Have a good grasp of grammar or the ability to learn as you go.
Be disciplined.
Be determined.
Understand the importance of editing your work to make it as 'clean' as possible (refer to the chapter on editing).

Have you realised that there is not one characteristic in the above list that you cannot cultivate? All are achievable and are taught in this book.

Successful Australian author, Christos Tsiolkas, said that he aims to write 1,500 words each day, five days a week. But he says, sometimes trying to reach the 1,500 is 'forced' and he knows the next day he will have to return to the work and have more rubbish to edit out.

1

Anybody can write if they apply themselves. There is nothing mysterious or elitist about writing. I know many who became frustrated and closed because they were told that they had no talent and would never amount to much. Invariably, these students got so despondent that they rejected what they formerly loved.

In the writing courses or circles that I run, I forbid negativity to come from any quarter. We always look for the good in each other's' writing. Yes, I may return to a student after an assignment and say that I feel their work is not as good as they are capable of, and perhaps they should try this or that to improve it. But I make a point of always encouraging them, and so you must encourage yourself.

Digressing a bit more, I have writing-coach friends who can be harsh on their students if they think that they have no talent. Their rationale is that the student is better off doing something else. I disagree. If a person enjoys writing, why spoil it for them? All people can improve their writing, regardless of their standard, and so I would rather encourage than destroy their interest.

Writing ability is not a gift given to a few. It is for everyone, much the same as the air we breathe. All it takes is the willingness to try and persist.

Stephen King again… "I was ashamed. I have spent a good many years since – too many, I think – being ashamed about what I write. I think I was forty before I realized that almost every writer of fiction and poetry who has ever published a line has been accused by someone of wasting his or her God-given talent…"

Elizabeth Gilbert started writing as a child. All she wanted to do was to write. She wrote as an adolescent, and into adulthood. She submitted dozens of articles to various publications in the hope that she would be published. Of course, at first, she was not, but persisted, until she was. Her biggest seller was *Eat Pray and Love*.

You can become a skilled writer if you pay your dues.

> Rebecca by Daphne du Maurier (1938): "Last night I dreamt I went to Manderley again. It seemed to me I stood by the iron gate leading to the drive, and for a while I could not enter, for the way was barred to me. There was a padlock and a chain upon the gate. I called in my dream to the lodge-keeper, and had no answer, and peering closer through the rusted spokes of the gate I saw that the lodge was uninhabited."

Rebecca is a classic psychological thriller with hauntingly beautiful prose, filled with suspense and intrigue. This opening passage sets a tone of mystery and foreboding, drawing readers into the gripping narrative.

A writer's job is to present the readers with an alternative of the world. Margret Geraghty, writer and author.

Many writing coaches suggest that new authors write about what they are familiar with. That may make sense, as it is easier to focus on the writing. But also what makes sense is to expand your writing into what you do not know. That way you grow as an individual and your store of knowledge can be drawn from a wider field.

Discipline is an earmark of a good writer.

1

Norman Mailer, author of the *The naked and the dead*, had this to say about discipline: "I used to have a little studio in Brooklyn, a couple of blocks from my house — no telephone, not much else. The only thing I ever did there was work. It was perfect. I was like a draft horse with a conditioned reflex. I came in ready to sit at my desk. No television, no way to call out. Didn't want to be tempted.
There's an old Talmudic belief that you build a fence around an impulse. If that's not good enough, you build a fence around the fence. So, no amenities, just writing."

Your first book

But What to write? When you have been writing for a long time, the question changes to what to not write about?

Stephen King: "The scariest moment (when writing) is always just before you start. After that, things can only get better."

Why write a book?

- Gain credibility.
- Inform, teach, and share information.
- Improve your status in your field.
- Gain recognition as being a writer.
- Find other work, such as seminars and consulting.
- Earn money.
- For the love of writing.
- To publish research you have conducted.

Part One – About Writing

Irrespective of the reason, you need to be clear about your intentions. If not, you are unlikely to get past page twenty. A strong motive will help get you through. Keep in mind the questions and answers of the quiz you started with – Are you ready to be an author?

How can you distinguish your writing amidst the myriad works that explore the same subject you intend to delve into?
This inquiry frequents my interactions with new authors and it holds truth – the topics you aim to address have likely been explored extensively. However, the key lies in trusting your distinctive voice and perspective shaped by your unique life experiences. It is the fusion of your individuality and the passion you infuse into your work that sets it apart.

 *A book from the heart is better than one from the head.*

I receive many manuscripts on positive thinking and motivation. Sadly, most are not written from the heart. Many are also not written from experience. They are written from a misguided belief that 'I can also do this and make money from it,' which is the wrong attitude to have.

I speak of the need to be the guru who writes, not to write to be seen as the guru. These people who regurgitate what others have written without heart will never make it. They have not infused their experience or voice into the work, and readers will know it.

It comes back to the fact that when you write from the heart, on a subject that you love, and use your unique voice and experience, only then will the work have the seed of promise.

What follows is a short meander through some of the subjects, or themes, that you could write about that interest and affect modern society. Remember though, trends influence reader selection, so if you write with a plot or sub-plot that has a current trend, then you are likely to gain more readers. But as books can take a long time to write, and coupled with an average two-year publishing time, the trend may have shifted by the time your book is released.

Insights into humanity: The meaning of life, realising your potential, coming of age, the underdog overcoming adverse circumstances, redemption, finding one's identity, traditional family values, moral dilemma of society integrity, corruption, current affairs, political machinations, international intrigue, the playing on the public's fear for events such as global warming, viruses, war, and terrorism.

Revenge: vendettas, a wrong corrected, betrayal overcome, sense of justice.

Love: to love or the need to be loved, fulfilment, the need to be part of a community, acceptance, loyalty, and friends, to make life more beautiful for all, self-expression.

Any of the above themes can be woven into your work as the main plot or as sub-plots.

Part One – About Writing

About writing

Story telling: to believe in magic, and fairies, where hope springs eternal, to challenge limitations, to see what is possible, create new life that does not yet exist. Storytelling is the power you give yourself – to listen to your inner child at play.

As a writer you will often hear the term creative writing. It usually refers to novels and short stories, as opposed to academic or journalistic writing.

Creative writing is writing to add 'colour', where characters, place, events, and plot are expressed to create interest beyond the story. It employs play and imagination.

Throughout this workbook there are many examples of creative writing, from dozens of authors, enough for you to gain a good appreciation of what the term means. Do not just read them – study them. Study them and apply all the skills that this book offers. It is safe enough to say, *to be a master, you must study the masters!*

I hope these geniuses that I have selected inspire you as much as they inspire me.

Chinese writer/poet, Li Sen in his book *Drifting Skandhas* says: "At the same time, great writers find it necessary to formulate concepts to enable expression of the grand ideas that swell in the human heart. Not liable to set rules, a good piece of writing moves on freely and smoothly like floating clouds or flowing water. Clouds drift and form new skyscapes every other day; a good writer develops most fitting styles for different purposes. Water shapes its course according to the nature of the ground over which it flows; a good writer works out his excellence in relation to the material about which he is writing. Thus, is created the natural unity and coherence of writing with rich spontaneous creativity."

> Thomas Mann wrote beautiful creative prose in his work *Bashan and I*. If you love dogs and creative writing, then you will love this book. It was written in 1918 in Germany and translated into English by Herman Scheffauer.
> The opening of the story begins: "When spring, which all men agree is the fairest season of the year, comes around again and happens to honour its name, I love to go for half an hour's stroll in the open air before breakfast. I take this stroll whenever the early chorus of the birds has succeeded in rousing me… …I long to draw a few draughts of young morning air to taste the joy of the pure early freshness of things…"

Notice the sparse use of words in the excerpt above; the elegance of the author's writing.

See how he describes Spring: "…When spring, which all men agree is the fairest season of the year, comes around again and happens to honour its name…" Notice how he makes the season a tangible, almost a living being, when he writes "comes around again and happens to honour it's name" What a wondrous way to depict something so mundane as a season of the year.

The entire book is a delight, and that is because it is more about the writing than the story.

Part One – About Writing

> Words as things, tangible as the fibrery paper and the liquid ink, almost like small objects, rocks, or gems. Words as stones, as stars, as seed, tracks, doors, words as mountains, words as skins. Words as colours....
> J Ruth Gendler

Reading

To be a good writer, you must read widely. Reading with the 'writers' attention to detail: analysing characterisation, plot, dialogue, flow, and metaphor, opening, resolution, etc..

When you read with awareness it will bring a greater appreciation of good writing, much the same as a wine tasting course gives you even greater delight in the taste of fermented grapes.

HELPFUL TIPS

"Before I compose a piece, I walk around it several times accompanied by myself." Ian Satie (composer)

Write down the heading What do I want from this writing Course? For six minutes, write without pausing. Be ambitious, such as stating I want to write a book – in fact, many books.

1

Creativity, and that mysterious connection!

Slowly, the idea comes to you, hardly noticeable at first, but gradually momentum builds, and you know you must write it. As you do, there are no thoughts of it not being good enough. The ideas hurtle through you like a high-speed train. You do not know where it comes from, but it consumes you, until there is no self, or computer, just compelling ideas.

Although impassioned, the words lay on the page with ease, ready to enthral all who read them. Later, when finished, you check it and know it's good. Your words will inspire men, making them commit to an idea. It will bring lumps to throats as you expound on some social injustice or laugh at your observations of political issues; you amuse and entertain. Readers will glance to the bottom of the page to see who wrote this piece that roused them. This time it's not the artist or the singer who inspires to action… it's you.

You ponder, how can I have written with such force and elegance?

You did it because you did not let your logical mind get in the way, and so your creativity was abundant. You trusted that wherever it came from, that it was good, powerful, and brimming with integrity.

You may be wondering where that place is that you fell into, that place of intuition where creativity dwells? With a flash of understanding, a smile crinkles your eyes and breaks your normally serious face. It doesn't matter where as you know you are welcome to enter that chamber any time you wish.

● ● ●

Part One – About Writing

> We must accept that this creative pulse within us is God's creative pulse itself.
> Joseph Chilton Pearce

There is no doubt that writing is a mystical process. There is too much in my writing (and that of many famous creatives) that cannot be explained in any logical way. For instance, I have written material that at the time of writing I thought I understood, only to learn what it really meant later. Where would this have come from?

> The position of the artist is humble. He is essentially the channel.
> Piet Mondrian (Famous Dutch modern artist)

Another intriguing indicator is that on occasions I use words that are not part of my vocabulary. Sometimes these words have long since drifted out of use, but suddenly come back to me in the moment.

Certainly, when writing with enthusiasm, there is union between you and your higher self. I do not know what that higher self is or where it resides.

Alice Walker, author of *The Color Purple* wrote "of spirits calling to her" in dreams. She said, "I felt called to write a book about black women and feminism. It is difficult to explain the nature of this calling—what it means to be called by that unseen force I call divine grace."

1

Songwriter and author Willie Clayton (two of his books were adapted to movies) had this to say when asked where his ideas derive: "It's mysterious, I just run into them. I can't explain it."

Writer and poet Dorian Haarhoff says, "As writers we listen to the subject that has chosen us."

> The outer teacher is merely a milestone. It is only your inner teacher that will work with you to the goal, for it is the goal.

With your pen firmly on a page of your journal, don't lift it off the page until you have written four lines that come from your soul. Connect with your higher consciousness and ask it to tell you what it's feeling.

Colum McCann was awarded The National Book Award for his novel *Let the Great World Spin* (2009). His fiction has been translated into thirty languages. He said it took four or five months to get the tone of one of the main characters, Tillie's, voice. He told his wife he was on the verge of giving up, he didn't think he could do it. Then one night this line came to him: 'The skinniest dog I have ever seen is the one on the side of the Greyhound buses.' "It was a simple line," he said, but he recognised it as the voice that would work. He wrote all night. Australian author Suzanne Falkiner was not looking to write a story about Rose de Freycinet. "Whilst touring", she said in an interview on

Part One – About Writing

Australian's Radio National, "I read a notice on a beach I stopped at – it was about Rose de Freycinet.

Sitting on the beach I was set upon by a mental image of Rose walking up the beach". She started her research, and the book *Rose* is the result.

Elena Ferrante explained in a rare interview with her publisher that if some difficulty occurs in a manuscript, amazingly the answer arrives from a classic. "It is uncanny how this always works. I will be reading a classic for leisure and the answer pops up, as if ordered."
Ferrante has gained international fame with *My Brilliant Friend*, and many other books.

> To Kill a Mockingbird by Harper Lee (1960): "Summer was on the way; Jem and I awaited it with impatience. Summer was our best season: it was sleeping on the back screened porch in cots, or trying to sleep in the tree house; summer was everything good to eat; it was a thousand colors in a parched landscape; but most of all, summer was Dill."

This excerpt from *To Kill a Mockingbird* captures the essence of childhood nostalgia and the anticipation of summer, evoking a sense of warmth and longing. Harper Lee's timeless prose beautifully portrays the innocence and simplicity of youth against the backdrop of the Southern setting.

The angel for writing and creativity is Archangel Gabriel, and so if you believe in Gabriel, ask him to help you when you are about to write.

Bell Hooks, the author of twenty published books, wrote an article for the *Lionsroar* website: "Oftentimes men have evoked the muse, whether real or fictive, to talk about those forces beyond the realm of human reason that drive the imagination. This perhaps is a more acceptable way to talk about 'spirits' and the creative imagination. Few men attempt to link their muses to spiritual practice."

> I myself do nothing. The Holy Spirit accomplishes it all through me.
> William Blake

The word enthusiasm comes from the Greek based word enthuse: to be filled with God. And so when you write with enthusiasm you are likely to be filled with (your) God.

> Straightaway the ideas flow in upon me, directly from God.
> Johannes Brahms (composer)

Tom Keneally, arguably Australia's most prolific author with over sixty novels and a bag of awards, spoke about his inevitable connection to the 'Collective Consciousness' in an interview. He elaborated about how, when writing a novel, the Collective Consciousness seem to absorb him and his entire writing process, and how he allows it to support his creative process.

Australian author, Jamie Marina Lau runs writing workshops where she teaches her students Automatic Writing. "Automatic Writing," she says, "...is writing from the subconscious mind... to honour what that is deeper within us all... to allow it to emerge."

I was watching TV one other night and caught a documentary on the

Part One – About Writing

South African poet Lebo Mashile. She confirmed what I know to be true when she said, "Writing is like listening, as I hear the words that I am to write."

Gail, a writing student of mine, wrote a lovely piece and only towards the end did she put in the boy and girl's ages. One of the other students asked, "Why did you only give the ages at the end? Would it not have been insightful to offer them at the start so that the age could be worked with throughout the story?"

Gail answered, "I don't know why I did it this way and not your way, but there was a tugging that I followed."

When it comes to the silent voice, no teacher can teach you this, as the voice is filtered for each writer. Become aware of it and trust it.

I remember in the early days of my writing when I first became aware of the silent voice. I was amazed at how it only whispered when needed. Its voice is always gentle with wisdom. It is as if I have my own personal writing guru standing quietly behind me.

> Rilke in his Book of Hours – We're listening to silences too. To the great silence around the subject, to what is not being articulated for whoever is silent touches the roots of speech.

In her book *Mozart and the Whale*, artist and composer Mary Newport wrote about her 'connection': "Sometimes (when painting) I'd tie a bandana over my forehead so my eyes were blocked, and I couldn't see a thing. And I'd continue painting, slowly feeling my way over the wall, pulled, and directed by whatever that force was that had always been there for me for as long as I could remember whenever I picked up a brush or set out to compose music. As long as I got out of the way, it always did the rest. Blindfolded, all I saw was blackness. Yet I knew where every single curl, wavy brushstroke needed to go."

Vygotsky, (pioneering Russian psychologist, had the view that the mind extends beyond the skull. Therefore, thinking is not confined to our physical form. I leave it up to you to determine, that if thinking is not contained in our physical brain, then where does thinking come from? But I know for sure my thinking is helped when I have a pen in my hand.

The book of form and Emptiness (2022 Woman's prize for fiction) by Ruth Ozeki uses meditation to form characters. Ozeki is a Zen Buddhist priest who also teaches Creative Writing at an American university. She says that meditation and writing are synergistic. When writing a book, in meditation, in the moment, just taking in the world, with open sense-gate, and she places her mind into the position of the character, the place, the activity, and what is going through the mind of the character – then writes from that place.

Sogyal Rinpoche wrote, "I think of a great work of art as like a moon shining in the night sky; it illuminates the world, yet its light is not its own but borrowed from the hidden sun. Art (and writing) has helped many towards glimpsing the nature of spirituality. It is one of the reasons for the limitations of much of modern artistic expression…"

Science fiction writer Ray Bradbury offers, "I do not write. The other me demands emergence constantly."

• • •

Part One – About Writing

To access that mysterious connection is simultaneously the easiest and the hardest thing to do. Riding a bike is easy, unless you have never ridden one before. As many of the above well-known creators have indicated, the connection is not a forced thing – it just happens. But it can only happen when you are open to it, when you enter the writing as if nothing else exists, without pressure or expectation, and only when you write for yourself – when you *are* the words and the story. Writing is a form of meditation. But the minute we stop writing, the connection is broken.

> Creativity is seeing something that doesn't exist already. Your need to find out how you can bring it into being and that way be a playmate with God.
> Michelle Shea (writer)

HELPFUL TIPS

I am sure you have heard of an 'Aha' moment, where the perfect idea seems to have just 'dropped in' without rational explanation. It is that mysterious most perfect connection.

Every child is an artist. The problem is how to remain an artist once he grows up.
Pablo Picasso (painter)

"Write for yourself," says Elizabeth Gilbert. When writing her next book after her mega successful *Eat Pray Love*, she wondered how to write

1

the next book for the millions of adoring fans. For this new book she had written 500 pages but felt it did not work. Perplexed, she realised that she did not write *Eat Pray Love* for millions, but only for a few and mainly for herself. In her own words, "I had needed to write that book for my own personal reasons…" Pondering that next book, she realised that she was writing for the masses, and it was not working. She reverted to writing for herself, and I may add: that if *she* liked it, then it was probably good for the masses.

When you write for others, your voice changes, and you put pressure on yourself to write what you think the audience wants to read, not what comes naturally to you. And if you have read any of her work (I have not read *Eat Pray Love* but I have read *The Signature of all things*) her writing is wonderful, probably so because she is relaxed and writes in her own voice.

Stephen King feels the same. He wrote in his book *On Writing*: "let's get one thing clear right now shall we? There is no Idea Dump, no Story Central, no island of the Buried Best Sellers; good story ideas seem to come quite literally from nowhere, sailing at you right out of the empty sky… … your job isn't to find these ideas but to recognise them when they show up."

- How do different writers generate their ideas?

or

- How do you know if your book idea is the right one?

J.K. Rowling visualised her first *Harry Potter* book when it flashed through her mind when on a train from Manchester to London.

> Part One – About Writing

Apparently, time stood still, for the determined but unknown author, as she witnessed it, film-like within her mind.

Many brainstorm. Others 'feel' a book. Recently an idea came to me of a book – it was just a whisper. Three days later I was talking to someone who started to discuss that very topic of my potential book, and when she said, "I would love to write this but I can't", I took notice.

A few days later, as I was walking a bush trail, it came to me again, this time not as a whisper but quite forcibly. Thereafter, for the duration of my walk my mind played with the ideas of the book. When I returned home, I sat down for an hour with an A3 sheet of paper and outlined the work (topics, research, interviews, etc.). I was excited but have put it aside – to sit with it for a while. I am still sitting with it – it can take some time!

 *"Imagination, our highest faculty" says the poet Coleridge.*

From the introduction of the book, *The Intelligence*, "Whilst researching this story, I learnt that a story finds a teller and it will not rest until told.
Creating a story entails 'deep' listening. To hear beyond the conscious mind – avoiding rational mode – past prejudges – beyond conforming – circumventing our hypnosis – through left brain limitation – to listen to that which is beyond us – to gain the 'power' of what bubbles below – to feel the story. Therefore, you 'listen' a story into existence. I have heard of people meditating or dreaming book concepts into life, or often they might be reading something else when an associated idea bursts into their mind. Many authors pick up ideas for new books from research they conducted from a past book. Others have gleaned a lead

1

for a book from a newspaper article.
Experienced and practical authors know that these are exciting moments and acknowledge them by writing them down before they disappear.

And how do you know if your book idea is the right book for you to write? The answer is that most often you do not until you start writing it. It is then that you realise how much you resonate with the work and how much information you have on the topic. Usually, you do not have to write for too long to come to this realisation.

Another way to know is when it will not let you go, much like that extract from the introduction above. It will nag at you like a dog with a ball. At first the dog may drop the ball some meters from you. If you don't respond he'll pick it up and drop it closer, until in the end he will put the slobbery thing right on your feet, and do those funny little dancing shuffles that dogs do when they want you to do something for them – this is hard to ignore.

When you have a book idea that does that to you, you can be sure this is one that you must look into. Another indication that this is the right book for you is when you keep realising you are already writing it in your mind, such as when you're in the shower, riding a bike, driving your car, or awakened at 3 AM with more ideas on the book.

American writer Tracy Chevalier wrote, *The Virgin Blue* (1997), which was a moderate success, but her second book (written in only eight months), *Girl With a Pearl Earring* (1999), was a best-seller. Speaking about writing, Chevalier said, "Don't write about what you know — write about what you're interested in. Don't write about yourself — you aren't as interesting as you think."

Part One – About Writing

To eliminate a dud idea, is to do market research to see if it has been done, or rather how many times it has been done.

Hanya Yanagihara who wrote A little life and To Paradise, advises new authors "Only write a book when you are compelled (burning) to write it, and one that no one else has written."

But, Amor Towles, author of the successful novel, *A Gentleman in Moscow*, said he does not get an idea, research the idea, and then write it. He first has affection for a subject, then researches it, whilst writing it. He writes what he knows, and does not write what he does not know.

How do I start?

You start today – right now! You start in the middle of the work, you start at the end, you start at the start. It does not matter. What matters is that you start today. Vincent Van Gogh said, "Great things are not done by impulse, but by a series of small steps."
It does not matter where you start because starting is the key. Starting shows intent. Creative awakens with action.
When you start, what you write may not go into the finished manuscript, but that does not matter, because you will warm up to the process and achieve more momentum with each day of writing.

1

Be disciplined

Write one hour per day and you will accomplish all that you need and want from writing. Within this hour you do your research, your plotting, and the actual writing. Of course, if you have more time to dedicate to your writing, you will get things done faster.

I suggested one hour a day because most of you are novice writers and probably hold down a job, have families to support, and other commitments. But if you write for only one hour per day, you would have a book in a year or twenty books over twenty years? It works like this: even a bad typist can type 1000 words per hour. The average book is 80 000 words and therefore would take roughly 80 days to complete. Yes, you need research, say 30 days (all still at one hour a day). Your first draft should be complete after 110 days. Later in the book, I give the stat that the editing process will take (roughly) 60% of the time, so you do the math. Anyway, a book a year is possible, at an hour a day.

Your first book is not likely to be very good. But still, you must write it as that is the start of your career. By writing bad books, you learn to write good books. John Steinbeck (*Of Mice and Men*) said, "I think I shall write some very good books indeed. The next one won't be good, nor the next one, but about the fifth, I think will be above the average." He became well above average with his writing skill.

A Woman of Substance (1979) sold thirty million copies. When Barbara Taylor Bradford was asked what she likes to write about, she says; "I think women like to read about other women who succeed. When I was growing up, I was always interested in reading about

Part One – About Writing

people who made something of themselves, women who made a difference."

Knowing that if you start today, you could have your manuscript ready for publishing this time next year, what are you waiting for?

The only other thing is to get into a routine. That is, organise a comfortable desk space to work from, allocate undisturbed writing-time every day, and lastly, make a big sign saying I WILL WRITE AN HOUR A DAY! This will help you keep the goal at the forefront of your mind.

So, go on, get started!

Your novel as a journey

The Dagara people of East Africa do not have a word for sex. Sex is a concept; a journey with the partner. It is not seen as a one-off situation, but a journey together that lasts for the rest of their life. Like all journeys there are twists and turns, but the mere fact that the journey is together is what really gives them an interesting framework for sex.

Writing a story is also a journey, with its twists and turns that you were not aware of at the outset, and that you also grow along with the story. As Australian writer Michelle de Kretser states, "Art (and writing) is about risk.

1

> Moby-Dick by Herman Melville (1851):
> "Call me Ishmael. Some years ago—never mind how long precisely—having little or no money in my purse, and nothing particular to interest me on shore, I thought I would sail about a little and see the watery part of the world."

J.K. Rowling said in an interview with Oprah, that from the age of six all she ever wanted to do was to write. She wrote through all her school years, and into her early twenties. There were many periods of frustration where her words were not appreciated – until she had that mammoth success with her first Harry Potter novel, *The Philosophers Stone*. Thereafter, there were another twelve mega-releases.

When asked by Oprah, "What is the likely reason for your success?" Rowling answered, "Even from an early age I believed that I would be a successful writer. I believed I could write a good story, and never gave up, so I didn't."

Elizabeth Gilbert goes on to say, "I don't know how to write a best seller, especially on demand." And, John Boyne said, "When you feel passionate about the work, then it is likely to be interesting."

You need to pick a story that you are passionate about, otherwise you are not likely to produce your best work and your readers will know it. Also consider that you and the story will be teammates for a long time, and so you should strive to become the best of mates.

Part of that journey is to 'own the work.' Most new writers are fearful when their work is about to make an entrance. It crawls to the surface for a myriad of reasons. I well remember the panic I felt when my first book (a self-help book) was about to emerge. I had the none-

Part One – About Writing

too-helpful thoughts such as – *hell no, people are going to see my exposed thoughts* Or, *what if the market doesn't like my work?"* Or worse, *Will I be ridiculed?* The panic escalated when I thought of my close friends and associates scrutinising the regurgitations of my mind. It is the same when I consider people reading my early work – it was not very good. I cringe. Yet, there is no reason to do so, as I now call that time my apprenticeship. But we writers do not stop and continue regardless. Trust yourself. You will you be okay.

Writing and planning

Before you get too far into the book it is a good idea to:

- Write the back cover synopsis first as this will help with your focus. This must be compelling.
- Write a testimonial from a fictitious authority on the subject. This will help you get clarity and pinpoint the core.
- Lastly, write a magazine review of your work, around 800 words.

This will get you thinking as to what the general market really wants.

The above are used as guidance, much the same as a mission statement guides a company.

When writing a long work, such as a book, it is natural to wander and over-write. Your back cover and review will help keep you on track.

Production methods for your book

When managers operate a factory they set up a production line to produce faster and more efficiently.

For your book it helps to set up a production line. For this, you need your own space that will not be interfered with by others. Better still, have a large table on which you can lay out piles of papers that represent the different chapters and research.

As I write this, my table is strewn with reference materials and piles of paper that are all used in the creation of this book. There is not one thing on the table that has nothing to do with this book.

Insert each chapter idea or topic into a plastic sleeve, and add to this information you have accumulated on different topics such as:

- Front cover.
- Back cover.
- Introduction.

Testimonials or credits.

- Research one, research two, etc.
- Chapter one, chapter two, etc.
- Bibliography.
- Research.

Then there will be sleeves for:

- Character sketch.
  Characterisation of the first protagonist (the hero or heroine).
  Characterisation of the second protagonist, and so forth.
- The opening, the end-resolution.
- Various dialogue types.
- Place and setting.
- Plot.

The production model will help identify what is missing.

Part One – About Writing

Benefits of the production line are:

- Helps with the planning of the work, as information can easily belocated or moved to a more appropriate sleeve.
- As most people are visual, the brain more readily sees the work. That is why I prefer this manual and physical method as opposed to the apps you can use.
- If everything is captured on a computer, it is not so easy to see the components fitting together. The constant scrolling up and down, changing data-files is clumsy, time-consuming, and annoying.
- It gives clarity and also creates a feeling of control, whereas a lack of control creates stress.
- In your house, you do not have the sugar in the tool shed, the tea in the lounge and the milk in the bedroom. You have it all in one convenient area. The same applies to all the components of your book.
- A book is a massive jigsaw puzzle in as much as pieces fit together creating a homogeneous whole. Some information may fit in several chapters. However, there is that one perfect place for it. By playing with the piece (as if a jigsaw) you will find the best fit.
- A production line helps with the logical sequence that the book must ultimately take.
- Once you have set up the sleeves, you build the book, rather than just write it.

You can also insert your plastic sleeves into a file, or get yourself a zip-up or sealable folder. This represents a portable production line you can take with you, allowing you to work while waiting for appointments, or wherever you may travel. It also means that if you come across an idea or have that 'break-through' thought, you can add it to the file in the relevant sleeve.

A sealed folder is practical as you will not lose any work. Plastic is also a good idea as it will keep everything dry if you get caught in a thunderstorm.

1

Plot

Plot is what happens in your story. Do you have one? Remember, even if the work is not a novel, there must be some sort of overriding theme.

The following are some brief plot scenarios:

- Boy meets girl; likes her but pushes her away.
- Boy meets girl, loses girl, gets girl back again. All ends in happiness.

With romance, what kind of boy/girl will attract the interest and loyalty of the reader?

- Suspicion makes for intrigue.
- All seems smug for the for the protagonist, until, it comes crashing down...
- Faith moves mountains and is a great motivator, especially when the protagonist achieves the almost impossible. Make it formidable but credible.
- The development of the character. People love people, and each person's favourite person is themselves. And so, if you have a character that the reader can identify with, and have that character grow, and develop, readers will feel the growth – as if they have grown. An example is where a meek character wins over the world with her public speaking.
- Villains must oppress your main character. Villains often seem invincible.
- Opposites create interest. Out of the strong and uncompromising springs sweetness. Or, from soft and sweet, to strong. The timid becomes inflamed. Another theme on opposites is where the villain becomes the saviour (*Gone with the Wind*). Sincerity and thievery are good opposites.
- Anguish sells, and is usually directed at the protagonist, or a character emotively close to the protagonist.

Part One – About Writing

More suggestions for what you could write about:

- Write on your favourite hobbies and perhaps earn a living from doing so. What skills do you feel you can contribute?
- Look for a column to write for. What skill or knowledge do you have to offer? (see the section below on writing for magazines).
- Self-help is a massive field, and you could make your mark there if you have something different to offer and have a compelling voice. This book is an example in the self-help category.
- A burgeoning genre on the rise comprises works centered around the LGBTQ+ or non-binary experiences. It is evident that authenticity in these narratives is best achieved when crafted by individuals who personally 'identify differently.' Such works play a crucial role in normalising and legitimising the existence of non-binary identities.
- You could write yours or someone else's biography, but these do not normally sell very well, unless the person is famous.
- Travel is a good topic and always in demand, providing it is done in a fresh way.
- Perhaps you could start an in-house company magazine for the company you work for, or the novel that has been tickling your mind. Or you could write them all!

The plot is the sequence of events that make up the storyline of a narrative. It typically includes the introduction of characters, the establishment of setting, the development of conflict, and the resolution of that conflict. Plots can vary widely in complexity and structure, from simple linear narratives to intricate webs of interwoven storylines.

Example: In J.R.R. Tolkien's "The Lord of the Rings," the plot revolves around Frodo's journey to destroy the One Ring, accompanied by various subplots involving other characters like Aragorn, Gandalf, and Sam.

In addition to plots, there are sub-plots, twists, foreshadowing and flashback.

Subplot: A subplot is a secondary storyline that runs parallel to the main plot, often involving different characters or themes. Subplots can serve to add depth and complexity to the narrative, provide contrast or relief from the main storyline, or enhance character development.

Example: In "Harry Potter and the Goblet of Fire" by J.K. Rowling, while the main plot follows Harry's participation in the Triwizard Tournament and the return of Voldemort, there are several subplots involving Hermione's efforts to promote elf rights, Ron's insecurities, and the budding romance between Harry and Cho Chang.

- **Plot Twist**: A plot twist is a significant change or revelation in the plot that alters the audience's understanding of the story or characters. Plot twists are often unexpected and can dramatically shift the direction of the narrative, adding suspense, tension, or surprise.

Example: In "Gone Girl" by Gillian Flynn, the revelation halfway through the novel that Amy is not only alive but has orchestrated her own disappearance and framed her husband for her murder is a major plot twist that completely changes the reader's perception of the story.

- **Foreshadowing**: Foreshadowing is a literary device in which hints or clues are dropped early in the narrative that suggest future events or developments. Foreshadowing can build suspense, create anticipation, and provide subtle insight into the direction of the plot.

Example: In "Romeo and Juliet" by William Shakespeare, Romeo's premonition of his own death before attending the Capulet's party foreshadows the tragic outcome of the play.

- **Flashback**: A flashback is a narrative device in which the story shifts to a scene from the past, providing context or backstory for the current events. Flashbacks can help to explain character motivations, reveal

> ### Part One – About Writing

important information, or deepen the audience's understanding of the plot.

Example: In "The Great Gatsby" by F. Scott Fitzgerald, the narrator, Nick Carraway, frequently flashes back to events from his past, offering insights into his relationships with other characters and the events leading up to Gatsby's demise.

These elements can be combined and manipulated in various ways to create engaging and compelling narratives.

Readers want to read about people, not things.

Escapism Writing, like reading can be a form of escapism. So, let's escape...
Finish the following:
The vault of untold stories
"Shhh," I whispered cautiously, ensuring our conversation remained secret. My lips brushed against her ear as I divulged, "Yes, there exists a vault of untold stories."
Before she could blurt out a response, I preemptively silenced her with another gentle yet firm "shhhhhh."
Despite her attempt to convey an apologetic expression, the glint of possibilities gleamed vividly in her eyes.
Speaking with a conspiratorial tone, I continued, "This vault resides on the brink of enchantment, just beyond the realms of intuition. To access these untold stories,

• • •

> you must navigate the uncharted territories of imagination…"Have fun with this.

Mind Maps

    A great way to develop a plot and open you up to that mysterious creativity is to make a mind map. The process of mind-mapping is like removing the plug from a genie's bottle.
Start with a large, blank piece of paper, and in the middle write down the core idea. Let's say it is an idea for nine-year-olds. The words 'nine-year-old' are written as the core subject and associated ideas are attached to it with lines connecting and radiating out, spider web like.
    Brainstorming is the soliciting of ideas, and mind mapping is the organisation of those ideas for later reference and development. Both rely on and stimulate the other. Take your time with your plot.
When doing mind maps, there are important things to remember:

- When starting a mind map, open yourself up to your 'higher self' —as that is the main source of creativity.
- Write everything down even though it may seem silly. Sometimes the silliest ideas turn out to be the best.
- Totally immerse yourself in the brainstorm – there are no other thoughts.
- Develop ideas and sub-ideas, follow all threads.
- Use different colours for different associations.

Mind maps work because:

- When you focus on the subject you become more connected to it.
- There is a link between the association of ideas and creativity.

Part One – About Writing

- They stimulate your creativity.
- They eliminate lineal thinking.
- Many people are visual and so being able to see the vision on a piece of paper helps them.
- Mind maps are easier to assimilate than lists of unconnected phrases or words.

Some authors spend enormous amounts of time on the plot. The preparation, for them, pays in the long run.

Below is a sample mind map for a story that I thought that I would write, called *Little Red Riding Hood* – sadly, it has already been used.

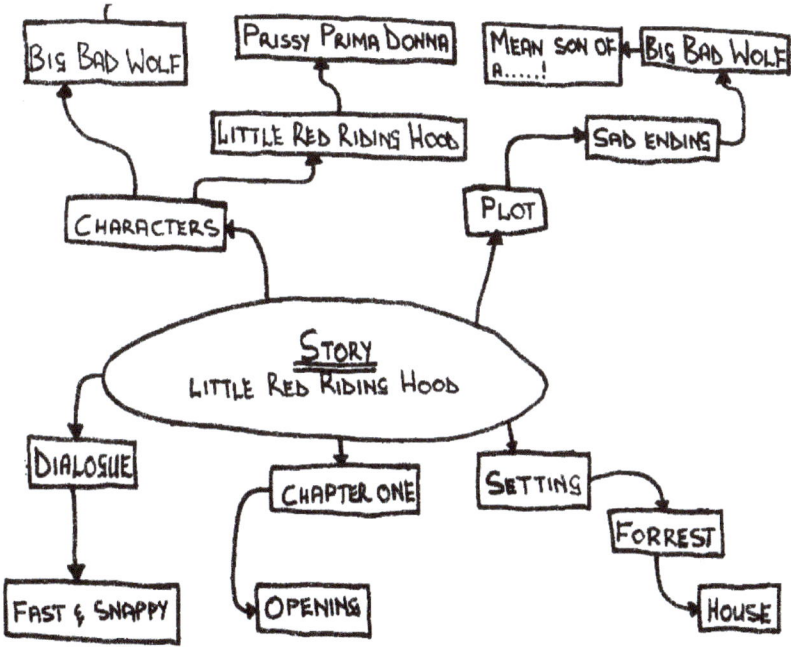

Mind maps are also an effective tool for integrating plot and structure in your work.

When completed, redraw it, bigger, on an A3 page, and sticky-tape it in you writing work room.

American author Colm Tóibín said of planning a book, "You're operating tactically all the time. You're thinking a number of years ahead. You're planning and plotting and then you're allowing the textured work to emerge without all that plotting."

Not all authors follow the plot:

Elif Shafak says that she prefers the mystery of not knowing where a story is going as she writes it. For Elif, the illusive nature of her characters actions makes for more interest for her and her readers.

Stephen King has a 'rough' plot or direction, which is not fixed – he feels a fixed plot limits the story.

Many of my short stories had no plot. It is a bit like going on a journey, but not knowing where I will end up. As a guideline I may want to go north, perhaps it's warmer that way, but as I 'feel' my way I could end up going north-west, as that is a better direction.

Is intuition and instinct more important than plot?
Defining plot only using a linear and conscious method can limit the work. Intuition and instinct open the door to greater creativity.

Don't Ramble
Deviation from the core concept usually starts when you commence the planning process – you get excited and lost in detail and ideas. Before you know it, you have a cumbersome book. Stick to the core concept that you wrote for the review and back page, and synopsis as suggested above.

Part One – About Writing

Best not to tell friends about the book idea as it could sound half-baked and discourage you.

The opening pages

The opening pages are important as they will govern whether a browser in a bookstore (or online) buys the book or puts it back on the shelf.

These entail:

- The introduction.
- Testimonials.
- The first chapter.

> Gathered in little groups around three or four candles, some of the women were sewing, others were spinning; several were idle, their necks stretched, their heads and eyes turned towards an old peasant who was relating a story…

This is the opening sentence of the story The Country Doctor by French novelist Balzac (1799 – 1850). It is a great opening and an example of tight writing, as in only one sentence, he has set the scene and prepared the reader for what is to come. Balzac was called the Shakespeare of the novel by his contemporaries.

Stuart Turton, author of The Deaths of Evelyn Hardcastle said: "The first chapter of this book is the last thing I wrote…… The beginning of the book needs to hook the reader… I wrote a billion different versions of

1

the beginning."

Enjoy the opening of Stuart Dybek's book *We Didn't*.

> "We didn't in the light; we didn't in darkness. We didn't in the fresh-cut summer grass or in the mounds of autumn leaves or on the snow where moonlight threw down our shadows. We didn't in your room in the canopy bed you slept in, the bed you slept in as a child, or on the backseat of my father's rusted Rambler, which smelled of the smoked chubs and kielbasa he delivered on weekends from my uncle Vincent's meat market. We didn't in your mother's Buick Eight, where a rosary twined the rearview mirror like a beaded, black snake with silver, cruciform fangs.
>
> At the end of our lover's lane – a side street of abandoned factories – where I perfected the pinch that springs open a bra; behind the lilac bushes in Marquette Park, where you first touched me through my jeans and your nipples, swollen against transparent cotton, seemed the shade of lilacs; in the balcony of the now defunct Clark Theatre, where I wiped popcorn salt from my palms and slid them up them up your thighs and you whispered, "I feel like Doris Day is watching us," (it was a Doris Day movie) we didn't.
>
> But we didn't, not in the moonlight, or by the phosphorescent lanterns of lightning bugs in your back yard, not beneath the constellations we couldn't see, let alone decipher, or in the dark glow that replaced the real darkness of the night, a darkness already stolen from us, not with skyline rising behind us while a city gradually decayed, not in the heat of summer while a Cold War raged, despite the freedom of youth, what does it matter? – we made not doing it, a wonder, and yet we didn't, we didn't, we never did…"

Part One – About Writing

So intriguing. Why didn't they 'do it' when they were clearly in love? A hundred questions shout upon reading, and what happened to her?

Did you notice that Stuart Dybek imbued his work with the cultural period? That is, "the place", where the young love occurred and, how astute the first person experience was.

Hooking the reader (the opening pages)

For any storytelling, novel or factual, captivate your audience by mastering the art of hooks. D.W. St. John, in his insightful work, *The Nasty Little Book on Writing* emphasises the critical role of setting the hook to grab the reader.

In the realm of bestselling authors, the 'hook' is an indispensable tool to ensnare the reader's interest. While Dickens could leisurely engage his audience, today's successful author must skillfully 'set the hook' within the opening paragraph, ideally within the very first line. Failing to do so risks losing the reader's attention entirely.

The strategies for 'grabbing' the reader are as diverse as the bestselling authors themselves. Some wordsmiths effortlessly seize the reader's attention right from the first sentence. While St. John advocates, "...for an immediate hook, there's room for assurance – the hook can be meticulously crafted over several paragraphs."

The essence lies in understanding the significance and timing of this narrative 'grab.'

The grab manifests through various means, such as compelling narration. For instance, Michael Crichton achieved a gripping hook with the opening of Airframe.

1

Michael Crichton - Airframe

Emily heard a low rumbling sound, almost a vibration that seemed to come from the wing. She snapped her head around.

"What was that?"

"Take it easy, Em," Tim said, still laughing.

Sarah laughed, too, giggling delightfully.

"We're almost home, honey," Tim said.

But even as he spoke, the plane seemed to shudder, the nose of the plane turning down. Suddenly everything tilted at a crazy angle. Emily felt Sarah sliding forward off her lap. She clutched at her daughter, pulling her close. Now it felt like the plane was going straight down, and then suddenly it was going up, and her stomach was pressed into the seat. Her daughter was a lead weight against her.

Tim said, "What the hell?"

Abruptly she was lifted off the seat, her seat belt cutting into her thighs. She felt light and sick to her stomach. She saw Tim bounce out of his seat, his head slamming into luggage compartments overhead, the camera flying past her face.

From the cockpit, Emily heard buzzing, insistent alarms and a metallic voice that said, "Stall! Stall!" She glimpsed the blue-suited arms of the pilots moving swiftly over the controls; they were shouting in Chinese. All over the aircraft, people were screaming, hysterical. There was the sound of shattering glass.

The plane went into another steep dive. An elderly Chinese woman slid down the aisle on her back, screaming. A teenage boy followed, tumbling head over heels. Emily looked at Tim, but her husband wasn't in his seat anymore. Yellow oxygen masks were dropping, one swinging in front of her face, but she could not reach for it because she was clutching her baby.

She was pressed back into her seat as the plane descended steeply, an incredibly loud whining dive. Shoes and purses ricocheted across the cabin, clanging, and banging; bodies thumped against seats.

Part One – About Writing

> Tim was gone. Emily turned, looking for him, and suddenly a heavy bag struck her in the head – a sudden jolt, pain, blackness, and stars. She felt dizzy and faint. The alarms continued to sound. The passengers continued to scream. The plane was still in a dive.
> Emily lowered her head, clutched her infant daughter to her chest, and for the first time in her life, began to pray.

Within a few lines the story is set, the reader projected along a path of intensity.

From now on, get into the habit of studying the opening of every book or story that you read.

Similarly, Maya Angelou's memoir, *I Know Why The Caged Bird Sings*, begins with a poignant statement, "What you looking at me for? I didn't come to stay..." The very title of the book serves as a hook.
Consider Claire Kendal's thriller, *The Book of You*, where the opening paragraph reinforces the genre's essence, "It is you. Of course, it is you. Always it is you." This instant engagement is crucial in hooking the reader into the unfolding narrative.
In merely nine words, Gabriel Garcia Marquez captivates with the introduction of *One Hundred Years of Solitude*, "Many years later, as he faced the firing squad..." These concise yet powerful words set an irresistible hook, inviting readers to delve further into the tale.
Andrea Camilleri's *The Shape of Water* expertly weaves a hook into its

opening paragraph, skillfully introducing the setting, humor, and the distinctive style that defines the book. "No light of daybreak filtered yet into the courtyard of splendour..." instantly draws readers into a world both mysterious and captivating.

In mastering the art of storytelling, understanding and implementing the hook not only captivates the reader but also serves as an invitation to explore the rich depths of a well-crafted narrative.

Lastly, two more intriguing openings;

From *The Night Circus* by Erin Morgenstern**:** "The circus arrived without warning. No announcements preceded it. It was simply there, when yesterday it was not. The towering tents were striped in white and black, no golds and crimsons to be seen. No color at all, save for the neighboring trees and the grass of the surrounding fields. Black-and-white stripes on grey sky; countless tents of varying shapes and sizes, with an elaborate wrought-iron fence encasing them in a colorless world. Even what little ground was visible from outside was black or white, painted or powdered, or treated with some other circus trick."

From *The Shadow of the Wind* by Carlos Ruiz Zafón: "I still remember the day my father took me to the Cemetery of Forgotten Books for the first time. It was the early summer of 1943, and we walked through the streets of a Barcelona trapped beneath ashen skies as dawn poured over Rambla de Santa Monica..."

Structuring your work

When you build a house, you have a plan which incorporates the foundation, the rooms, and the roof. Your book must also have a plan;

> Part One – About Writing

a structure which comprises of the introduction, the main body, and the ending or resolution.

Award winning American novelist John Irving said: "The building of the architecture of a novel – the craft of it – is something I never tire of."

The introduction

This usually sets the scene for the place, people, the situation, the period, and tells the reader where the story is going. As just mentioned, the first sentence must hook.

> Roald Dahl – *Lamb to the Slaughter* (a short story)
> The room was warm and clean, the curtains drawn, the two table lamps alight – hers and the one by the empty chair opposite. On the sideboard behind her, two tall glasses, soda water, whisky. Fresh ice cubes in a Thermos bucket.
> Mary Maloney was waiting for her husband to come home from work. Now and again, she would glance up at the clock …

Makes you want to read on, doesn't it?

The introduction is normally around ten percent of the book, but there are no hard and fast rules for this.

> Develop a story in your mind and set out its plot. Write an opening sentence or paragraph. Next, do another opening for the same story. Lastly, do a third opening for the story.

The body

The body contains the bulk of the writing and is the most difficult to keep going whilst retaining interest. This is where most writers lose their way. The body needs a definite structure as all writing must further the story.

When writing the main body of the work, keep the core concepts alive.

Resolution

The ending or climax gives the reader resolution. This can take up as much as ten percent of the book or it may come down to the last page. Not only must the plot be finalised, but all loose ends tied up as well.

American author Colm Tóibín said of the resolution, "Ending a novel is almost like putting a child to sleep — it can't be done abruptly."

For nonfiction works, build the story up in a 'step-by-step' manner, so the reader will trust you to lead them to a 'clean' finish.

> Select your preferred introduction from the previous exercise. Now write the body and the resolution. Make a note in your diary to go back to it in a week and re-work it, making any improvements you deem necessary.

Part One – About Writing

Writer's block

You drag your listless body to the keyboard knowing you *should* write a 1000 words for the fifth chapter. Before starting you decide, *I'll quickly phone Joe and see why he left a message*. Thirty minutes later, again you return to the keyboard, looking at it like it's a rotten pizza... We have all been in this state of mind with a task. For writing you think that it is writer's block, and it could be, but even so you must further the work in another way.

Take the pressure off yourself and write something else. Know that it will come in its own good time. But until then, work on another aspect of the book: design the cover, conduct research, write a different chapter, one that offers more fun, or one that is shorter and easier to write.

To my mind there is no such thing as 'writers block', as there is always something else that can be done to further the book.

Perhaps it is not writers block, maybe the concept you want to write is floored or needs expansion. The subconscious mind could be holding you back as the idea needs maturing.

Sometimes, writing is like baking bread, you cannot rush it. Perhaps you need to explore another aspect of the story.

The egg hatches when ready.

Each painting has its own way of evolving. When the painting is finished, the subject reveals itself.
William Baziotes (artist)

1

Writing a book, any book, is not easy – sometimes it is downright daunting. Know this and keep going. Journalists are 'not allowed' to have writer's block, if they did, they would get fired.

Elizabeth Gilbert (the author of *Eat Pray Love*) says; what got her through difficult times was always the returning back to what she loved, and that was writing. It was writing that allowed her to work through the difficult times when she was not being published, or when she wondered if she was able to produce a book again as good as *Eat Pray Love*. She has a belief that for her, writing is her 'home' and that for her to be successful she always returns home. She believes that everybody has a 'home' of sorts, whereby their ability and talent is housed within this home.

Irrespective of your muse when things do not seem to come so easy, go back to the basics, go back home, open the door and go within and get stuck in.

Sting was given a guitar at the age of five. From that time on the guitar became a friend for life. 'When the songs stopped coming' he always knew it was time to go back to himself, to his roots, the quiet in that space the songs derive – the words would come, as would the rhythm.

John Steinbeck: "When I face a block, I gradually write one page, and then another. One day's work is all I can permit myself to contemplate."

If you do feel desultory, and your pen is listless, try the mind-mapping exercise that I just gave above. The playing with ideas, immersing in creativity may inspire you enough to get you going. In mind mapping, remind yourself of your goals, how much you love writing, and why you need to 'tell that story', or 'give that message'.

• • •

Part One – About Writing

Try writing half a page, as to why you feel separated from your writing. See what insights occur to you.

What is inspiration? To be a proficient writer you do not rely on inspiration. South African author and writer Peter de Vries said, "I write when I am inspired, and I see to it that I'm inspired at nine o'clock every morning."

It happened on holiday.
Think about this concept for one minute. Write the introduction for two minutes, the body for four minutes, and end for two minutes. Use your creative writing skills.
Why not insert a twist? (refer above).

Attitude

Many successful writers know disappointment, having received one or more manuscript rejections. Were these rejections failures?

No, you only fail if you give up. Either rework the manuscript or put it away for a time and start another. Be a 'stayer', do not give up – ever. But you may need to learn more about writing.

The brilliant philosopher Goethe was know to say, "In the making of art, there can be no question of suffering."

Another form of rejection is a carry-over from our early days, where perhaps we wrote something and some well-meaning but misguided person told us it 'could be better' and tried to cloak the rejection in niceties, but essentially that is what we hear. It could have been in the classroom, or a drunken parent telling you, "I don't like your ending." Maybe a report you wrote was scorned by people in the board room. In the early days of my writing, when I was enthusiastic but vulnerable, I shared a piece to a friend who had been writing for many years. She quickly scanned it, scoffed in a superior way and asked, "What makes you think you can write on that subject?" She went on to lecture me on the need to stick to the subjects I have experience with. At first I was crushed, but on later reflection I asked myself, 'Surely I'm likely to learn the craft better the wider I write'.

When you write a piece, there will always be detractors, but there will also be people who will like it. There will be others who will not give a hoot one way or another. So irrespective of how good the work is, there will always be mixed messages.

There are times though when the criticism is valid. You must be open minded and think about what has been offered to you as there could be sage advice for you.

Autobiographical Fiction
How do you separate yourself from your characters? Or how do you use empathy when writing a scene? Often, even without knowing it – we insert ourselves into our lines. When this is done consciously it is called autobiographical fiction, which is a genre of its own. Conversely, there has been research that suggests if a full

Part One – About Writing

novelis 'reversed engineered'(analysed), it is possible to have a basic character sketch of the novelist.

To be a person is to have a story to tell.
Isak Dinesen (Out of Africa)

Jane Eyre by Charlotte Brontë (1847): "I am no bird; and no net ensnares me: I am a free human being with an independent will, which I now exert to leave you."

Finding your voice

The amalgamation of your life's experiences – whether infused with a sharp sense of wit or marked by its absence – coupled with your overall knowledge and the sentiments you wish to express, collectively shapes your writing voice. Much like a well-crafted white wine that captivates the palate with nuance, your voice undergoes gradual maturation. Similarly, akin to the development of self-confidence, it requires guidance and encouragement to reveal its true essence.

We are all unique, and as writing is an expression of who we are, your writing will also be unique, if you allow it to be. The famous Chinese dancer, Jin Xing, was born a man but transgendered to a woman. She wrote in her biography *Shanghai Tango*, that as an adolescent and young man he strove to be the best ballerina in China. However, in middle age, after achieving world acclaim with many travails along the way, she said, "Don't aim to be the best – aim to be unique."

Perhaps now is a good time to refer to that piece where you wrote about who you are. Now you have a better idea as to why I suggested that piece. Add to that piece what you think makes you unique.

In an interview, Booker Prize winner Damon Galgut, said, "Each book has an ideal voice in which it wants to speak. A major part of the writing is finding out what that voice might be. Then it requires working out if it will be first person, third person, what tone it might be, the emotional range. You have an obligation that the book speaks as fully as it can".

As a writer, you write, but not all of your work will be good. Remember, even the best marksman has an off day.

Part One – About Writing

The following part-story is given to help you identify your writing voice. When you read it, read with awareness of metaphor, dialogue, characterisation, the flow of the story, and the introduction.

> Your roar is within you.
> Little Lion was only two years old and wanted to roar like her Daddy, Shumba. But her roar seemed not to be there and only came out as a squeak.
> Worried, Little Lion said, "Daddy I can't roar. I have tried and tried."
> Shumba was wise and said with love in his voice, "Your roar is inside of you... you don't have to try and force it out. It will come when needed..."

When you write, know that your **roar** is powerful and within you. You do not have to look for it, but you do have to develop it.

> Write down (in no fewer than 300 words) what you consider voice to be. Also address these four questions:
> Do you think voice is valuable?
> In a sentence or two, do you think your voice is active or passive?
> Can you identify your voice?
> What would you like your voice to become?

From a writing course I ran, I was given the following answers to the question, "What do I mean by voice?"

- It's your own footprint, shouted one student.
- It's your conviction about what you write and who you are.
- It's your essence, your soul expressing itself.
- The difference between writing that 'speaks' to the reader and writing that doesn't.

1

 *When you become aware of metaphor, dialogue, characterisation, the flow of the story, introductions and resolutions, and where you can weave them into text, you are learning to write.*

> Great Expectations by Charles Dickens (1861):
> "I loved her against reason, against promise, against peace, against hope, against happiness, against all discouragement that could be."

Lynette, a life coach, has a wonderful exercise, normally done in a group that shows individuality. It goes like this: Hold a piece of A4 paper, close your eyes. Fold the paper in half, then in half again. Next, tear the bottom left-hand corner, then the top right-hand corner. Do one more fold and tear at the bottom left-hand corner. Unfold the paper and open your eyes.

When done in a group, each paper will be different. The reason for the differences is the way in which we interpret the instructions – some fold horizontally, others vertically. Some tear off the entire corner, whilst others will just make a tear.

This reflects our variation of voices. It is your unique voice that will attract readers.

New ideas?

This may shock you, but almost nothing that you write will be new, as it has all been written before. But what is new to the readers is your voice.

Part One – About Writing

This book on writing is probably one of many thousands on writing. I have made sure that this one is unique. My voice is in it, as is my emotion and vulnerability. Some will resonate with it, some will not. But all will recognise a difference.

A book is like a garden carried in the pocket –
Chinese proverb.

The Picture of Dorian Gray by Oscar Wilde (1890):
"The only way to get rid of a temptation is to yield to it. Resist it, and your soul grows sick with longing for the things it has forbidden to itself, with desire for what its monstrous laws have made monstrous and unlawful.

Neil Gaiman – "The one thing that you have that nobody else has is you. Your voice, your mind, your story, your vision. So, write and draw and build and play and dance and live as only you can."

Agatha Christie – The Adventure of the Christmas Pudding (excerpt)

"You mean someone's killed the girl... what's her name... Bridget?" demanded Desmond. "Who on earth would want to kill her? It's unbelievable!"

"There are many things that are unbelievable," said Poirot. "Especially before breakfast, is it not? Please wait here, all of you."

Carefully making a circuit, he approached Bridget and bent for a moment over the body. Colin and Michael were now both shaking with suppressed laugher. Sarah joined them, murmuring, "What have you two been up to?"

"Good old Bridget, "whispered Colin. "Isn't she wonderful? Not a twitch!"

"I never seen anything look so dead as Bridget does," whispered Michael

Hercule Poirot straightened up again. "This is a terrible thing," he said. His voice held an emotion it had not held before.

Overcome by mirth, Michael and Colin both turned away. In a choked voice Michael said, "What... must we do?"

"There is only one thing to do," said Poirot. "We must send for the police."

"I think," said Colin, "I think... what about it, Michael?"

"Yes," said Michael, "I think the jig's up now." He stepped forward. For the first time he seemed a little unsure of himself. "I'm awfully sorry," he said, "I hope you won't mind too much. It... er...it was a sort of a joke for Christmas and all that, you know. We thought we'd... well, lay on a murder for you."

"You thought you would lay on a murder for me? Then this... then this..."

"It's just a show we put on," explained Colin, "to... to make you feel at home, you know."

Part One – About Writing

> "Aha," said Hercule Poirot. "I understand. You make me the April fool, is that it? But today is not April the first, it is December twenty-sixth."
>
> "I suppose we oughtn't to have done it really," said Colin, "but... but... you don't mind very much, do you, M. Poirot?... Come on Bridget," he called, "get up. You must be frozen to death already."
>
> The figure in the snow, however, did not stir.
>
> "It is odd," said Hercule Poirot, "she does not seem to hear you." He looked thoughtfully at them. "It is a joke you say? You are sure this is a joke?"
>
> "Why, yes." Colin spoke uncomfortably. "We... we didn't mean any harm."
>
> "But why then does Mademoiselle Bridget not get up?"
>
> "I can't imagine," said Colin.
>
> "Come on, Bridget," said Sarah impatiently. "Don't go on lying there playing the fool."
>
> "We really are very sorry, M. Poirot," said Colin apprehensively. "We do really apologise."
>
> "You need not apologise," said Poirot, in a peculiar tone.
>
> "What do you mean?" Colin stared at him. He turned again. "Bridget! Bridget! What's the matter? Why doesn't she get up? Why does she go on lying there?"
>
> Poirot beckoned to Desmond. "You, Mr. Lee-Wortley. Come here."
>
> Desmond joined him.
>
> "Feel her pulse," said Poirot.
>
> Desmond bent down. He touched the arm... the wrist. "There is no pulse ..." he stared at Poirot. "Good God, she really is dead!"

Agatha Christie was famous for her distinctive voice. This work contains suspense and good storytelling. Note the dialogue – no words are wasted, and all words further the story.

• • •

1

A powerful expression of the value of words by Gail Godwin in her novel *The Old Woman*, where she wrote, "What she wanted was a metaphor and she believed in them deeply. The articulation, interpretation, appreciation and preservation of good words. She believed in their power. If you truly named something, you had that degree of control over it. Words could incite, soothe, destroy, exorcise, redeem."

HELPFUL TIPS

Your personal narrative truly resonates when infused with your pain and emotions, breathing life into your words. This requires a deep connection to yourself and you craft, allowing emotions to unfurl unabashedly. That is voice.

Different styles of writing

What follows are two stories on the painting below (you saw this painting earlier). They are taken from a spontaneous writing drill, where students were shown the painting and asked to write about it. The first version does the job as there is flow and a story line, but it is flat. Knowing that the student could do better, I asked him to have another go, but this time give it power. The difference in passion between the two is remarkable, as you will see.

Part One – About Writing

The Man in the snow – Version one:

A solitary man, warmly dressed, stick in hand, a knapsack on his back, is walking purposefully away from town. It has snowed all day; everything is covered with a soft white blanket, the ground, the shrubs, and the roof of the church tower, which is rising above the distant trees. It is late afternoon, and the wanderer has to hurry because it is still a fair distance to his home, way outside of town at the edge of the forest. He is looking forward to getting home to his wife and children, to the warmth spread by an open fire, and a good meal. These are the thoughts raised in his mind from the stillness of the snow-covered landscape. This profound stillness is even deeper than the stillness in the church, which he visited before he left town. He wanted a word with the priest to clarify his thinking on some of the difficult questions of life. Now he has the time to ponder what they discussed. The wanderer is content, his world is in order, and he is thankful for that, and he brings this home as a gift to his family.

The man in the snow – Version two

"Even the weather's against me," mutters the solitary man as he thrusts himself into the drifting snow. He's marching away from the town he hates, where he scrapes together a living; this hateful town with its self-important 'gentlemen' and their overdressed wives who keep him in bondage. As he walked past the church, a symbol of oppression, he sees the heaven-pointing spire mocking him, as if to say, 'It is all from God, accept it!'

"I will be damned if I do," he grumbles to himself and pushes even more forcefully ahead against the cutting wind. His thoughts leave no room for the beauty of the snow-enlightened landscape. "I want more," he shouts. He is heading to meet mates for a beer and to talk about how to change the world, or maybe it is more to talk himself out of his frustration. He's in no hurry to get home to the noisy kids and the complaining wife.

Know the style

This book is written in a conversational style. Later, in the chapter on magazine writing, you will learn that style is important, as each magazine has a different style, and if you intend writing for a magazine, you must fit their style.

It is good to understand what your personal style is, but you need to be able to select and use other styles to suit the purpose, much the same as selecting the correct golf club for a particular shot.

Here is another style of writing, where the dialogue puts you in the story, and takes you along:

● ● ●

Part One – About Writing

> LeAnne Hardy – Glastonbury Tor
>
> It was Matilda who broke the spell. "Porridge is ready." Using her apron to protect her hands, she lifted the heavy iron pot and swung it away from the coals.
>
> "You shouldn't be doing that," said Father Bede. "Not a woman in your condition."
>
> Nicholas glanced up quickly. "Condition?"
>
> Father Bede looked slyly at Matilda from under half closed lids. "Your wife didn't tell you she's expecting a child?"

Why do you need to acquire good writing skills?

- If you write less creative work, such as textbooks or manuals, you still need to convert your knowledge, wisdom, and research into a book that is read with interest and communicates that information clearly.
- With several million new books published per year, you must compete on all fronts, not just with a good idea.
- You can turn dry information into entertainment.
- To stimulate readers.
- To add colour and expression to your work.
- Gain the confidence to write anything anytime

All the writing you have done in the past, such as reports for work, or school and university assignments, will have helped in developing basic writing skills. All types of writing need to flow coherently, otherwise the reader will not be able to follow your argument. It is not a large step to take from report writing to creative writing. Though it does take a mind-set change.

1

Manifest a mentor If you write crime, perhaps use Michael Connelly or James Patterson (for intrigue), Charlotte Brontë (historical romance), Charles Dickens (historical sociology), or Stefan Zweig or Hemingway (story telling).
When you start to write, ask them for help, as if they were there with you… "Ernest, what do you think of my dialogue?" "Charlotte, is the period correct?" Of course, you need to know their work. Although you like their style of writing, you must remain authentic with your own voice and style.

Spontaneous writing (Six minutes)
Take your journal to a garden or park. Settle into the natural surroundings and immerse yourself in the sensory details of the environment. Resist the temptation to merely state the presence of red flowers and green leaves; instead, strive to vividly portray the garden's vitality. Offer readers a canvas for their 'mind-sight' with descriptive images. Let your words not only depict what your eyes observe but also convey the genuine emotions pulsating within your heart.

Some time ago, I read out loud to a writing group an excerpt from *Stephen King On Writing*. It is a great volume of writing wisdom. I read, "I'm convinced that fear (being timid) is at the root of most bad writing." He talks about the form of writing, where writing for yourself is less likely to be timid. "Good writing," King continues, "is often about

Part One – About Writing

letting go of fear..."

In understanding King's assertion that "fear stops us from writing well," the impact of this idea settled more so with Daphnie who later wrote, "King's passage was significance for me as I realised that much of my writing lacked boldness. Fear had become a barrier, hindering my willingness to play with metaphor and stifling my creative flow. In the realm of Salvador Dali's surreal artistry, my clocks would have been meticulously structured."

Try and make your words stand tall, proud, infused with meaning.

As writers the challenge draws us along, like a horse pulls a cart. But be gentle, this must not be considered work, it is play – wordplay, storyplay, metaphorplay. By doing so, the stories will run like honey from a warm spoon, phrases will skim across the page as a skater skates across the ice.

In the introduction of this section where the comments on Anton Chekhov said, "and certainly without moral judgement". Often, in fact too often the moral judgment of the author gets in the way, and his or her emotions are reflected in the piece. Chekhov had the ability to *write without moral judgement.* He taught us that if the writer is just the reporter, the channel, and they must report without emphasis. They must report without an agenda or the need to influence.

However, this depends on what is being written about.

1

Part Two –Creative Writing

Part Two – Creative Writing

In this section:

- What is creativity?
- Creative visualisation.
- Tight writing.
- Show, don't tell.
- Metaphor.
- Flow – the rhythm of sentences.
- Sensory writing.
- Writing a motion.
- Inventing experience.
- Tension.
- Characterisation.
- Narration.
- Dialogue.
- Place (where the action happens).
- Detail.
- Humour and fun.
- Comic relief.
- Storytelling.

2

People often ask, "What is creative writing?" Creative writing is the pigment in the paint, the hum of the strings after the last pluck. It is the smell of coffee and the flowers in the panoramic view.

> Write half a page on what you consider creativity to be. Describe times when you have been creative. It could be when you got your way as a ten-year-old, or perhaps how you created a garden, or arranged the furnishings in your house. You could also have designed a wedding dress. List as many things as possible, and you will see that you have called upon your creativity numerous times in your life.

What is creativity?

Creative writing is a skill and a challenge – the challenge to make your work more captivating.

It involves the genesis of something novel, born from the unexplored or unconventional. This may entail pioneering uncharted territories or refining existing methods. According to actor Jose Ferrer, "The creative artist is a restless person, consistently contributing new dimensions to the richness of their work." Award-winning author Vera John-Steiner, in *Notebooks of the Mind*, asserts that creativity resides in the ability to perceive with heightened clarity and insight what one already knows, even uncovering hidden facets at the peripheries of awareness. It is, as Rilke suggests, the act of "churning the mind."

Part Two – Creative Writing

> In 1794, a small boy underwent surgery for a tumour with no antibiotics or anaesthetics) To distract his attention, he was told a tale so intriguing that he later avowed he had felt no discomfort. The boy was Jacob Grimm.
> George Burns – 101 Healing Stories

Creative writing has power to it, irrespective of the work being fiction or fact. The following is an excellent example of creative writing:

> Mark Twain - The Adventures of Huckleberry Finn
> The sun was up so high when I waked that I judged it was after eight o'clock. I laid there in the grass and the cool shade, thinking about things and feeling rested and rather comfortable and satisfied. I could see the sun out at one or two holes, but mostly it was big trees all about, and gloomy in there amongst them. There were a few freckled places on the ground where the light sifted down through the leaves, and the freckled places swapped about a little, showing there was a little breeze up there. A couple of squirrels sat on a limb and jabbered at me very friendly. I was powerful lazy and comfortable and didn't want to get up and cook breakfast. Well, I was dozing off again, when I think…

This piece has wonderful flow, interest and creative writing describing someone doing … well, nothing!

Here is a back cover description of Anton Chekhov – Selected Stories: "Chekhov is truly the grand-master of the short story. With supreme delicacy constructs stories where the action and the drama are often implied rather than described, and which rely on the intelligence and imagination of his readers. All are written with an

2

extraordinary compassion and with a view of life that, though tragic, is tempered by his delight in the farcical situation and the incongruities of human behaviour. Chekhov presents life as he sees it, with no apology, and certainly without moral judgment."

As a writer you can order your world in a way that suits you, where it is more or less, predictable. You can control the outcome, make the world fair, or chaotic so it conveys the message you want.

When writing, what is it that you are not seeing? Look beyond the obvious, as this is the creative component and that excites your readers.

HELPFUL TIPS

Observation, a writer's best friend, says novelist Jon Hassler: "I've always thought of the Red Owl Grocery Store in Plainview, Minnesota, as my training ground, for it was there that I acquired the latent qualities necessary to the novelist, namely ... the fun of picking the individual out of a crowd and the joy of finding the precise words to describe him. I dare say nobody ever got more nourishment than I did out of a grocery store."

You can probably write nice characters. Can you write nasty characters? Try it now. To do so takes a real ability to understand human nature. Two pages.

Part Two – Creative Writing

Human progress has been propelled by the force of creativity, a driving engine that has steered mankind to its current state of advancement. Similarly, your prowess in writing is propelled forward by your creative ingenuity. Whether you are concocting a culinary masterpiece, designing an architectural marvel, or innovating a state-of-the-art creation, the key lies in inventing, forging, and shaping it in a distinct manner. Elevating oneself above the ordinary demands of not just skill but the infusion of ingenuity, imagination, and foresight. The realm of the arts, encompassing writing, specifically relies on the bedrock of creativity. Any artistic endeavor necessitates not only technical proficiency but also the interplay of connection, enthusiasm, curiosity, insight, and imagination to achieve true creative excellence.

In *The Novel of the future* by Anias Nin, she maintained that: "The core of creation is to summon an image and the power to work with the image". It took Nin time to trust her images.
William Burroughs, American writer and product of Harvard, knew that he had to silence the inner talk and let his imagination expose itself, that it was a conscious process to develop his imagination. He said, "When you start thinking in images, you are well on the way."

> Dostoevsky's *The Brothers Karamazov* (1880): "Above all, don't lie to yourself. The man who lies to himself and listens to his own lie comes to a point that he cannot distinguish the truth within him, or around him, and so loses all respect for himself and for others. And having no respect he ceases to love."

Creativity therefore, is giving the unexpected. The Literary Zone website writes, "Creativity implies that you maintain a balance between surprise and believability. To do that, surprises (if they come first) should be followed by reason (whys) and vice versa."

• • •

2

Creativity is central to the meaning in our lives. When we are in creative mode, we feel fulfilled and complete – more alive.

It is my belief that by utilising our creative talents we are happier and remain younger than our biological years suggest. The well-known Canadian neurologist Wilder Penfield wrote of the exhilaration of creative pursuits.

You do not have to be a professional performing artist to be creative. When you tap into the creative source, it is food for the soul, and when the soul is nurtured by these exquisite creative energies, it is equipped with what it needs to serve and to guide. When you open the 'Mind's Eye', as Eugene Newmann says, "It is the material that informs the world, and it is soothing to me that it does."

 *Curiosity is linked to creativity, and often creativity is the result of curiosity.*

Amy Tan, who has published approximately thirty books, wrote that she gains her best creativity through asking questions about an issue. She creates half a dozen questions around it. From the questions, she derives answers that suit her. When writing fiction she notes that fiction by its very nature is not real. Therefore, to maintain objectivity, she aligns herself with the story. For her to have that objectivity, she must believe in the story.

Part Two – Creative Writing

Imagination is not mine to horde. It comes from something far grander than I am – Author unknown.

Also from Fyodor Dostoevsky: *Crime and Punishment* by (1866): "He was one of the numerous and varied legion of dullards, of half-animated abortions, conceited, half-educated coxcombs, who attach themselves to the idea most in fashion only to vulgarize it and who caricature every cause they serve, however sincerely.

Imagination and creativity

Imagination is the ability to mentally visualise or generate ideas, while creativity involves the application of those imaginative ideas to produce something novel and valuable. They interact symbiotically, with imagination providing the raw material and creativity shaping it into unique and meaningful expressions. One is the hammer, the other is the nail that secures two pieces of wood together. But I am not sure which is the hammer or which is the nail!

Unlike some other artistic pursuits, writing may seem like it has less room for expression. For instance, the skilled painter can show pain or bemusement on a face; a sculptor offers realism in body shape or expression. A writer must bring the work to life by creating the mind's-eye image with words.
You can't depend on your eyes when your imagination is out of focus. (Mark Twain)

2

Being artistic is your God-given right. It is a skill that can be learned and perfected.

Creative writing is a combination of things that all come together to make the reading experience more enjoyable, whilst giving the reader a better view of what the writer sees in their mind's eye.
Creativity is harnessing universality and making it flow through your eyes, says artist *Peter Koestenbaum*.

Movie makers can use a combination of the senses, enhancing the viewers' experience through sight and sound. Radio has a lesser ability to stimulate and uses sound to add to the creative words that are spoken, words that have originally been written!

It is difficult to write about music, whereas film and radio play the music to affect the audience at pivotal moments.
In a movie/soap/etc., when an actor indicates that some harsh words have been spoken, there is a camera-pan to the actor, at first a frozen face, then the eyes may dart to the floor, and perhaps a tightening of the mouth (all are well choregraphed).
As a writer you can 'show' the effect of the music through your words.

Here is one such example from *Captain Corelli's Mandolin*; the scene is set as the Italians invade the Greek islands: "Nothing was as anyone had anticipated. Those who had thought that they would be filled with rage were afflicted instead by sensations of wonder, curiosity, or apathy. Those who knew that they would be terrified felt an icy calm and a rush of grim determination. Those who had long felt a terrible

> Part Two – Creative Writing

anxiety became calm, and there was one woman who was visited by an almost venial apprehension of salvation."

The challenge of creative writing is to mimic all the other artistic forms by stimulating all the senses. For the accomplished writer this can be done easily as there is so much expression to be crafted from words.

Poet and storyteller Garth Greenwell, who wrote the novels *Mitko*, *What belongs to you* and *Cleanness*, offers the opinion that literature is the best technology to communicate the consciousness of an action or thought process. To express what life really feels inside. To place an action under a microscope, to reveal all its complexity.

> *Walden* by Henry David Thoreau (1854): "I went to the woods because I wished to live deliberately, to front only the essential facts of life, and see if I could not learn what it had to teach, and not, when I came to die, discover that I had not lived."

For creative writing to flow, there must be no censure or attachment to the outcome. It flows because the writer is connected, passionate and unafraid. Remember, in an earlier example it was Stephen King who told us not to be afraid. At this stage the writer is writing for himself, not with the reader in mind. Yes, later it can be tidied up, but first one must put the flavour on the page, along with the tears.

The painting has a life of its own. I try to let it come through. Says abstract artist, Jackson Pollock.

• • •

2

At a writing course I conducted, these words were suggested to describe creativity:

- Artistic.
- Inventive.
- Intuition.
- Exploring.
- Imaginative.
- Inspired.
- Visionary.
- Original.
- Innovative.
- Ingenious.
- Resourceful.
- Clever.
- Fertile.
- Unique.
- Tangential.

Creativity is also:

- Non-linear.
- Lateral thinking.
- Having no expectations.

A business perspective on creativity is that an entrepreneur is creative, whilst (often) a manager is linear and works according to set patterns.

An awareness of your writing skills is a great place to start with the development of your own creative voice. Read widely and with

> Part Two – Creative Writing

awareness and you will discover a world of wonder through creative writing is.

> From *A Sand County Almanac* by Aldo Leopold (1949):
> "Acts of creation are ordinarily reserved for gods and poets, but humbler folk may circumvent this restriction if they know how. To plant a pine, for example, one need be neither god nor poet; one need only own a shovel. By virtue of this curious loophole in the rules, any clodhopper may say: Let there be a tree – and there will be one."

Our cat was about four years old when I showed it that it had a tail. It took several instances of stroking, lightly pulling the tail and waving it in front of her eyes. Now she loves her tail, she rolls and plays with it, and attacks it as if it is an alien creature. Her best though, is where she waives it in the air, much like a blown windsock, whilst she is mesmerised. I am sure she wonders how on earth she got on without one.

Creativity is like this. You must discover yours.

 *Practice is the best teacher of creative writing, but I would suggest you enrol in several creative writing courses as there are many skills that you can learn.*

Creativity is a vast world of potential possibilities, and it is a source of important growth. When creativity is blocked, inspiration dries up and everything appears mundane, and difficult. Creative work takes you out of your head and into your heart. It is like a child discovering its world for the first time, completely focused on what it is observing. When you are in that space of feeling good, immersed in the creativity that you are indulging in, you are not bound to the debilitating aspects of negativity, you are tapped directly into 'The Source', and that is when you are at your most receptive, that is when you engage that mysterious connection. Try it out, experiment with the many aspects of being creative and the many dimensions of creativity and allow it to play with you, to lead and guide where it will show you how best it can be expressed.

When to write creatively?

Once you understand how to write in a creative way, you will always write creatively. However, not all your writing will use metaphor or be experiential, as you need to select the form for the message.

Newspaper, magazine, and report writing uses less creativity. They do, however, require good writing skill.

In a 1995 National Geographic article, Maney, a shy young Cherokee soapstone carver of great creativity, said when asked about his work: "You have to let it tell you what it wants you to do. I can feel it talking tome."

> Part Two – Creative Writing

> A humorous piece from "My Family and Other Animals" by Gerald Durrell (1956):
> "Outside the rain beat down like the cudgels of a dunderheaded policeman; the wind howled like a pack of wolves storming a museum of violins; thunder tore at the air with the fury of a croupy Viking."

Writing with creativity is like that, you must listen to what it.

Writing with expression is not as concise and clipped as academic writing. Nor is it report writing, which mainly focuses on fact. Most newspaper and trade-magazine writing can be dry, whilst speeches are written with the motive of making the speaker look good.

Although your book may not be a novel, you need to give it colour, and your descriptions must be alive. By using 'show, don't tell' interesting dialogue and descriptions, you write creatively (there is a section on show, don't tell below).

Go within to find your creativity

Throughout this work I talk about connectivity. The best way to get connected is to go within.

I shut my eyes in order to see. Paul Gauguin (painter)

2

I believe that creativity comes from the same place as intuition. Both are expressions of our natural-given spirituality. We are told that we are created in God's image, and as God is the creator then so must we be. This has nothing to do with religion. Everything is a vibration, and creativity is a vibration. You tap into that vibration and it expresses from that vibration. If your mind is in the wrong place, buzzing in another vibration, you will not arrive at the right vibration. That is why you need to 'let go', be calm, and allow yourself to drift into the right vibration.

> It is the creative potential itself in human beings that is the image of God.
> Mary Daly

Learning to write creatively will help your painting or interior design. Conversely, your creative painting is likely to help your creative writing. It is all expression, and it all comes from the same place.

> Why should we all use our creative power? Because there is nothing that makes people so generous, joyful, lively, bold.
> Brenda Ueland

Words make up sentences, sentences describe mind pictures. Your mind sees the picture and sprouts the emotion, the syntax automatically comes as you conceive the perfect words to maximise the effect. Most of this is done on an intuitive level and does not require too much thinking. The more you practice, the better the intuitive process, and the easier it will become. You can practice by doing the spontaneous writing drills.

> **John Steinbeck – *Sweet Thursday***
> In the Pan Books Limited London addition they wrote the following about Steinbeck, "One of the greatest American writers of this century, winner of the 1962 Nobel Prize for Literature.
> Uninhibited in his choice of material, insatiably curious about the human race, Steinbeck is a natural storyteller. The sinewy strength and realistic harshness of his writing, lit by flashes of humour and poetry, make unforgettable reading."
>
> And from HG Wells when referring to Steinbeck; "That tremendous genius."
>
> The following are short exerts, in three categories from Steinbeck's Sweet Thursday.
> *Wisdom*: "Doc was changing in spite of himself, in spite of the prayers of his friends, in spite of his own knowledge. And why not? Men do change, and change comes like a little wind that ruffles the curtains at dawn, and it comes like the stealthy perfume of wildflowers hidden in the grass. Change may be announced by a small ache, so that you think you're catching a cold. Or you may feel a little wind that ruffles the curtains at dawn, and it may even take the form of a hunger that peanuts will not satisfy."
> *Philosophy*: "… For what can a man accomplish that has not been done one million times before? What can he say that he will not find in Lao-Tse or the Bhagavad-Gita or the profit that Isaiah? It is better to sit in appreciation of contemplation of a world in which beauty is eternally supported on a foundation of ugliness; cut out the support, and beauty will sink from site. It was a good thing Doc had, and many people wished they had it to…"

2

> "... Thought is the evasion of feeling. You're only walling up the leaking loneliness."
>
> "... He liked himself again as he once had; liked himself as a person, the way he might like anyone else. The self-hatred which poisons so many people and which had been irritating him was gone for the time. The top voice of his mind sang peacefulness and order, and the raucous middle voice was gentle; it mumbled and snarled but it could not be heard. The lowest voice of all was silent, dreaming of a warm, safe sea."
>
> Humour: "Thinking is always painful, but in Hazel it was heroic. A picture of the process would make you seasick. A grey whirling furore of images, memories, words, patterns. It was like a traffic jam at a big intersection with Hazel in the middle trying to get something to move somewhere…"
>
> "... Hazel's thoughts were not complicated. It was just remarkable that he had them at all…"
>
> ... She had taken up astrology because she found that people who won't take advice from a wise and informed friend will blindly follow the orders of planets – which by all reports are fairly remote and aloof."

Right and Left-Brain Garbage

In the past, it was believed a human brain, at birth, and through the influence of environment, tend be either more right-brained (creative) or left-brained (logical). This, however, is not fixed, and you can train yourself to be both creative and logical. You can be a creative artist (right-brained), but also manage a business (left-brained). You can landscape your garden and design the interior of your house (both right-brained), whilst at the same time design computer software (left-brained).

Part Two – Creative Writing

By believing that you are predominately one-sided, you limit yourself. As a writer, you must develop the right side of your brain. However, you must also be logical. As an author you need the ability to be logical, but open to expansion. It requires practiced awareness, and confidence to do both. When you do this you will liberate many skills that you did not know you had.

Russian composer Tchaikovsky said: "One of the most neglected areas of the study of creativity is that of discipline…"

Male – Female Energy

Another limitation is to only use your feminine energy if you are female or masculine energy if you are male. You need to be aware of your polarities and develop the one you do not use. The energies are opposing but complementary. Creativity is more of a feminine energy.

When you develop and understand the other gender side of your psyche, you are more rounded. It gives you a new range of abilities and skills. And, you have greater empathy for those who identify themselves differently to yourself. You will see things from a different perspective. It does not mean women have to become hard as we sometimes see in company management, but it does mean that a man can express emotion if he feels so inclined.

Why harness only 50% of your ability? Of course, when you develop the other side of your nature you move away from conforming to what some consider socially- accepted norms. You may lose friends, but you will gain new one's who, like you, will be inclined to non-conformity and are likely to be thinkers in their own right.

To develop your other gender side, develop an awareness of it and let go of your culturally invoked beliefs. It may take you a while to let your other half emerge but the balance will be worth it.

> This writing is to be creative and cathartic. If male, write about being at a 'hen party' from a woman's point of view. If a woman, write as if you were a man on a boy's night out.

Creative visualisation

The book of form and Emptiness, 2022 Woman's prize for fiction by Ruth Ozeki uses meditation to form characters. Ozeki, a Zen Buddhist priest also teaches Creative Writing at university. She says that meditation and writing are synergistic. When writing a book, in meditation, in the moment, just taking in the world, with open sense-gate, and she places her mind into the position of the character, the place, the activity, and what is going through the mind of the character – she writes from that place.

Sometimes creativity hits you between the eyes, other times you must go out and drag it in with a rope. When the latter is required, it helps to know what you need to be creative about:

- Is it a character? If so study people in a park or café.
- A place? Look at maps, magazines, travel shows.
- A chapter?
- What about a plot? Meditate and it will come.
- Sub plots.
- Humour.

Part Two – Creative Writing

HELPFUL TIPS

When you are creative, you are alive. Creativity is playtime, childlike and fun.

Finally, regarding creativity – when I immerse myself in the process of writing a book, my creative mind enters a realm where distractions fade away, leaving only the book. This solitary communion can extend for months on end. I willingly allow the book to envelop me, creating an environment where creative thoughts not only flood my consciousness but are actively encouraged. Even after the so-called end of the workday, whether I'm with my partner, watching TV, or driving, the book is an ever-present undercurrent in my thoughts.

At night, after I turn off the light and succumb to sleep, my creative mind often awakens, offering precious gems of inspiration. I diligently record these nocturnal musings, sometimes staying awake for hours to process the influx of ideas.

The following morning I may greet the day an hour later than usual, having relished the rich tapestry of creative exploration during the night. This process, though unconventional, is a source of profound inspiration for me.

Subsequently, my mind transforms into a repository of 'book' information, surpassing the capabilities of a computer. It is as if my brain hosts an intricate system of ledger cards, with each new thought or piece of information finding its place on one of these mental cards. As I continue to gather thoughts or write, the most pertinent information, sourced from the relevant mental card, effortlessly presents itself.

While the complexity of this multi-channeled mental process might seem unconventional, creativity by its very nature defies convention. For me, this unique and seemingly intricate journey is not only effective but also essential to my creative output. I suspect that fellow authors and individuals across various artistic genre share in a similar, albeit idiosyncratic, creative process.

What follows are various topics that will guide you in your search for expression.

Tight Writing

Concise writing or tight writing aims to offer maximum meaning with minimal words. It thrives on short, succinct sentences, ensuring a pleasant reading experience while sustaining steady momentum. For example:

> *The Beggar* (a short story by Anton Chekhov. This is the opening paragraph. "Kind Sir, have pity; turn your attention to a poor, hungry man. For three days I have had nothing to eat; I haven't money for a lodging, I swear it before God. For eight years I was a village schoolteacher and then I fell a victim to calumny (false statements)."

Not one wasted word, and within that paragraph, four lines, we are appraised of the beggar's situation and how he came to be so.

Part Two – Creative Writing

Brevity – if the words do not enhance the story or the plot, leave them out.

The following is an example of writing with brevity.

> Rudyard Kipling – *The Jungle Book*
> "It was seven o'clock of a very warm evening in the Seeonee Hills when Father Wolf woke up from his day's rest, scratched himself, yawned, and spread out his paws one after the other to get rid of the sleepy feeling in their tips. Mother Wolf lay with her big grey nose dropped across her four tumbling, squealing cubs, and the moon shone into the mouth of the cave where they all lived. "Augrh!" said Father Wolf, "it is time to hunt again"; and he was going to spring downhill when a little shadow with a bushy tail crossed the threshold and whined;' Good luck go with you O Chief of Wolves…

The next creative writing insert is by Danish writer Karen Blixen. Although good writing, there is an added intrigue because of her European influence.

2

Karen Blixen (Isak Dinesen) – *Out of Africa*
"The chief feature of the landscape and of your life in it was the air. Looking back on a sojourn in the African highlands, you are struck by your feeling of having lived for a time up in the air. The sky was rarely more than pale blue or violet, with a profusion of mighty, weightless, ever-changing clouds towering up and sailing on it, but it has blue vigour in it, and at a short distance it painted the ranges of hills and the woods a fresh deep blue. In the middle of the day the air was alive over the land, like a flame burning; it scintillated, waved, and shone like running water, mirrored and doubled all objects, and created great Fata Morgana. Up in this high air you breathed easily, drawing in a vital assurance and lightness of heart. In the highlands you woke up in the morning and thought: Here I am where I ought to be.
The mountain of Ngong stretches in a long ridge from north to south, and is crowned with four noble peaks like immovable darker blue waves against the sky. It rises eight thousand feet above the sea, and to the east two thousand above the surrounding country; but to the west the drop is deeper and more precipitous – the hills fall vertically down towards the Great Rift Valley.
The wind in the highlands blows steadily from the north-north-east…"

Trained journalists have perfect tight writing, and with practice so can you.

Part Two – Creative Writing

Show, don't tell

Show, don't tell, is universal advice that most writing coaches give to authors. Show, don't tell is like cooking practice to a chef – a necessary and basic skill.

From the above excerpt: "*...with four noble peaks like immovable darker blue waves against the sky*". This is showing the reader as opposed to telling, "*...four big peaks stood up...*" Showing is more visceral for the reader than telling.

You show through writing skill, through metaphor, through dialogue.

When you get to the point in a story where you introduce another person by saying 'he is tall,' or 'she is sad,' or 'she smelled chicken,' is telling. It helps the reader if you show it in a different way, such as, 'His long frame could not fit comfortably in the chair,' or 'The odour of the roast chicken bought back memories of family dinners, dinners that were so long ago'.

When 'showing', the use of metaphor is important. An example from a student: *She felt depressed* became *She felt like wilted flowers of midsummer heat.*

It is your job as a writer to show the readers, so they see it just as you saw it.

You could say, *He took his hat off*, which is telling. The following extract is from *Great Expectations* by Charles Dickens: "Taking his hat up carefully, with both hands, like a bird's-nest with eggs in it." That's showing.

2

 *Anton Chekhov – "Don't tell me the moon is shining; show me the glint of light on broken glass."*

> J.K. Rowling – *Harry Potter and the Prisoner of Azkaban*
> "Harry's euphoria at winning the Quidditch Cup lasted at least a week. Even the weather seemed to be celebrating; as June approached, the days became cloudless and sultry, and all anybody felt like doing was strolling into the grounds and flopping down on the grass with several pints of iced pumpkin juice, perhaps playing a casual game of Gobstones or watching the giant squid propel itself dreamily across the surface of the lake.

The above is a good example of showing, as opposed to telling. It is also offering a skilful way to lead the reader into chapter sixteen.

 Describe one of you parents, using 'show and not tell'.

 *When showing, you only need to add a few extra words to transform the imagery.*

• • •

116

Part Two – Creative Writing

You could write, 'nature is wonderful and mysterious'. That is telling. Or you could write, 'Gardeners marvel at the mystery of growth, while dirt cakes their hands and blackens their fingernails'.

The back page of Anton Chekhov short stories reads: "...he constructs stories where the action and drama are often implied rather than described..." That is showing.

> Convert the following phases from 'telling' to 'showing': 'He touched her', and 'She tasted salt'.

As I was writing this, a friend asked me if I wanted to run with her in the park. As my mind considered the idea, she followed up with, "Come and see the autumn leaves."

As she said this, I had the evocative image of crunching through a soft carpet of curled-dry-crisp leaves displaying different colours of decay. "Hang on," I said, "let me get my running shoes ..."

You do not always have to show, but showing the important phrases highlights enlivens the reading. Like the phrase: "You shouldn't be doing that," said Father Bede. "Not a woman in your condition."

It is best to show the emotions, sensations, and descriptions for main characters. For your characters, show who they are through their emotions and thoughts, not by telling with explanation.
American journalist and novelist Chuck Palahniuk says, "Dump verbs, such as, thinks, knows, understands, realises, believes, wants; replace adjectives with images."
Stephen King said, "I believe the road to hell is paved with adverbs."
Showing is describing – telling is explaining. Telling is the recipe. Showing is savouring the cooked meal.

• • •

2

You could tell the reader, "After Fred kissed Jill, he was so happy…" (telling – boring). Now for showing: "After that kiss with Jill, all day Joe could not keep the glow off his face. Even his sister asked, "Why are you looking so smug?"…"

Emotions are best conveyed through body language and action; "…as Fred hurried home, he skipped the entire way… even Mrs Wentworth got a happy, "Hullo"…" Or "as Megan left, the door slammed behind her" is better than saying "Megan was angry."

There are times however when telling is required – "The clocked chimed! It was exactly 8:00pm when she rang the door" as it transitions into a new scene. And there are readers who want to be told. You must direct them.

Yet, telling has its place in keeping the pace brisk. There is economy in telling. It is a balancing act. If you want the reader to know the character, then show, but many things require telling, for example "he tied up his shoelaces as he spoke…"

Being specific is a way to show: "the bird swooped…" is telling. There is more imagery in, "the magpie swooped…"

Or the specifics of "eight men, all experts in their own field, in their own way examined the evidence…"As opposed to "numerous experts examined the evidence." Or later in the story having to belabour that there were eight men – always look for efficiency.

Other examples:
You can show excitement or dread:
"Pam's eyes shone with determination, she was going to win the prize."
"Pam cringed when she saw the state of his bedroom, not wanting to touch a thing…"
"Angel breath, that's what came to Pam's mind with that first kiss.""Vulnerability coursed through Pam's stomach like hot lava."

● ● ●

Part Two – Creative Writing

Nature Farmers have a sense of it; it is unlikely that it is money keeping them on the land. Stargazers are awed in her presence. Gardeners marvel at the mystery of growth, while dirt cakes their hands and blackens their fingernails. Yet, to explain it is difficult.

The ancient tribes of the world knew it, as a brother, and you can as well, if you have the intent.

I have spent many hours in the bush, hiking and camping on my own. Always, for the first half-day, I feel alone but then I listen and realise that I am accompanied by nature's presence. When bedding down at night, the connection, her energy, and unity, are there.

Nature can be spectacular in her scenery, but communing with nature on a deeper level is the lesson. The sweet aromas of pollens and flowers after a summer storm is only a façade, as is the colour display that nature puts on for us in a field of poppies. As delightful as it all is, there is so much more. This is just Mother Nature's make-up, her rouge and perfume. She is like any woman whose outer beauty doesn't reveal her true self. They are enticements to draw us closer – her charms to attract and seduce. Once enchanted, there is a universal desire to look deeper. Underneath her countenance, her smile, there is a depth of untold riches to be discovered.

Giving yourself over to nature is like sitting next to your lover and, although not talking or touching, still feeling one another's energy. The connection is likely to be strong but if asked to explain that force, you would find it difficult. Our language is just not rich enough. Yet you know it and knowing is the key. And so, with nature, when you allow her to creep into your being, you will recognise her. She will evoke hidden feelings of past times, when in some other form you were coupled closer to her. It is much the same as a dog barking at a full moon. He doesn't know why he barks but senses an affinity…

• • •

2

Use an observer in showing

A method many authors employ is where an observer notes: an action or situation to 'show' meaning. Let's look at two examples.

Wife to husband, "Now dear. Tell me about what you did when I was away," enquired Hilda. "Nothing much really" Paul said with a trace of hesitation. "It was quiet without you…" It was at this moment that Ella, the young fresh-faced secretary came in with some documents, and without waiting to be invited said, "Paul, I need your signature."

Paul, with a touch too much willingness to please, reached for the documents.

Hilda, seemingly forgotten in the exchange, had a chill up her spine.

The observation was enough for Hilda to know of her husband's infidelity."

And,

"When questioned by the detective, her son kept rubbing his hands together. An action he did as a child when caught fibbing. Upon seeing this, his mother knew her son was the killer.

Both of the above create intrigue because we can only guess Paul is sleeping with Ella, and that the son is the murderer. However, the observations voice the implication, which is usually enough evidence for the reader, showing, not telling, that furthers the story.

Writing can be dream time in action.

"You must be an outsider to be able to write about people," says Kevin Kwan author of *Crazy, Rich, Asians*, "otherwise how can you observe them without compassion?"

Part Two – Creative Writing

> Intangibles.
> Take five minutes and write about mosquitoes bothering you at night. Do this before you continue reading any further.

How did you go? Not easy, is it? Other intangibles could be writing about the taste of chocolate cake or the scentalising (my own word) the smell of a rose. What about feelings and emotions? How would you show and not tell about the sadness of a major break up, or the death of a loved one?

Using an analogy to explain is an effective technique, as readers will recognise the frame of reference. Remember the analogy of Stevie the eight-year-old soccer player. Readers remember stories – I am sure you remember Stevie's story at the start of this workbook.

Another method to write about an intangible is metaphor.

I wrote the above excerpt, *Nature*, to describe how nature is often intangible. As you read be aware of the similes.

Metaphor

Metaphor is:

- Comparison conveyed in a single word (*The Kings English Dictionary*).
- A way of describing something by referring to it as if something else.
- For example, referring to a lot of tears as 'a river of tears' (*Longman*).
- A simile, allegory, image, symbol, figure of speech, analogy (*The New Penguin Thesaurus*).
- It sees a characteristic of something in another thing.

2

Play with metaphors like you would play with children. Run and bounce them across the page, laugh and giggle until you fall over. See them float across your mind like sheep-clouds sliding across the sky.

 *Metaphor, a 'showing' device offering evocative images.*

> ...the air was alive over the land, like a flame burning.
> (Karen Blixen; Out of Africa)

There are two metaphors in the above.

Shakespeare said of Juliet, "Juliet is the sun." Only four words to describe how he felt about her.

A metaphor is a thought first before it is a word. But as the thought it must be a mind picture, and that is what you are trying to convey to your reader – a picture of the mind.

Metaphor is mentioned some eighty-eight times throughout this workbook, so keep an eye out.

Recently I read a manuscript, good story but too many metaphors. So many it clogged the flow and deviated from the story – so don't overdo them.

Novelist, Dashiell Hammet says his style of writing is called "hard-boiled" and it contained almost no extraneous detail. In one story, he described a woman: "Her eyes were blue, her mouth red, her teeth white, and she had a nose. Without getting steamed up over the details, she was nice."

Flow – The rhythm of sentences

Chinese poet Su Shi famously summarised the secrets of literary writing: "A good piece of writing moves on freely and smoothly like floating clouds or flowing water. Clouds drift and form new skyscapes every other day."
Flow makes for easy reading, where the concepts fly off the page. Bad flow is where the work is disjointed and difficult to follow. A lack of flow is usually the result of long clumsy sentences.
Sentences should make appropriate used of conjunctions, comas, and dashes, as these give the reader a continuous contextual feed into the next thought, so that the thought is uninterrupted, without a new sentence start. Did you notice that last sentence was extraordinarily long, with about forty-two words? Although it does work, just because of the punctuation, the flow is not great. It would be better in three sentences.

The clarity of a sentence is:

- A clear expression, no fumbling.
- The use of the least number of words to eloquently express an idea.
- The use of the right words.

Management of the sentence.

Consider this 181 word sentence that shows what is possible. It is from an essay by Virginia Woolf – *On Being Ill* (read it slowly).

2

"Considering how common illness is, how tremendous the spiritual change that it brings, how astonishing, when the lights of health go down, the undiscovered countries that are then disclosed, what wastes and deserts of the soul a slight attack of influenza brings to view, what precipices and lawns sprinkled with bright flowers a little rise of temperature reveals, what ancient obdurate oaks are uprooted in us by the act of sickness, how we go down the pit of death and feel the waters of annihilation close above our heads and wake thinking to find ourselves in the presence of the angels and the harpers when we have a tooth out and come to the surface in the dentist's arm-chair and confuse his "Rinse the mouth – rinse the mouth" with the Deity stooping from the floor of Heaven to welcome us – when we think of this, as we are so frequently forced to think of it, it becomes strange indeed that illness has not taken its place with love and battle and jealousy among the prime themes of literature."

It is clear enough, but not easy reading.

Consider the following:

- The driver of the train (four words). Better to write the train driver (three words). Simplified text facilitates flow.
- Detective Jones had Bill Jackson jailed because he wanted revenge. Becomes: Detective Jones, out for revenge, jailed Jackson.
- The teacher looked at his student coldly. His lips were curled in a sneer. Becomes: The teacher, his lips curled in a sneer, coldly looked at his student.
- More quickly becomes quicker.
- Have to becomes must.

Flow-stoppers:

- The following is from a manuscript I recently reviewed, "I was maybe making money and living comfortably…"The word 'maybe' disrupts

the flow. Read it aloud, with and without *maybe*, and you will see what I mean.
- If it is not clear and concise there will be no flow.
- Sentences should only have one or two phrases, and a paragraph should have sentences that fit one focused idea. New ideas should start in a fresh paragraph.
- Avoid sentences and paragraphs with too many subjects.
- '*Of the*', can normally be left out of a sentence, as given above: 'The driver *of the* train' can just be the 'train driver'.
- It was *ever so* lovely, is a flow stopper unless it is in dialogue.

The book, Elements of Style by Strunk and White is a powerhouse of ideas. One paragraphs advises; "In general, remember that paragraphing calls for a good eye as well as a logical mind. Enormous blocks of print look formidable to readers. Breaking a long paragraph in two, even if it is not necessary to do so, is often a visual help."

> Excerpt from "*The Elements of Style*" by William Strunk Jr. and E.B. White (1959): "Vigorous writing is concise. A sentence should contain no unnecessary words, a paragraph no unnecessary sentences, for the same reason that a drawing should have no unnecessary lines and a machine no unnecessary parts. This requires not that the writer make all his sentences short, or that he avoid all detail and treat his subjects only in outline, but that every word tell."

But firing off many short paragraphs in quick succession can be distracting. Moderation and a sense of order should be the main consideration in paragraphing.

The above is sensible when we consider the rhythm and flow that we want from our writing.

2

Another paragraph test: think about when a reader is to pick up a coffee for a sip. Usually it is at a paragraph break – why?
Or, when the reader wants to digest aspects, perhaps a brilliant phrase, or something to do with the plot, it is usually at the end of the paragraph – why?
In both incidents it is because the paragraph contained a complete concept, and I suspect the mind is happy with that consolidation before continuing.

Flow, to me, is as important as grammar. As suggested above, sentences should generally not be long and clumsy. Yet you do not want to be prosaic because you stick with rules. Remember, you are entertaining your reader, not just furthering a story. There are times in your creative writing where you will ignore the so-called 'rules' with elegance, humour, and interest, where the writing thrills the reader, in addition to the story.
Consider the following two sentences from Thomas Mann's *Bashan*: "I have a great love for brooks, as I have for all bodies of water – from the ocean to the smallest, scum-covered puddle. When I happen to be in the mountains during the summer and chance to hear the secret splashing and gossip of such a streamlet, then I must follow the liquid call, even though it be distant, and I cannot rest until I have found its hiding place."
Both sentences are interesting. The second is longer than one would normally suggest. That is creative writing, where the writer's wit is on full display to admire, laugh at, and be amused by.
You could write *"The boy kicked the stone, which broke his toe."* Or you could write *"The boy kicked the stone. This broke his toe."* Or you could write *"The boy kicked the stone and broke his toe."*

Part Two – Creative Writing

All three are correct, but the first, *The boy kicked the stone, which broke his toe* flows better (read all three aloud and decide for yourself).

The below writing is a good example of brief writing, where an entire life is described in 106 words. The writing could be seen as characterless but shows you how words can be eliminated, whilst retaining meaning.

> Palms – A Natural Biography
> The palms of my hands chart a life of events. Events of joy and sadness, success, failure, loves, hopes, hurts, and fears.
> Spider-webbed lines, with lumps and striations, blemishes, like a parched river pan – a biography of fornications and drunken exploits, of friends, compassion, children raised, of love, sweet romances, brutality, brawls, tranquillity, regrets, arguments, anger, attitudes, addictions, optimism, and happiness – all are represented.
> Although my palms are cluttered and packed like an over-stocked graveyard, I revel in thoughts of lines to come and thrill in the prospect of new etchings. After all, an unblemished palm would indeed reveal a boring life.

Getting technical...

Some words are passive in that that they slow down the pace of the writing by interrupting the flow. Passive words *offer nothing to the work – they detract from it*. I could have said ... *in fact, they detract from it*. The *in fact* being passive. Active writing supports flow.

'By' is usually a passive word:

The dog was hit by a man with a stick. In this example, the by is passive.

A man with a stick hit the dog. This is the active voice and more direct. If you read both aloud, you will see the second flows better.

There are also fewer words in the second example, which makes for tighter writing.

Another example of the difference between the active and passive voice:

The clock was set this afternoon (passive).

The man set the clock this afternoon (active). By telling the readers that the man set the clock, you are inserting an active voice.

My trusty *Editing Made Easy* by Bruce Kaplan explains that voice is the characteristic of a verb (a doing word) that tells us whether the subject of the verb is performing the action of the verb (active voice), or whether the subject is acted upon (passive voice). He gives this example and explanation..:

"A man with a stick chased three people in a city park last night."

Here, the subject (a man with a stick) performed the action (chased three people).

The grammar book *Elements of Style* by EB White states: "The active voice is usually more direct and vigorous than the passive.

I shall always remember my first visit to Boston.

is much better than:

My first visit to Boston will always be remembered by me.

Passive phrases derive from our verbal speech. *Gees, are you sure, mate?"*

> Spend time with your grammar book, becoming familiar with active and passive voices. When you think that you have a good understanding, create a sentence that is passive. Rework it to make it active.

Part Two – Creative Writing

The next part-story, by Henry Lawson, includes metaphor, humour, tight writing, and dialogue. Henry Lawson (1867 – 1922) was an Australian and is regarded in some literary quarters as one of the most accomplished Australian writers of all time. Read the following and you will understand why (it is longer than the other readings, so you can get a good feel of all the elements):

Wonderful dialogue, metaphor, humour, and of course, tight writing. As is the following:

> Poisonous Jimmy gets left by Henry Lawson in Joe Wilson's Mates
> ...they had brought the cattle down from the north and were going no further with them; their boss had ridden on into Mulgatown to get the cheques to pay them off, and they were waiting for him.
> "And Poisonous Jimmy is waiting for us," said one of them.
> "Poisonous Jimmy kept a shanty a piece along the road from their camp towards Mulgatown. He was called 'Poisonous Jimmy' perhaps on account of his liquor, or perhaps because he had a job of poisoning dingoes on a station in the Bogan scrubs at one time. He was a sharp publican. He had a girl, and they said that whenever he saw the shearers coming along the road, he'd say to the girl, 'Go, run and get your best frock on, Mary! Here's the shearers comin' .' And if a chequeman wouldn't drink he'd try to get him into his bar and shout him till he was too drunk to keep his hands out of his pockets.
> "But he won't get us," said another of the drovers. ...

2

We were burned to bricks and ragged and dusty and parched up enough, and so were our horses. We only had a few shillings to carry us four or five hundred miles home, but it was mighty hot and dusty, and we felt that we must have a drink at a shanty.

Just before we reached the shanty I got an idea. 'We'll plant our swags in the scrub,' I said to Jim.

'What for?' said Jim.

'Never mind – you'll see,' I said.

So we unstrapped our swags and hid them in the scrub by the side of the road; then we rode on to the shanty, got down, and hung our horses to the veranda-post.

Poisonous came out at once, with a smile on him that would have made anybody home sick.

He was a short nuggety man, and could use his hands, they said; he looked as if he'd be a nasty, vicious, cool customer in a fight – he wasn't the sort of man you'd care to try and swindle a second time. He had a broken nose, and a cunning, sharp, suspicious eye that squinted, and a cold stony eye that seemed fixed. If you didn't know him well you might talk to him for five minutes, looking at him in the cold stony eye, and then discover that it was the sharp, cunning little eye that was watching you all the time. It was awful embarrassing. It must have made him awkward to deal with in a fight.

'G'day, mates,' he said.

'G'day," we said.

'It's hot.'

'It's hot.'

We went into the bar, and Poisonous got behind the counter. 'What are you going to have?' he asked, rubbing up his glasses with a rag...

Part Two – Creative Writing

To everything there is a season, and a time to every purpose under the heaven. A time to be born, and a time to die; a time to plant, and a time to pluck up that which is planted. A time to kill, and a time to heal; a time to break down, and a time to build up. A time to weep, and a time to laugh; a time to mourn, and a time to dance. A time to cast away stones, and a time to gather stones together; a time to embrace, and a time to refrain from embracing. A time to get, and a time to lose; a time to keep, and a time to cast away. A time to rend, and a time to sew; a time to keep silence, and a time to speak. A time to love, and a time to hate; a time of war, and a time of peace….
(Ecclesiastes 3. 1-13, one of the books of the Old Testament).

2

I like Allen's writing because it is expressive, whilst being as direct as writing can be.

> *As a Man Thinketh* by James Allen is an essay published some 120 years ago. The essay deals with the power of thought, and particularly with the use and application of thought for a happy life. He wrote, that "... each man and woman holds the key to every condition, good or bad, that enters into his life, and that, by working patiently and intelligently upon his thoughts, he may remake his life, and transform his circumstances." And indeed he did as some of the following reflects.
>
> "As the plant springs from, and could not be without the seed, so every act of a man springs from the hidden seeds of thought and could not have appeared without them. This applies equally to those acts called 'spontaneous' and 'unpremeditated' as to those, which are deliberately executed.
>
> Man's mind may be likened to a garden, which may be intelligently cultivated or allowed to run wild, but whether cultivated or neglected, it must, and will, bring forth. If no useful seeds are put into it, then an abundance of useless weed-seeds will fall therein and will continue to produce their kind.
>
> Men do not attract that which they want, but that which they are. Men are anxious to improve their circumstances but are unwilling to improve themselves."

Sensory writing for creating images (Representational systems)

From a writing perspective, there are three main senses to address. These are visual (seeing), auditory (hearing) and tactile (touch, taste, smell).

Part Two – Creative Writing

The words you use and the way you write will enhance or detract from the way a reader absorbs the information. There are methods that will support readers of different processing abilities to best receive the information. Visual readers, for instance, do better with more drawings or illustrations, so for them, use visual imagery or metaphors. By doing so, you will be using representational systems.

Visual people may say: 'We don't see eye to eye', 'Point of view', 'Crystal clear', 'That's a different perspective', 'Sketch me an outline', or 'Clear as mud'. All these are clichés, which below I comment on.

To write for visual people, give visual descriptions such as 'show, don't tell', as well as sketches and visual images.

Auditory people: 'Sounds good to me', 'I hear you', 'That work gives me a buzz', 'Music to my ears', 'Tone it down', 'We are on the same wavelength', 'We are in harmony', 'It was drummed into me', 'Calling the tune', 'Shouting the odds'.

For auditory people use words and phrases that they 'hear'.

Tactile people: (physical sensations) 'Rubbed me up the wrong way', 'Gets up my nose', 'He is such a pain in the neck', 'It left a bad taste in the mouth', 'It's on the tip of my tongue', 'I can get my teeth into that', 'Was hard to swallow', 'It's just a different flavour to this', 'A bitter pill to swallow', 'Chew it over'.

Tactile people feel sensation and so use metaphor to evoke physical sensation.

By sending sensory messages according to different peoples' preferences you are more likely to have better results. If you are to write a report, access the general sensory type of the reader. For instance, engineers are more likely to use a different sensory type than artists.

You will not always know what your readers' processing abilities are, so it makes sense to include an array of different techniques, without cluttering the work. As People are a mixture of senses and perhaps one of them is sharper.

Try not to use any of the above phrases given above in your writing, as they are all clichés. Clichés are the lazy writer's pick, and they usually tell and don't show.

Look at the picture below of Faith, the hero dog. The poor little girl was born without front legs, but as you can see, Faith overcame the odds and learnt to walk upright.

Part Two – Creative Writing

> For ten minutes write about the emotion (and wonder) that Faith is likely to evoke in seeing her for the first time. When you write, show me, don't tell me, what emotions are being felt.
> You can learn more about Faith by visiting www.faiththedog.net.
> And yes, Jude, the owner, was kind enough to give me permission to use the picture.

Writing emotion

> Crime and Punishment, by Dostoyevsky, translated by David McDuff; "My dear respected Sir," he began with almost ceremonial formality, "poverty is not a sin – that is a true saying. I know that drunkenness is not a virtue, either, and that's an even truer saying. But destitution, dear Sir, destitution – that is a sin…"

Writing emotion is best done if you use your existing emotions, or the emotions that you have felt in the past. If you do not tap in and use your past hurts or experiences, the emotions you write could be hollow.

> Write a page on how you felt after a fight with a friend. I'm sure this has happened to you. In the piece examine the emotions that you felt and do your best to 'show' them on the page.

For acting/drama, there is the well-known Stanislavsky System of dramatic training, named after 20th century Russian actor Stanislavsky.

Using this system, an actor, in an attempt at greater realism, recalls and invokes past experiences and emotions from which to draw on the emotion or pathos required for the part.

You have seen actors producing memorable scenes, where their vulnerability, fear, panic, hate, anguish, love, silliness, and other emotive expressions are served in their facial, hand and body movements. They do not say, *I am sad*, they show it.

How can they evoke such feeling into a scene? How do you, as a writer, show and convey so much feeling in your message to your reader, without telling?

This is not an easy skill, but like all skills you get better with effort and practice. Do not be afraid – try, test, fail and then succeed.

> *Cry, the Beloved Country* (1948); by Alan Paton
> "Cry, the beloved country, for the unborn child that is the inheritor of our fear. Let him not love the earth too deeply. Let him not laugh too gladly when the water runs through his fingers, nor stand too silent when the setting sun makes red the veld with fire. Let him not be too moved when the birds of his land are singing, nor give too much of his heart to a mountain or valley. For fear will rob him of all if he gives too much."
> *Cry, the Beloved Country* (a novel) was written in deceptively simple prose, but it incorporated a lot of themes that were critical to South Africa (and the world) at the time (and even today).

Below is a sample of convincing and compelling writing by novelist Fay Weldon. She appeals to the emotions to provoke a desire to address financial issues.

> "Lack of money causes misery, anxiety, and early death: the cramping of personality, the limiting of human potential.
> Lack of money prevents us eating properly when we are children, ruins our health, and rots our teeth. Lack of money makes our parents quarrel and take to drink. A lack of money stops us having the clothes we want, the friends we like, the parties we long for. Lack of money stops us having tuition, which would enable us to get an education – makes us end up street sweepers and not doctors. Lack of money induces women to have babies because there is no money for travel or entertainment, or to leave the parental home any other way. A lack of money humiliates us all our lives.
> Lack of money makes us live with husbands or wives we no longer love. Lack of money makes us age earlier than we need. Lack of money makes our hands rough with toil and our brows crease with worry.
> Lack of money keeps us weeping by day and sleepless by night: the terror in our lives is the bill, which can't be paid. Our lives close in the knowledge of failure, we failed to make enough money. We never did what we wanted with our lives. How could we? We didn't have the money. We tell ourselves 'money isn't important,' but it is, it is. We couldn't afford this, we couldn't afford that, and our lives and our friendships and our marriages and our children were thereby curtailed, limited."

Exclamations and emotion

You can add exclamations to your work, such as: "when Meggie saw the size of the ice-cream she blurted, 'Wow'." These are sounds or utterances that exclaim. They are usually not real words as such, but can be use in dialogue to reduce word count. The writer could have said, "Boy, this a very big ice-cream," but "Wow" says it better.

2

Words expressing emotion or amazement are called interjections. Here are more:

yuk, arch, ugh for not nice.
phew, whew for escape.
tut, tsk for annoyance.
brr for cold.
grrr for angry.
sh shoosh, pssst for be quiet.
hmm, mmm for thinking or contemplating.
oww, ouch for hurt.
wheeeee! for speed or excitement.
aaaah for understanding.
eeek, yikes for I need to get out of here.
hmpg, humph for okay or to interrupt.
oops, whoops made a mistake.
phwoar when boy sees stunning girl.
duhh for when something dumb happens.
gulp for fear.
whooppy, for delight.
ooo aarh for surprise
(Different countries or cultures have different interjections.)

When using interjections make sure you are in the right period, as words drift in and go out of use, and using the wrong word can date the work. For example, the word spiffy was in vogue over one-hundred years ago and means good or cool. Make sure they are used for the right character, as I would not expect the President of the United States to shout, "Whoopy… I won the election".

Part Two – Creative Writing

Be aware that some of the above examples have become clichés, such as wow!! so use them sparingly.

The following is a few ways to show emotions through gesture:

She put her knuckles to her mouth and lightly bit on them in thought.

With a slightly tipped head in contemplation, she gave him a withering glare.

His sigh showed his frustration.

She gently touched him on the arm and said...

... patting him on the back, like he was some cherished pet.

Her eyebrows narrowed in concentration.

Her slight side-smile said all he needed to know.

Upon hearing this, he looked towards the ceiling in thought.

In concentration he lightly bit his lower lip.

Many of the above have become clichés. In the section below on Place, there is a section on too little or too much detail. You will learn that authors fill novels with details, just like some examples in the above list. But readers will not remember them, and they become arbitrary. Perhaps there is a better way. Instead of saying "As the killer approached, Joe's heartbeat was so strong..." You could say "As the killer approached, Joe, panicked and wet himself." Readers will remember the fact that Joe wet himself, not the strong heartbeat.

To create your own gestures, observe, and continually observe. Go to different settings and watch people. Write down what they do in a little book. Analyse and understand them. Watch movies and soaps and take in the actors' gestures. Watch people when they are caught in the rain; or how they walk against a strong wind; or how the father addresses the young waitress, while his wife and children watch him make a fool of himself; or a young boy feeding the pigeons in the park.

2

Thoughts after something is said can reveals a lot. "You could have done better!" Could prompt the following:

- She squirmed inside.
- She smiled a knowing smile.
- She looked at the traffic and pretended she couldn't hear him.
- A defiant gleam filled her eyes as she stared at him.
- Screw him, she thought.
- "Oh me. Look at the time" as she avoids the issue.

Lastly on emotion:

> Mother Earth
> I'm dying, slowly dying. Yet nobody listens, nobody cares. The tragedy is not only about me, or humans. It's about all the animals that live on me. All will perish with me – all species will be gone, forever.
> And what about me? I have a soul and I have feelings. I don't want to die. Yet my veins are full of your poisons and my air, which was once clean and pristine, is now murky and heavy. Not to mention the toxins that have killed the goodness of my soil. The aura that surrounds me is lifeless, all colour gone. The trees and plants are dwarfing and suffocating, dying of the same cancer as I am.
> We had a deal, you, and I – I would let you live here, but only if you respected me. Part of our deal was that you would bathe in the enchantment of what I had to offer, glory in my beauty and abundance. I am the Creator's art. But you have destroyed me. You have whored me, brutalised me and left me to lie in my own vomit, too weak and sick to help myself. You changed the environment so what was once controlled is now out of control. Yes, it is you, man, who has caused the wind to destroy, rain to flood and sun to dry, desecrate and burn.

> I cry tears of anguish for the lost future – do you not realise what you have done? How can you be so shallow in your outlook? Your law of Thou shall not kill is ignored when it comes to me, your mother, as every day the stake is driven deeper, the gases more intoxicating. My death is slow and full of pain. I am not meant to die. Not yet anyway. I trusted you. I did not know that you were without a soul, callous and uncompromising. In generations to come when I am a lifeless, barren ball of darkness, sombrely floating through the universe, the annals of history will show that man was the selfish race.

Inventing experience

As a novelist, there is no way you can experience everything you want to write about. This is when you have to invent experience. All great novelists do this well.

Do you think those cowboy authors spent thousands of hours chasing real bandits across hundreds of miles of desert countryside? How many sci-fi authors have lived in outer space? Not many, I'm sure. And what about those steamy bedroom scenes… no, let's not go there.

So how do you invent experience? Research is a starting point, as is reading the work of others who have been 'there'. Then with that information, settle yourself down, quieten your mind, and in a half meditative state do a mental 'daydream' and put yourself in the position you are to write about it. Feel it, see it, and be it. Have a recorder with you and record all that you see and feel, and then write it down.

You may have to do this several times to get all that you need to make a great experience for your readers.

When bestselling author **Barbara Taylor Bradford was** asked what advice she would give new novelists, she said, "You can't be a novelist if you can't imagine things happening that have never happened; you need to be a really good liar. A **novel** is a monumental lie that has the ring of truth."

> From *The Grapes of Wrath* by John Steinbeck (1939):
> Man, unlike any other thing organic or inorganic in the universe, grows beyond his work, walks up the stairs of his concepts, emerges ahead of his accomplishments. This you may say of man—when theories change and crash, when schools, philosophies, when narrow dark alleys of thought, national, religious, economic, grow and disintegrate, man reaches, stumbles forward, painfully, mistakenly sometimes. Having stepped forward, he may slip back, but only half a step, never the full step back. This you may say and know it and know it.

Tension

Storytelling tension is what keeps readers buying novels as we all like a little bit of adrenaline.

Look for the hope and the despair. One juxtaposed against the other gives that tension. If one of your characters has a plan to achieve a result, such as stopping the theft at the last minute, do not tell the reader beforehand. However, if the character is set to fail, then outline the plan beforehand. If the plan is to succeed there is more tension in not knowing the plan beforehand. Conversely, tension is created if you know the plan, and also know it will fail.

I recently finished *Sunday Times Bestselling Author* Stephen Leather's novel *Slow Burn*. *Slow Burn* is a thriller but some sixty pages before the end, the resolution was so obvious that the thrill went out of it for me, and *Slow Burn* became a *Slow Read*. The only reason why I continued reading because in my mind there had to be a twist. There was no twist. I was disappointed.

Ask yourself hundred times, who is this character that I am writing about? Try and get into their head.

Over-writing kills tension stone dead.

There are many ways to increase tension:

- You can use dialogue: "touch that and you're dead..."
- You can tell the audience, such as when Lawson told us in advance that "Poisonous Jimmy was a nasty character".
- You can show: "then, she slapped his face..."
- You can use an observer. As given above, Paul is (seemingly) sleeping with Ella, and the son is the likely murderer, but we are not certain, and it is this uncertainty that creates tension.

How are you going to transport your readers? That is what creative writing does.
Do a mind-map on how tension is created in the above reading, *Mother Earth*. This is also a good time to add sub-plots and story-twists.

2

Characterisation

If our characters are to be real, then it follows that they mimic real people. Real people are spontaneous and unpredictable. Real people do not live to a plot – their plans usually do not go to plan because of the nature of cause and effect in normal life. For your characters, and the events that happen to them to be real they do better if 'free' of plot. Their lives and the story must unfold naturally and spontaneously, according to what has previously occurred, where the chain of events is not known at the start. There can be a rough approximation of this, but the freedom is what makes a story and character real. Is the character all that he seems to be? Is he a wolf in lamb's clothing? Is the virginal girl as innocent as she pretends? Is the loving father 'overly' loving with other little boys? Creepiness creates interesting characters and tension.

Stories need characters. Good or bad characterisation can break a story. A bad story can be enlivened with good characterisation. If you want your stories to be interesting you need to craft good characters.

As many stories are mini-lives, characters are prone to change, grow, and develop. Behind facades lay the opposite traits. The motivational speaker who is a narcissist to those who are close to him – the swindler who regularly donates to animal shelters – the warrior general who is afraid of spiders – the beggar who is selfish – the cold-hearted priest – the mother of the murdered girl forgives the culprit...

How do you create such characters? What I have learnt from reading well over a thousand books is that authors who write great characters have a wonderful grasp of human nature. They are observers of people and have a natural affinity for psychology. They find people fascinating and can dismantle and reassemble the way people think and act. They are able to offer physical traits that match the mindset of the character

Part Two – Creative Writing

in all their various moods, displaying the complexities that we humans have.

The Brontë sisters were particularly adept at this. From Anne Bronte's *Agnes Grey*: "Often she would stubbornly refuse to pronounce some particular word in her lesson; and now I regret the lost labour I have had in striving to conquer her obstinacy."

And from the same book: "She certainly looked charming as she strolled lingeringly, with her closed book in one hand. In the other, a graceful sprig of myrtle which served her as a very pretty plaything... her bright ringlets escaping profusely from her little bonnet, and gently stirred by the breeze, her fair cheek flushed with gratified vanity, her smiling blue eyes, now slyly glancing...."

But I suspect we know more of human nature than what may immediately be expressed. Observe, read, watch people on TV and in movies and you will get better at creating characters. It helps that if your main character is a plumber, that you know something about plumbing. You could look like a bumbling fool if your main character is a neuroscientist, and you failed elementary physics, as he or she is likely to be inauthentic.

Try this. Watch a soap on TV for a month. Have a character card for each person in the show. On each card write down the character traits and the inconsistencies of each character. At the end of the month, compare all the characters. By doing so you will have 'reverse engineered' what is likely to be a well-planned human sketch in all its complexities. Where the modest girl has a series of sexual relationships, or the shy boy fronts up to the thug. Even if, like me soaps are not your thing, you will find there are characters you despise, and some you like, and that is why people are entranced by long running soaps. It is not so much the story – it is the 'real' human frailty that draws.

• • •

2

Author of The World Behind, Rumaan Alam, says that he is poor at describing his characters. He feels it is more pragmatic to 'show' them through the things they buy, the items they surround themselves with, the books they read or don't read, their clothes, the suburbs they live in, the TV shows they watch, their opinions, what they drink and eat, who they vote for. Alam spends a lot of time describing these things to the reader. He visits their cupboards, raids their mind, surveys, their lounge room.

> Reread the above and try writing a character script for two pages where you 'show' the reader who the character is through his or her actions/habits/desires.

Individualistic characters are remembered. A good character is so distinct in his behaviour from other characters that it becomes his style. Even a mostly passive character like Jane Eyre is still remembered for her strength in restraining herself. She is remembered because she fought with her desires. Here is an examples that exemplifies Jane Eyre's strength in restraining herself and fighting with her desires. One notable passage that illustrates this is when Jane confronts her feelings for Mr. Rochester despite the societal and personal obstacles she faces: "I am no bird; and no net ensnares me: I am a free human being with an independent will, which I now exert to leave you." - Charlotte Brontë, "Jane Eyre"

In this quote, Jane asserts her independence and strength of will by refusing to succumb to her romantic feelings for Mr. Rochester, despite the intense emotional turmoil it causes her. This demonstrates her ability to restrain herself and to stand firm in her principles, even in the face of desire and temptation.

Most are familiar with Scarlett O'Hara's (spoiled brat) and Rhett Butler's (playboy) characters in Margaret Mitchell's *Gone with the Wind*. However, I wager that many can't recall the actual story line. Not that the story line was lacking – it was quite compelling, but the characters were just so captivating.

> *To Kill a Mockingbird*" by Harper Lee (1960):
> "Jem and I found our father satisfactory: he played with us, read to us, and treated us with courteous detachment."

Character Sketch

For each main character it pays to do a character sketch as this is how you will get to know your characters, make them interesting, and keep them consistent. Perhaps you could write something like:
"Joseph hated being called Joe and was miffed each time it happened. He'd aggressively reprimanded the culprit – who invariably enjoyed the rise from Joseph."
"Although he tried to find his feminine side, he was too entrenched in the 'men don't cry' culture of the time. This resulted in vacillating from one aspect to another without rationality."
"Christina, a no-nonsense girl doesn't care who she hurts, as by her own confession she must be brutally honest to be true to herself."

2

The name of the character must help the reader recognise the character. Ethnicity, period, and culture can all affect character and the name. Remember, some cultures allocate meaning to names, such as this snippet from *The secret under the mahogany tree* by Feng Ping: "As Xiaomei played her music with Wang Jing's child, she felt her heart miss a beat. Only then she understood why Wang named his son Xiaosong (pine), as her name was Xiaomei (plum flower). In Chinese culture, both the plum flower and pine tree belong to the three evergreen plants and were regarded as auspicious. Wang Jing still remembered her and kept her name in his mind. She..."

Be careful when using names from cultures other than your own. Do your research. For example, in China, until the mid-1900s, a person usually had three names besides his or her surname: the name given by their parents; the name granted to a person at the beginning of adulthood; and a less formal name chosen by the person themselves. Sometimes there is even a fourth name, an English name, such as Bill, for their English contacts.

Do you want a name that no one can pronounce and is so clumsy that it slows the reading? Maybe you give them the name because it fits their character, like plain Jane. In the Western world, names like Paul, John, Susan, Christina are common, is your character common? And there are period names, for example the 90's saw many Kylies' filling up nurseries.

There is a history of extravagant names that seem to be enjoyed. Double barrel names like Esme-Rose could give a powerful and unique quality that may sound right to the reader.

Many authors take a lot of time and thought into their name selection, perhaps more so than new parents do for their newborns.

Part Two – Creative Writing

Thomas Harris's *The Silence of the Lambs* was made into a spine-chilling psychological thriller movie and for good reason. His main character (Hannibal) was created with such brilliance it is breathtaking. The mind of Harris and the way that the story was put together, in my mind, is beyond a mere mortal. There is so much wisdom, philosophy, understanding of human nature, all crammed into one masterfully told story that it gave me goosebumps.

Early in the story when FBI agent Clarice Starling is sent to interview Doctor Hannibal Lecter. Lecter, a psychopath who had mutilated numerous people and was incarcerated in a high security asylum for life. It is believed that Doctor Lecter, with his abnormally high intellect and deep knowledge of psychology could help in discovering who the current serial killer is and what drives him. Here is an excerpt from the work:

"...when he spoke again, his tone was soft and pleasant. "You'd like to quantify me, officer Starling. You're ambitious, aren't you? Do you know what you look like to me, with your good bag and your cheap shoes? You look like a rube. You're a well-scrubbed, hustling rube with little taste. Your eyes are like cheap birthstone – all surface shine when you stalk some little answer. And you're bright behind them, aren't you?...

... Starling raised her face to him. "You see a lot, Doctor Lecter. Here is the question you're answering for me right now, whether you mean to or not; are you strong enough to point that high-powered perception at yourself? It's hard to face. How about it? Look at yourself and write down the truth. What more fit or complex subject could you find? Or maybe you're afraid of yourself?"

"You're tough, aren't you, offices Starling?"

"Reasonably so, yes."...

... "Has anyone ever sent you a Valentine, offices Starling?"

2

"Yep."

"I've been thinking about Valentine's Day. It reminds me of something funny. Now that I think of it, I could make you very happy on Valentine's Day, Clarice Starling."

"How, Doctor Lecter?"

By sending you a wonderful Valentine. I'll have to think about it. Now please excuse me. Goodbye, Officer Starling."

"And the study?" Asked Starling.

"A census taker tried to quantify me once. I ate his liver with some fava beans and a big Amarone. Go back to school, little Starling."

Hannibal Lecter, polite to the last, did not give her his back. He stepped backwards from the barrier before he turned to his cot again, and lying on it, became as remote from her as a stone crusader lying on a tomb.

Starling felt suddenly empty, as though she had given blood. She took longer than necessary to put the papers back in her briefcase because she didn't trust her legs."

Both characters are marvellously revealed through dialogue, showing the complex Lecter, with his ingenious and evil mind, and the simpler, non-conniving Starling, in stark contrast. Lecter enjoys the drama. Starling is focused and driven.
The interaction, which is early in the book, revealed the personalities and their drives. It supports the characterisation that the narration is in third person.
Books with great characterisation requires lots of dialogue, so they tend to be larger books than most.

• • •

> "Mr. Bennet was so odd a mixture of quick parts, sarcastic humour, reserve, and caprice, that the experience of three-and-twenty years had been insufficient to make his wife understand his character."
> *Pride and Prejudice* by Jane Austen.

Embracing the Fun of a Foreign Character in Your English Novel

In your character sketch, you have eight main characters plotted for your novel. How to create eight unique and believable characters? One way is to take one of the characters and make him or her a foreigner.

Crafting a foreign character can be an exciting and creative process, especially when playing with accents, pronunciations, and common tense errors.

Showing Through Actions and Dialogue

It is easy to "show" (not telling), when it comes to multilingual characters. Consider how different native speakers might distort English words, adding an extra layer of authenticity and humour to your characters. For instance:

New Zealand: "iee" instead of "e" (e.g., "fish" sounds like "feesh").

- **Vietnamese:** "o-pp-en" for "open."
- **French:** "sink" for "think."
- **German:** "vater" for "water."
- **Spanish:** "esport" for "sport."
- **Russian:** "ze" for "the."
- **Japanese:** "riber" for "river."

- **Chinese:** "sree" for "three."
- **Indian:** "wery" for "very."
- **Brazilian Portuguese:** "eez" for "is."

A German or Swiss character might say, "I have looked everywhere for a 'chob'" instead of "job," or use incorrect tenses, adding to their charm.

Accents and Pronunciations

When writing dialogue, accents can be a powerful tool to reflect a character's background. However, it's essential to do this with care and authenticity. Research and understand the phonetic traits of the language you're portraying. For example:

- **French Accent:** "Zis is not what I 'ad in mind. Why must you always do zis?" (Dropping the "h" sound, using "z" instead of "th.")
- **German Accent:** "Zis is a very good idea. Ve should go to ze market now." (Pronouncing "w" as "v" and "th" as "z.")
- **Italian Accent:** "Ah, you make-a me laugh! Let's-a go to da store." (Incorporating the rhythmic and melodic qualities of Italian speech.)

Common Tense Errors

Another way to reflect a character's foreignness is through common tense errors. For instance:

- **Russian:** "I go yesterday," instead of "I went yesterday."
- **Chinese:** "He go to school every day," instead of "He goes to school every day."
- **German:** "She didn't knew," instead of "She didn't know."
- **French:** "I have 20 years," instead of "I am 20 years old."
- **Spanish:** "I am agree," instead of "I agree."
- **Japanese:** "He is work," instead of "He is working."
- **Italian:** "I no understand," instead of "I don't understand."
- **Turk:** "She will can do it," instead of "She will be able to do it."

- **Brazilian Portuguese:** "I have saw him," instead of "I have seen him."
- **Arabic:** "She coming tomorrow," instead of "She is coming tomorrow."

These linguistic quirks can help make your character's dialogue more authentic and engaging.

Cultural Expressions and Gestures

Different cultures have unique expressions and body language that can add depth to your characters. Italian body language, for instance, is expressive and can enhance the dialogue with gestures like:

The Pinched Fingers Gesture
Raised Eyebrows and Wide Eyes
Hand Flick from the Chin
Leaning Forward
Pointing with an Open Hand

These cultural nuances help paint a fuller picture of your character's personality and background.

Language Switching and Code-Switching

Multilingual characters might switch between languages mid-sentence, or inadvertently use a word from their native tongue. This adds realism and can also be a source of humour. For instance, a native French speaker might say, "Merci," instead of "Thank you," or "Voilà," instead of "There it is."

Humour in Multilingualism

The potential for humour in multilingualism is vast. Characters might directly translate idioms from their native language, leading to amusing expressions. For example, a German character might say, "I have a stone in my stomach," instead of "I'm worried."

Be mindful, though that some idioms may require contextual explanations. Direct translations often need adjustments to fit the context of your story, ensuring they remain relatable to your readers. But if you have to explain, then the passage may become passive.

Language Barriers as Plot Devices

Language barriers can also serve as plot devices, creating conflict or opportunities for character development. A character might struggle to express themselves correctly, leading to misunderstandings, such as saying, "I want your bra," instead of "I want your bar."

While we've focused on the humorous side, a foreign mindset can also be an asset in your story. A character's unique cultural perspective might help them navigate situations that others can't, adding richness to your narrative.

Balancing Language Use

Balance is crucial. Overdoing accents or language differences can make the text hard to follow or seem caricatured. However, when done thoughtfully, these elements can enrich your characters' backgrounds and create a unique voice.

Dialects and Regional Variations

Don't forget that characters from different regions or counties within the same language group can have their own dialects and speech patterns. Portraying these accurately requires the same careful research and mindfulness.

Part Two – Creative Writing

Summarising

By following these guidelines and your own observations, you can create foreign characters who are not only authentic but also add richness and humour to your story. Why not take a character, make him/her foreign, and entertain your readers while deepening the narrative?

Must a character be endeared by the reader?

This question sparks my enthusiasm. Is it not more about crafting a compelling story, one where realism mirrors our shared imperfections, where each of us harbours some form of flaw? And as the author, must you have affection for the characters you create? Perhaps there is liberation and amusement in conjuring characters who are unwashed, rude, obstinate, egotistical, sexist, impatient, shallow, flatulent, or an arrogant know-it-all. Some authors revel in presenting charming yet sinister figures, possibly living vicariously through their characters' felonious deeds.

Consider the act of plunging a knife into soft flesh, feeling the squelch as blood makes the knife handle slippery, and staring into the stunned, horrified eyes of the victim. While humans possess the capacity for complete malevolence, societal norms usually prevent us from acting upon it. However, as a writer, you can explore these darker realms without real-world implications. You can delve into the freedom of imagination without moral consequence.

Characters who aren't necessarily likable often mirror the complexities of real individuals more accurately than we care to acknowledge. The creation of unlikable characters is akin to holding a mirror to the less savory aspects of humanity. In truth, an author who introduces a despicable character is, in essence, being authentic.

• • •

2

Bestselling author Francine Prose, when discussing if readers have to like a character? "No, but they must be intrigued enough to want to read more about them."

Some authors allocate to their main character a unique trait. Kojak ate lollypops; Columbo wore that hideous trench coat; Homer Simpson is fat and lazy; Rhett Butler had the smile of a cad; Shakespeare's Lady Macbeth is strong, ruthless, and ambitious. Some carry a walking stick; or have a wiggle as they walk; could be that she drools; or farts; or belches; or has a constant and slightly annoying laugh; a nervous twitch; a gap in the front teeth; extra-large ears; a fetish for feathers in a range of hats; has a lisp or emits a slight whistle when speaking; hunched back or military-parade-like posture; where she has the habit of adjusting her breasts in her bra, or that she constantly and absent-mindedly flicks her underpants' elastic through her dress to adjust for comfort.

One of my favourites was in the movie *As Good As it Gets*, where actor Jack Nickolson's portrayal of the obsessive-compulsive protagonist was brilliant. I remembered the obsessive behaviour, but not the character's name (Melvin Udall). I had to look it up.

The possibilities for traits are endless, but they must fit the character, and be uniquely yours; predictable and referred to in a timely manner. When done well, you will have endowed your protagonist with a memorable trait that will stay with the reader for years.

Allan Folsom in his book, *The Exile* started the book with protagonist John Barron having to change identity (as a survival tactic) to that of Nicholas Marten. So, for 232 pages we had John Barron. But then, until

• • •

Part Two – Creative Writing

page 690, it was Nicholas Marten. The transition was smooth and well-conceived. It could have been clumsy.

Literary Realism (warts and all) in writing shows the character without romanticising them.

What if you invented your characters first and then built the synopsis around the characters?

Or you start off with a basic idea of the story and then design the characters with their personality traits. This is an unusual way of creating a story, but it certainly means that the characters fit the story. Do not have your character so complex that they confuse the reader and slow the plot.

Have a look at the below character sketch that one of my clients inserted in the introduction for her book. The story idea was set in South America.

The characters are as follows:

<u>Wantago</u>: a young up and coming indigenous leader, too young to be catapulted into a position of intrigue, where his wit and passion clash with the European administrators.
Was he guilty of the murder that he was apprehended for?

<u>Johanne</u>: an anthropologist, who's canny mind links the past to the future with telling accuracy.

<u>Wayne Cartwright</u>: long deceased but his legacy still pulls the strings.

<u>Emanuel Semler</u>: the brilliant specialist who is caught between the authority of the government department he works for, and the respect for the people that he serves.

Joseph Stone; Director, Liaison Unit of indigenous affairs: an indigenous puppet of the administrators or a renegade in disguise?

Wantila: a drunk, but one who carries the secret that can unravel the past.

Edwardo Decastro; Chief Minister: Imperious in his belief of native management, and that 'white is right'.

Janita: beautiful, emotional, and fragmented from a life of racialism… Will she emerge triumphant or broken?

Gejont, a tribal Elder; a traditional who follows the guidance of the ancestors and ruthlessly disciplines all who dare to break 'the Lore'.

A powerful story with powerful characters set in a make believe country in South America. Culminating on top of the sacred volcano of the region … who will lose their nerve first?

As you can see, the author has created a story guide so that the story is easier to follow. I liked her method and think that it makes for intrigue.

Learn to visualise your players

As soon as you start putting your first words on paper, you need to see who you write into the story. In your mind's eye, include the details of your character. Close your eyes and try to think of the colour of his hair, the structure of his face, his eyes, nose, clothes, weight, height, skin colour, his way of walking and his peculiarities. Once you have his image in your mind, include those details in your narration. Remember at the start of this manual I spoke about the production table. Have a file for your main characters.

There are two aspects you need to blend to create the full essence of the characters of your stories:

- Physical appearance

> **Part Two – Creative Writing**

- Personality

While describing someone with a long nose may capture a physical trait, it falls short in revealing the essence of the person. Readers crave a deeper understanding – the glint in his eye, the melancholy smile, the reasons behind their whimsical gazes into the abyss.

Some authors prefer to show their character's personalities through their deeds and not description. Another way is by sharing the character's thoughts, for example as a blizzard approaches, a character may think: "This young girl has stayed in this house long enough… It's time she left, immediately." From these thoughts, the reader will soon determine the sort of person the character is.

Other thoughts that indicate character: "Oh, I am such a benevolent man. That dollar I gave the street person will make all the difference to his day." Meanwhile, the giver has many millions to his name. Or it could be, "I'm glad I gave the street person that dollar. Wish it was more!" Meanwhile this unemployed lady is going home to a virtually empty fridge.

Below is an introduction to a story – note the characterisation.

> **What would you do if you knew you could not fail (excerpt)**
> The applause was deafening as he ambled to the podium. Although stooped, he carried an air of confidence and distinction that age could not disguise. Somehow, he seemed larger than his diminutive self. Shaggy white hair flopped over his wide forehead. Enormous eyebrows sheltered eyes that twinkled with intelligence. His clothes were those of a gentleman who walks in the park – not dapper, nor pretentious, comfortable perhaps. Most notable was his smile, wide and authentic, the smile of a man who has had a satisfying life…

Did you see the man?

2

Just a phrase or word here and there can make all the difference.

The need for strong characterisation is so important that many writing teachers believe that plot should be dictated by the character, as opposed to the other way around.
This makes sense because if the writing is good, the characterisation and dialogue will be more entertaining and powerful than the plot. Think of some of those great stories by Charles Dickens. They are more about character than plot. Yes, his plots were always intriguing, but the characters make his stories.

Author *Isabel Allende* says: "Passion lives here. Isn't it always true? Heart is what drives us and determines our fate. That is what I need for the characters in my books: a passionate heart. I need mavericks, dissidents, adventurers, outsiders, and rebels, who ask questions, bend the rules, and take risks. People like all of you in this room.
Nice people with common sense do not make interesting characters – they only make good former spouses."
The above was delivered in a TED talk.

When writing about people, places, or events, beware of the stereotypes and contemporary views that may prevail. Each person, event, and place have a deeper story than meets the eye. Your job as a writer is to see that and tell the full story.

If the characters in your novel are only seen as stereotypes they will not be real. The same applies if you intend to do travel writing; look beyond the obvious, and report about the real human side of the people in those places.

Part Two – Creative Writing

Why not write a biography of your main character, and like all good actors, become the character? Include unique dialogue to help to build your characters.

Try not to introduce the reader to more than three characters in the first chapter. And do not introduce a character like dictating a police report about them. Rather, build up the character piecemeal, through dialogue and action, much the same as getting to know someone in real life.

Go to a café and observe a stranger. As the observer, think about how you would describe that person. Try and get a sense of that person through their actions, gestures, facial expressions, and voice (if you can hear them). Write that person into life, and like a caricaturist, think about what features you will exaggerate to give the image that you would like.

Gestures help to define an image or character. A movement, gesture or image adds depth to writing. Studying people and seeing what gestures they use as body language sometimes offers more information than the words. Perhaps the character picks his teeth after eating the cake and wipes the muck on the tablecloth.

Yet author Laura Jean McKay likes her characters to have an air of mystery, even to herself – an element of the unknown, the unpredictable. Within that is a sense of freedom for her writing.

2

Good characters play with our morals. They dismantle our long-developed code of conduct, where the absurd becomes possible – such as when the middle-aged woman falls in love with the wrong man, a man of poor-character she would normally avoid – a devil to most, but seemingly an angel to her. Her usual common sense is derailed by infatuation, her behaviour modified to the point of compromise. The reader can subconsciously mitigate her behaviour.

Here's a real-life example. Australian cricketer Shane Warne died this week. I'll not discuss his incredible ability on the field, but rather the effect of his exploits off the field. The tabloids loved him as he was an infamous news-making machine. His many affairs and controversies were legendary. Most people loved him, even though he was a rogue; the type of rogue they would not want their children to be. However, he was amazingly honest, and took ownership of his mistakes and his fans loved that.

Shane would have made a wonderful character in a book: incredibly talented, dedicated to his sport, intelligent, provocative, generous, and a devil may care attitude that could have derailed his life and career at almost any time.

Lastly on character

As I said at the start of this book, I cannot teach you how to write, but I can (and hopefully have) revealed to you the tools. Often, I have shown you a hammer, a club, and a mallet, as there are variations that suit different authors and stories. The same goes for character building. Each author will have their own method. Read a million books and you will see a million ways. You have got to find yours.

> Charles Dickens, *Great Expectations*
> "Mr. Jaggers's room was lighted by a skylight only, and was a most dismal place; the skylight, eccentrically pitched like a broken head, and the distorted adjoining houses looking as if they had twisted themselves to peep down at me through it. There were not so many papers about, as I should have expected to see; and there were some odd objects about, that I should not have expected to see—such as an old rusty pistol, a sword in a scabbard, several strange-looking boxes and packages, and two dreadful casts on a shelf, of faces peculiarly swollen, and twitchy about the nose."

Narration for Fiction Writing

Do you write your book in first person or as a narrator (third person)?

There are pros and cons for both choices. Some stories lend themselves better to one than the other. Francine Prose, author of the amusing and intelligent book *Reading Like a Writer*, wrote: "The story is choosing the point of view from which it wishes to be written."

I recently read a James Patterson novel written in the third person, except for one character, the protagonist, who was in the first person. I must say it was odd, and I'm not sure if it helped or hindered the readability of the story. The story itself was not affected by the change, but the protagonist was better able to express her thoughts, which was obviously what Patterson wanted.

The same for the book *Divisadero* by Michael Ondaatje (also author of the book {and movie} *The English Patient*). Essentially there were three characters who at the start of the novel were all living on the same farm and revealed in third person. But through circumstances they separated. As each journey was followed it was in their first person. This mechanism helped the reader relate to each character better than if in third person because *I felt this* as opposed to *he felt this*.

The last example is Ruth Ozeki's *The Book of Form and Emptiness*. Some sections of the book are narrated by the protagonist, but much of the story is where "the book narrates itself."

Although the book won the 2022 Woman's Prize for fiction (one of the UK's most prestigious literary prizes), *The Washington Post* described the narrative as cluttered.

When deciding which narrative voice to use, there are limitations to take into consideration. This section shows the many nuances of the two, and with good application much variation can add interest to the narration.

Conversely, when variation is used badly, it can kill the story.

For both first and third person, it can happen that the author's own personality or prejudices can inadvertently be imbedded in the work. Watch out for this.

The author may choose to have the first-person narrator to be as invisible as the writing allows. The other possibility is to let the narrator be a full personality and a joy to be with. The personality, as with all personality traits, can vary from humorous to serious, clever but understated, and knowledgeable. All of these give the author wide scope, and the ability to build interest.

The narrator may give colour by speaking in a local dialogue, or by using colloquial language. The narrator's age, upbringing, and cultural background can also be displayed.

Part Two – Creative Writing

Using an interesting narrator helps the reader get into the story faster. If done well, even before the story unfolds, the reader may relax further into their seat, savouring what is to come.

The following reflects the pros (first) and cons (second) of each narrative style. First is third person narration:

Pros:

- Easier to write dialogue.
- Improves tension as the narrator can hide characters' thoughts and plans.
- Better able to further action.
- The writer knows the psychology of each character and can manipulate the different psychologies of characterinteraction.
- More objective, as there is truth to character descriptions.
- The writer becomes all-knowing and therefore able to give more perspectives.
- Third person narration allows the reader to get more involved with each character.
- Readers have access to the thoughts and actions of all characters.
- Physical and character descriptions are easier to offer.
- Imagine how much power you could give to a protagonist who had a disability or was sightless if done in first person? If done properly, the reader will feel the frustration or success of the incapacitated person.
- Can be more direct.
- Emotion is owned and real.
- Often offers greater authenticity.
- More intimate.
- Can relate thoughts of events to come, evoking tension.

Cons:

- Often, too many pronouns; he, she, they, and them.
- Must be the expert on the ground.

- Often can be less objective.
- It can happen that the first person infuses itself onto the other characters, making the other characters weak.
- If the book has many characters, first person is harder to navigate.
- First person is usually the protagonist, but not always. When not, they are often an active observer that needs to be with the protagonist at all times, everywhere.
- First person only has assumptions about the other characters and cannot be all knowing.
- It is hard to kill off the first person, reducing the tension in some genres such as thrillers.
- Unless he/she has ESP: the first person cannot project the thoughts or actions of other characters like a narrator can.
- Unless the first person is relating a memory, it is in the current tense, whereas third person can offer past and current tense.
- First person must magically be everywhere, so he/she knows what action is happening. That is a limitation.
- Must have met all the characters or meet them at some point. This can be difficult to do.
- Tells the reader how he sees all other characters.
- A third person narrator can tell the reader about the baddy hiding behind the barrel, ready to stab the goody. A first person narrator cannot do that, unless he/she is the baddy hiding.
- Time frames within the story and distance perspectives are harder to navigate for first person.

I prefer to first write first person narration, then convert it to third person later if that is the way I decide to go. By doing so it gives a wider perspective of the story, whilst letting the creativity flow. I then finesse the characters later.

Within this workbook there many examples of good writing. Reread these and listen to the narrator or first person voice and style. This will help you decide which narrative style is best for your book.

> *Jane Eyre* by Charlotte Brontë:
> "I wept as I never had before; great, heavy tears, almost blood-red, fell in a torrent from my eyes; I thought that in another moment I should die if he did not look at me; I longed to embrace him, to press my lips to his, to tell him everything; and yet I dared not speak a word."

Dialogue

Dialogue kills or lifts a story.

- There must be no wasted dialogue; keep dialogue short, simple, never ramble.
- Mannerisms, such as speech patterns, accents, and slang can make for interesting dialogue.
- Reading your dialogue aloud helps to keep it lively.

If you want to write novels, you will need to perfect the skill of dialogue writing. So important is dialogue there are many books dedicated to it.

Good dialogue makes for fine writing. A reader should be able to assess the personality of the character, and see the direction of the plot from dialogue. It should give detail about the speaker, without having to tell. Good dialogue is a 'show' of the character.

The more you know your character the easier it is to make him or her sound natural. As people adopt different styles of speaking, your characters should also be given a different style of speaking to each other.

2

In non-dialogue writing you would usually use the full expression, such as cannot or would not. However, dialogue sounds more natural when abbreviated, such as can't or wouldn't.

Accents and dialogue can fill an important role in a story. They explain class and culture, such as:

"His first words were, 'The Zippy Electric Wheelchair has the performance and manoeuvrability to get yah where yah wanna go. I'm a country boy, coming from outside of Broken Hill in the outback of Australia... No, no, I didn't ride this all the way from there to get 'ere.'"

David Crystal, in his book *Spell It Out, The Singular Story of English Spelling* wrote, "Writers want to give local colour to what their characters say, so they adopt non-standard spellings to reflect the way they speak. The spellings can reflect a regional origin, as with yer (for your), reet (for right) or thowt (for thought). They can simply be a reflection of a rapid colloquial speech style, as with gotcha (got you), gimme (give me), wanna (want to), kinda (kind of) and outta (out of). They can point to a class distinction; people from any social backgrounds, pronounce wot (for what), where there can be a definite lower-class implication – and the same applies to; bin (for been), Missus (for Mrs.). We see hundreds of non-standard forms in the novels of Charles Dickens, Emily Bronte, Walter Scott, and Mark Twain... ...Artemus Ward (wrote) non-standard spelling – 'It is tru,' says Josh Billings, 'that welth won't maik a man virtuous, but I notis thare

• • •

168

Part Two – Creative Writing

ain't enyboddy who wants tew be poor jist for the purpiss ov being good.'"

Then there is the language of texting, such as BTW (by the way), OMG (oh my god) LOL (laugh out loud), BRB (be right back), TTYL (talk to you later).

However, on cultural representation, when using an accent or dialogue type be careful of stereotyping. Racism, sexism, and culturalism all must be avoided if your do not want to offend.

> Write a half page story of two people who want to buy the same donkey from a farmer. This is an opportunity to write dialogue, so use with flair!

> "'Well, I can tell you it made me all over trembly and feverish, too, to hear him, because I begun to get it through my head that he was most free—and who was to blame for it? Why, me. I couldn't get that out of my conscience, no how nor no way. It got to troubling me so I couldn't rest; I couldn't stay still in one place. It hadn't ever come home to me before, what this thing was that I was doing. But now it did; and it stayed with me, and scorched me more and more. I tried to make out to myself that I warn't to blame, because I didn't run Jim off from his rightful owner; but it warn't no use, conscience up and says, every time, 'But you knowed he was running for his freedom, and you could 'a' paddled ashore and told somebody.'"

This piece, *The Adventures of Huckleberry Finn* by Mark Twain shows wonderful (internal) dialogue.

2

Unfortunately, we humans can be banal when it comes to our speech. There is the rhetorical question when passing somebody on the street, "Howdy, how are you, brother?" "Okay... and you...?" Leave that for the street, not your novel. Leave (most) of the greetings out. Perhaps something like, "When she approached, a quick nod passed between them."

I receive many manuscripts where the author proudly announces, "The dialogue is natural, just like I speak." Noooooo!!!, I think to myself. Our day-to-day chatter, our rambling, and obsession to inform so we can be heard is like dousing your ice cream in mud.

We humans seem to have the need to fill empty space with drivel. The "How was your day?" question that is asked every day when the man comes home from work. And, the reply, "So so... and yours?" "We do what we can do, don't we?" "Blar blar, and all the other mundane stuff".

This is our culture and what we are conditioned to do if we are to be polite and fit in. In a book it is boring and slows the pace. Be direct, as each utterance shows character and develops intrigue, furthering the plot – that's it. That is the function of dialogue.

In keeping speech brief, there's no need to elaborate, "My sister died of cancer. It was leukaemia. It was horrible and she had it for three years." Unless the leukaemia or three years is relevant to the story, leave it out – "she died of cancer" should do it.

Do not talk about the weather, not unless the weather has an effect on the story, such as, "The search was called off because of the torrential rain…"

Yet we do not want to produce stilted and boring dialogue because of being too brief and concise. There must be a rhythm and be realistic for modern readers.

• • •

Part Two – Creative Writing

Lengthy dialogue tires the reader and slows the pace of the story. There may be times when a verbose character labours on about a topic close to his heart, or a character is giving a speech, and the topic of the speech furthers the depth of the character or the story. But short, snappy dialogue is better dialogue. Long stretches of dialogue can meander away from the consistent need to further of the story.

In novels, dialogue has another important function, which is to show emotion. The ups and downs as the book progresses – "She blurted out, 'If you walk out of that door now, I... I will...' And she burst into tears."

Dialogue is a perfect mechanism for the author to show the manipulation of one character over another. It can show the high stakes, the fear, the anger, the love, the frustration, the intelligence or lack of the speaker or receiver, sexual intentions, creepy, ego, class hierarchy, ranting, use of power, empathy, self-esteem, contempt, being flustered, giving reassurance, rivalry, despair. The surprise, wit and charm (real or pretend), to penetrate and discover or of keeping certain information to himself, conniving, of melancholy, and creates time-line pressures.

What has been left unsaid?

If you can contrive that the audience will recognise and ponder the implications of what has not been said, you will arouse intrigue.
Vary the way characters speak to different people. For instance, the husband has one mode of speak for his wife (loving or disapproving), and another for his daughter (gentle and supportive, or overbearing), another for his employees (stern, gruff), and a jovial, little-boy-speak, with lots of banter and laughing for his mates at the pub.
All of these do help to round out the character and inconsistencies – the tone, and help to bring realism.

• • •

2

Later, I talk about nuance. In dialogue, nuance is especially important. The right word or phrase can convey the perfect sub plot affect that the author wants; after being asked if Mary (his daughter) is happy, the reply of, "I guess so", is very different from "What's it to you?", or "Whatever!"

> "'I could easily forgive his pride, if he had not mortified mine,' Elizabeth said, with some warmth.
> 'Your resentment of his character?' Mr. Darcy replied.
> 'Yes,' she replied, 'even if he had been twice as good as he is, and had more than double his worth, I would not like him half as much as I do now.'"
> "Pride and Prejudice" by Jane Austen.

Place

It is helpful to give the reader a clear picture as to where the action is taking place. If you take your reader into a room where relevant action is to happen, give their mind an image.

The images do not have to be long-winded, for instance, "The killer chased him down the green rolling hill past fat Jersey cows."

There are stories where place and time are integral, such as historic novels. Perhaps London in the 1800s: dirty, cold, mist enshrouded, where the citizens are a product of their environment. For the reader to occupy the story they must be part of its history, to feel the time and place, as if they were there.

Charles Dickens was as much of a sociologist as an author, and his novels *David Copperfield* and *Great Expectations* are wonderfully explicit. The appeal for me, and I suspect for many readers, is as much about the setting as the plot.

Or perhaps a story is set in 1970s Bulgaria, where the close-knit populous was suspiciously conservative when compared to the West, and where the culture is deemed archaic. A story set in this environment must expose the intrigue that abounds – to correctly understand their identity.

The same goes for sci-fi. It would be hard to picture 500 years into the future without a good sense of time and place. The story may not be enough.

Sometimes plot can fit into almost any setting and the place is just a backdrop for interest. Other times, the place must be created for the plot, such as in the previous example, or if the story is in a detention centre.

Setting, like character given above is best if you know the place, the country, the jail, the police, the hospital. Some authors go out on a limb, describing, say Italy and Italians, when they have never been there, and it still works.

Place can provide a fascinating backdrop to a story. Hemingway was expert at this. His short story, *The Snows of Kilimanjaro,* could have been set anywhere. He starts the story, "Kilimanjaro is a snow-covered mountain 19,710 feet high, and is said to be the highest mountain in Africa. Its western summit is called the Masai ('Ngaje Ngai') the house of God. Close to the western summit there is the dried and frozen carcass of a leopard. No one has explained what the leopard was seeking at that altitude..."

Hemingway placed you in this exotic setting, and the story is launched.

Stefan Zweig's *Chess* was set on a... well, you read the opening, "The usual last-minute bustle of activity reigned on board the large passenger steamer that was to leave New York for Buenos Aires at midnight." That opening sentence gave the setting (passenger steamer), starting and ending locations (New York for Buenos Aires) and the time (midnight).

Setting allows for culture, climate, animals, poverty or riches, and dozens of other interesting aspects. But those interesting aspects often require deep research. If the setting is Spain in the 17th Century, you had better put them in the correct clothes, on the right horses, in the relevant dwellings, using the correct armament, and using the speech of the period. Then, with added subplots of the times (politics, social events, poverty), you enhance the interest even more.

The Newsreader, a captivating television drama/soap airing on ABC (Australia) delves into the intricacies of both personal and professional lives within the world of journalism. Set against the backdrop of the 1980s, the narrative unfolds within the dynamic realm of the fictitious 'News on Six' station. As is common in most TV dramas, the series is replete with elements of clandestine relationships, intrigue, tragedy, and corruption – themes that could be relevant in any era. However, what distinctly ties it to the 1980s and sustains viewer interest is the incorporation of precise historical context in each episode.

The uniqueness of *The Newsreader* lies in its meticulous portrayal of the 1980s, achieved through the inclusion of specific dates and numerous news bulletins from that period. This deliberate effort to anchor the story line in historical events imparts a sense of realism, offering viewers a glimpse into the authentic atmosphere of the era. Notably, the show goes beyond mere thematic elements by providing a genuine sense of historical grounding. For instance, it presents original footage capturing pivotal moments like the Cuban crisis or the return of

Part Two – Creative Writing

Halley's Comet, thereby enhancing the overall authenticity of the viewing experience.

> "It was a queer sort of place—a gable-ended old house, one side palsied as it were, and leaning over sadly. It stood on a sharp bleak corner, where that tempestuous wind Euroclydon kept up a worse howling than ever it did about poor Paul's tossed craft. Euroclydon, nevertheless, is a mighty pleasant zephyr to any one in-doors, with his feet on the hob quietly toasting for bed. 'In judging of that tempestuous wind called Euroclydon,' says an old writer—of whose works I possess the only copy extant—'it maketh a marvellous difference, whether thou lookest out at it from a glass window where the frost is all on the outside, or whether thou observest it from that sashless window, where the frost is on both sides, and of which the wight Death is the only glazier.'"
> *Moby-Dick by* Herman Melville.

There can be too much detail

Russian playwright and storyteller Anton Chekhov, considered by many to be one of the greatest Russian writers of all, opined: "Descriptions should be brief and relevant. Instead of long-winded descriptions of it being a dark night, rather; the round black shadow of a dog or wolf emerged and ran…" He also said, "Best to avoid depicting the hero's state of mind; try to make it clear from the hero's actions." And: "You understand it at once when I say; The man sat on the grass. You understand it because it is clear and makes no demands on the attention. On the other hand, it is not easily understood if I write; A tall, narrow-chested, middle-sized man, with a red beard, sat on the green grass, already trampled by pedestrians, sat silently, shyly, and timidly looked about him... The situation should be grasped at once – in a second."

Details, therefore must be relevant. Place and detail are important, but do not to clutter the work: "... and in the scuffle, the wife picked up his beloved walking stick, and cracked open his skull. Here, the relevant thing is his beloved walking stick." Readers will note the irony and remember the detail.

> *Anne of Green Gables* by L.M. Montgomery:
> "The lake of shining waters was blue—a blue so intense that it seemed rather to be the colour of the sky, reflecting the sun and not the sky itself."

Detail

Place for ambience – detail for relevance, nuance, and affect. It is the pin-pointed detail in a movie murder that the viewer will remember the most. Perhaps the smile on the murder's face, or the way the victim fell to the floor, dragging the curtain down with him. I remember, nearly sixty years later, the blood running down the bathtub in Hitchcock's *Psycho* shower scene.

And we all remember the music that played when the shark was about to attack in the movie *Jaws*. This music was never played at any other time of the movie, and you never really saw the shark. But the instant the first bar of the music sounded, shivers tingled along spines. And now, even if the movie is not on, and you hear the music, instantly you recognise it was from the movie *Jaws*.

Part Two – Creative Writing

Perhaps what makes Dr Spock so memorable are his ears. All of these things are detail.

To come up with these relevant details takes skill, but also perhaps a touch of luck. They could be likened to the punchline of a joke, where the telling is better than the actual joke.

The perfect exemplar of detail is crime author Lee Child. It is said one of his novels is sold somewhere in the world every nine seconds.

From *Die Trying*: "Go right through, sir, she said. The general will be along in a moment.

Webster walked into the chairman's office and stood waiting. He looked out through the window. The view was magnificent, but it had a strange metallic tint. The window was made of one-way, bulletproof Mylar. It was a great view but the window was on the outside of the building, right next to the River Entrance, so it had to be protected. Beyond was a view of the Capital, across the Potomac. Webster could see sailboats in the Tidal Basin, with the last of the evening sun glinting low on the water…"

> Julian Barnes' – *Arthur & George* (shortlisted for the Man Booker Prize 2005). When describing Authur (an author): "Arthur believed in looking – at the glaucous eye of a dying whale, at the contents of a shot bird's gizzard, at the facial relaxation of a corpse who was never to become his brother-in-law. Such looking must be without prejudice: this was a practical necessity for…

The advice is just as relevant now as it was in the 20th century.

2

Humour and fun

Will the humour land at your reader demographic? For instance, an old bricklayer's joke is, "He lays as many girls as bricks." To a bricklayer that's funny. To everyone it misses the mark. Your humour could miss the mark if the joke is too old for young people (dad jokes) or too current for old people. Understanding the demographic of your audience is important in humour.

This next reading demonstrates how humour can draw the reader into a story:

> Allan Weisbecker – *The Calling*
> Setting the scene – Malcolm was twelve and hid in the boat under a net to go fishing with his father, the captain.
> "Malcolm's breath was coming easier now but the cramps in his legs were even worse, and the cold felt deeper, down into his bones. Then, suddenly, his teeth started chattering.
> "What in 'ell is that?' It was Ted, who was only four feet away. "That clickin' sound." Malcolm felt the net stir; Ted was poking around.
> "Sounds like something in the twine."
> Malcolm gritted his teeth to stop the chattering. Joe spat and said, "Prob'ly a crab clicken' his claws."
> Then they hit a deep rut and Joe farted something spectacular.
> Malcolm almost laughed and thought maybe he'd made a noise trying to hold it in. He found it hilarious when grown-ups farted ...

Humour can increase the interest that the reader has for your writing, as just about everybody loves humour. Be careful because failed humour will render the section passive. Because humour has the potential to fail, go in gently. It is also a good idea to run it by some of

Part Two – Creative Writing

your friends before it goes to the publisher, or worse, the market. There is no perfect formula, but as you continue practicing humour you will get better at it. Author Henry Green advises: "Laughter relaxes the characters in a novel…'And if you can make the reader laugh, he is apt to get careless and go on reading."

Try your hand at writing humour. The work must be half a page on anything that you would like to write on. Before you start, here are some tips:

- Think about an incident that made you laugh and then develop the theme from there.
- Approach humour with child-like glee.
- It doesn't matter if it does not work right away, as you can tweak it.
- It must be funny to you, otherwise it will not be funny on the page.
- Good dialogue supports humour.
- The editing process can add to the humour.
- John Boyne (author of *The Boy in Stripped Pyjama's*) suggests, "Have fun and enjoy yourself when doing humour. You will get better as you go along."

Now go ahead and give yourself some laughs.

HELPFUL TIPS

In your journal record anything you hear or see that is funny. You will see how easy it will be to insert in a story, perhaps with slight amendment to fit the story and characters.

2

> **Yogi**
> He is cunning, mean, and ruthless. A dog of the world, that is, he probably has all the dogs of the world within his genes. His sandy-coloured fur seems to propagate itself throughout the house as it clings to everything he touches. He is below knee height and looks a bit like a feather duster but with a shaggy tail inserted into one end and a floppy eared muzzle at the other, whilst four legs support the bushy undercarriage. Yogi was endowed with an amazing ability to remain puppy-like, even with the passing of years.
> Yogi believes that he is master of the house and in his canine evolutionary scale, cats are at the bottom of the chain. According to Yogi, felines are one-cell brained creatures of little worth. Next are postmen and meter readers, who have been put on earth for sport. Female dogs are second from the top and paramount are male dogs. Yes, you guessed it, Yogi is a male dog and so all are subservient to him.

Damon Runyon wrote tongue in cheek humour. This snippet is from his short story *Butch Minds The Baby*.

Big Butch is peeled down to his undershirt and pants, and he has no shoes on his feet, as Big Butch is a guy who likes his comfort. Furthermore, he is smoking a cigar, and laid out on the stoop beside him on a blanket is a little baby with not much clothes on. This baby seems to be asleep and every now and then big Butch fans it with a folded newspaper to shoo away the mosquitoes that wish to nibble on the baby. These mosquitoes come across the river from the Jersey side on hot nights and they seem to be very fond of babies.

"Hello, Butch," I say, as we stop in front of the stoop.

"Sh-h-h-h!" Butch says, pointing at the baby, and making more noise with his shush than an engine blowing off steam. Then he gets up and tiptoes down to the sidewalk to where we were standing, and I am

Part Two – Creative Writing

hoping that Butch feels all right, because when Butch does not feel so good, he is apt to be very short with one and all. He is a guy of maybe six foot two and a couple of feet wide, and he has hairy hands and a mean look.

In fact, big Butch is known all over this man's town as a guy you must not monkey with..."

John Irving, the very funny author of *The World According to Garp,* in his *The Water-Method Man* when writing a letter to his friend, stated, "Couth, I have felt close to you ever since I caught your clap from Elsbeth Malkas..."

When your book cover, or testimonial suggest the book is written with humour then this is what your readers expect. Deliver what you promise. If the readers' expectations are not met by what's been either written on the cover or in the flap of the book, they'll certainly be disappointed.

Carry Fisher has many one-line funnies in her writing. Such as before being a successful actress she spoke of being broke, "...not even having enough money to buy things I did not need."

Your story though is not a joke book. If you pack it with one liners, you will lose the plot. Humour must flow, not clunk.

Comic Relief

Comic Relief is a literary and dramatic device employed to inject humor into a story, play, or narrative, thereby lightening the mood and alleviating tension. This technique introduces amusing characters, witty dialogue, or comedic situations, providing the audience or readers with a temporary respite from more serious or intense elements.

Key insights about comic relief:

Purpose: The primary objective of comic relief is to offer a break from the emotional or dramatic intensity of a narrative, contributing moments of humor to balance the overall tone of the work.

Contrast: The effectiveness of comic relief lies in creating a deliberate contrast between lighter, humorous elements and the more serious or dramatic aspects of the story. This contrast enhances the impact of both serious and humorous moments.

Character Types: Comic relief often manifests through specific character types, such as the witty sidekick, the bumbling fool, or the character with a humorous perspective on unfolding events.

Timing: Strategic placement within the narrative is crucial for effective comic relief. It is typically introduced to interrupt or follow moments of tension, conflict, or high emotion.

Genres: While commonly associated with literature and drama, comic relief is a versatile technique employed in various art forms, including film, television, and everyday conversations to break tension. Its frequent use at the end of TV dramas is notable.

Cultural and Historical Context: The nature of comic relief can vary based on cultural and historical contexts. Humor that resonates in one culture may not have the same impact in another. And, be aware of offending people of different cultures and be aware of sexism. Classic instances of comic relief can be found in Shakespearean plays, where humorous characters or scenes are introduced amid tragedies. In the tragedy, *Hamlet,* Shakespeare employs the character of the gravedigger to introduce comic relief. While digging Ophelia's grave, the gravedigger engages in witty banter with Hamlet, injecting humor into a play known for its dark themes and tragic events.

In modern storytelling, comic relief adds a touch of humor to diverse genres such as science fiction, fantasy, and crime. Notable authors like Kurt Vonnegut, Jodie Houston-Lau, and Arundhati Roy offer insightful examples through their works.

Where used in the Harry Potter Series by J.K. Rowling, Rowling often uses the character of Ron Weasley as a source of comic relief. Ron's humorous reactions, awkward moments, and comical observations provide a light-hearted counterbalance to the intense and sometimes dark events surrounding Harry and his friends.

The film *Thor*, Ragnarok incorporates comic relief throughout, with characters like the witty and sarcastic Loki and the scene-stealing rock creature Korg. The humor in this Marvel movie serves to alleviate tension, adding a playful and comedic element to the otherwise epic and dramatic storyline.

Remember, that while comic relief provides humorous moments, its effectiveness hinges on maintaining the overall coherence of the narrative. When well-executed, comic relief enhances audience engagement by offering moments of levity amidst more intense or serious themes.

Storytelling

Throughout this workbook you have read many stories. I have used stories to reinforce ideas and to offer tools that will help you to remember that point, such as Stevie telling us he is a soccer player, even though he is only eight years old. In this respect, stories are a valuable aid in teaching and influencing.

Storytelling and plot are intricately intertwined elements in narrative creation, each relying on and enhancing the other to craft a compelling and engaging story. Storytelling serves as the vehicle through which the plot unfolds, providing the narrative structure, context, and emotional resonance that brings the plot to life.

Through vivid descriptions, character development, and the artful use of language, storytelling breathes depth and meaning into the plot's events.

On the other hand, the plot acts as the backbone of the story, offering a sequence of events, conflicts, and resolutions that give purpose and direction to the narrative. It creates the framework within which the storyteller can weave their tale, offering a roadmap for the characters' journeys.

Together, storytelling and plot form a symbiotic relationship where the storyteller utilises plot elements to build tension, intrigue, and emotional investment, while the plot, in turn, provides the storyteller with the raw material and structure needed to convey a cohesive and impactful narrative. In this dynamic interplay, storytelling and plot collaborate to captivate the audience, making the storytelling experience richer and more immersive.

Part Two – Creative Writing

Ernest Hemingway – *The Old Man and the Sea*

'Now!' he said aloud and struck hard with both hands, gained a yard of line and then struck again and again, swinging with each arm alternately on the cord with all the strength of his arms and the pivoted weight of his body.

Nothing happened. The fish just moved away, slowly and the old man could not raise him an inch. His line was strong and made for heavy fish and he held it against his back until it was so taut that beads of water were jumping from it. Then it began to make a slow hissing sound in the water, and he still held it, bracing himself against the thwart and learning back against the pull. The boat began to move slowly off toward the north-west.

The fish moved steadily, and they traveled slowly on the calm water. The baits were still in the water but there was nothing to be done.

'I wish I had the boy,' the old man said aloud. 'I'm being towed by a fish and I'm the towing bitt. I could make the line fast. But then he could break it. I must hold him to give line when he must have it.'

'Thank God he is traveling and not going down.'

'What I will do if he decides to go down, I don't know. What will I do if he sounds and dies, I don't know.'

'But I'll do something…'

He held the line against his back and watched it slant in the water and the skiff moving steadily to the north-west.

'This will kill him,' the old man thought. 'He can't do this forever.' But four hours later the fish was still swimming steadily out to sea, towing the skiff, and the old man was still braced solidly with the line across his back.

'It was noon when I hooked him,' he said. 'And I have never seen him.'

He had pushed his straw hat hard down on his head before he hooked the fish and it was cutting his forehead.

2

> He was thirsty too and he got down on his knees and, being careful not to jerk on the line, moved as far into the bow as he could get and reach the water bottle with one hand. He opened it and drank a little. Then he rested against the bow. He rested sitting on the upstepped mast and sail and tried not to think but endure.
> Then he looked behind him and saw that no land was visible. 'That makes no difference,' he thought. 'I can always come in on the glow from Havana. There are two more hours before the sun sets and maybe he will come up before that. If he doesn't, maybe he will come up with the moon. If he does not do that maybe he will come up with the sunrise. I have no cramps and I feel strong. It is he that has the hook in his mouth.' 'But what a fish to pull like that. He must have his mouth shut tight on the wire. I wish I could see him. I wish I could see him only once to know what I have against me.'...

As this workbook is titled, *How to Transform Words into Stories*, I give you more on storytelling.

In the book *The Halo and the Noose, the power of storytelling and story listening in business life by* Graham Williams and Dorian Haarhoff, the authors offer the following advice:

"Recent research is showing that story is a way to engage the disengaged in the workplace, that listeners suspend disbelief and counter-argument, that people prefer reaching their own insights, that well told stories stick in the memory and stimulate action."

The Old Man and the Sea is a wonderful story, but Hemingway is really teaching the reader about perseverance and character. Yet, not once does he talk about perseverance or character. What better way to teach than through the medium of story? If you have never read this novella, do so.

Part Two – Creative Writing

If you have read this workbook with attention and done the exercises, you are probably on the way to be a good storyteller.

Mathew Fox reminds us, "We are all endowed as storytellers, there's a mystic in all of us."

> "It is only with heart that one can see rightly, what is essentially invisible to the eye."
> *The Little Prince* by French Author Antoine de Saint-Exupery

From now on it gets harder. Using your 'newly found' understanding of creativity, write a story no shorter than 400 words on: *Who was the mystery man?*

Here are some unique aspects of storytelling with examples:

Unreliable Narrator – utilising an unreliable narrator adds an intriguing layer to the narrative. The audience is presented with a perspective that may be distorted, biased, or incomplete, challenging them to question the authenticity of the story.

● ● ●

187

For example, in Gillian Flynn's *Gone Girl* (a chilling spine thriller), the alternating perspectives of the protagonists create ambiguity and keep the reader guessing about the true nature of events.

Nonlinear Narrative Structure – departing from a linear timeline can create an engaging and thought-provoking reading experience. Nonlinear storytelling allows for the exploration of different timelines, perspectives, or events, adding complexity to the narrative.

Example: Christopher Nolan's film *Memento* unfolds backward, revealing the story in reverse chronological order, forcing the audience to piece together the plot as the protagonist does.

Interactive or Participatory Storytelling – engaging the audience actively in the storytelling process allows for a personalised experience. This can be achieved through interactive fiction, choose-your-own-adventure formats, or immersive experiences.

In *Bandersnatch*, an interactive film from the *Black Mirror* series, allows viewers to make decisions that influence the protagonist's choices and the unfolding narrative.

Storytelling Through Multiple Mediums – expanding the story across various mediums creates a transmedia narrative, providing audiences with a more immersive and interconnected experience.

Example: *The Blair Witch Project* not only had a successful film but also used a website, fake documentaries, and additional media to create a comprehensive and convincing backstory.

As did the Australian soap, *Home and Away* when one of the characters was abducted from a campsite. For weeks after there was 'an authentic' missing-persons bulletin by the TV channel, supposedly broadcasting the disappearance, as if a true event.

Storytelling through Silence – sometimes, the absence of words can be a powerful storytelling tool. Allowing moments of silence to convey

> Part Two – Creative Writing

emotions or pivotal points in the narrative can create a profound impact. We spoke about this above but here is another example: In the film *The Red Turtle*, directed by Michaël Dudok de Wit, the absence of dialogue enhances the emotional resonance of the story, relying on visuals and sounds to convey its depth.

Storytelling with Cultural Integration – weaving cultural elements into the narrative adds authenticity and richness to the story. This can include folklore, traditions, or historical events specific to a particular culture. Salman Rushdie's *Midnight's Children* intricately blends Indian history and mythology, creating a narrative deeply rooted in the cultural tapestry of the subcontinent.

Each of these unique aspects contributes to the diversity and innovation within storytelling, offering fresh and compelling ways to

> Here are some quotations from well-known authors on the art of storytelling:
> George Orwell – "The best stories... tap into universal human emotions. People all over the world have the same heartbreaks."
> Ernest Hemingway – "When writing a novel, a writer should create living people; people not characters. A character is a caricature."
> Isabel Allende – "Write what should not be forgotten."
> J.K. Rowling – "There's always room for a story that can transport people to another place."
> Ray Bradbury – "We are cups, constantly and quietly being filled. The trick is, knowing how to tip ourselves over and let the beautiful stuff out."
> Maya Angelou – "There is no greater agony than bearing an untold story inside you."
> F. Scott Fitzgerald – "You don't write because you want to say something, you write because you have something to say."
> Margaret Atwood – "A word after a word after a word is power."

engage audiences across various mediums.

What follows is a brief introduction on Interactive fiction (IF). IF is a form of narrative that allows the audience, often referred to as 'players' or 'readers,' to participate actively in the storytelling process. It combines elements of traditional literature with interactive gameplay, enabling individuals to make choices that directly impact the progression of the story.

This genre often involves text-based narratives, where players navigate through a series of choices or commands to shape the outcome of the plot.

These quotes reflect the diverse perspectives and wisdom of renowned authors, emphasising the importance of authenticity, individuality, and the power of storytelling to connect with universal aspects of the human experience.

Developing and honing storytelling skills takes practice, feedback, and a continuous commitment to improving one's craft. Whether writing novels, screenplays, or any other form of storytelling, a combination of these skills contributes to creating engaging and memorable narratives.

Trust yourself to write compelling stories:

- Trust that your memory will supply you with a wide array of experiences that you can tap into.
- Trust that your general knowledge is good enough to supply facts.
- Trust that your intuitive powers and creativity will be there for you.
- Trust that your creativity will be on hand.
- Trust your brain to be methodical in its approach to the work.
- Trust your ability to learn and grow your writing skill.

> Part Two – Creative Writing

- Trust that you can write it well enough.

Thomas Maan (Nobel Prize for Literature) reminds us:
Follow the words:
Let them lead you
forget logic
A pen with freewill
is you unfettered
Can you trust yourself
if you don't
you'll never
   Reach what you can reach.

Trust that you can write a scene as well as Wilbur Smith does:

> Wilbur Smith – *A Time To Die*
> The sun rose above the papyrus and immediately the mist twisted into rising tendrils and then was gone. The water lilies opened their cerulean blossoms and turned them to face the sunrise. Twice they saw large crocodiles lying with just their eye-knuckles exposed. They sank below the surface as the dugout slid towards them.
> The swamps were alive with birds. Bitterns and secretive night herons lurked in the reed-beds, little chocolate-brown jacanas danced over the lily pads on their long legs, while goliath herons as tall as a man fished the back waters of the lagoons. Overhead winged formation of pelicans and white egrets. Cormorants and darters with serpentine necks, and huge flocks of wild duck of a dozen different species...

2

 Cartoon Character (have fun with this) Meditate on creating a new cartoon character for four minutes. Then for three minutes, write in what your mind created in bullet points. Mind map it for four minutes to develop the plot. Write the plot – pour it out, do not worry about grammar, spelling or flow, just get it out. Spend as long as you need on the writing.

 *2019 Pulitzer Prize winner, Richard Powers, when discussing authenticity said, "There is often the risk that a moral fiction becomes didactic. The solution though", he advises, "is in good storytelling and using compelling characters."*

By now you understand what is required for good story telling. To summarise:

Effective storytelling involves a combination of skills that engage and captivate the audience, such as:

Creativity – the ability to generate original and imaginative ideas, plots, and characters.

Importance – creative thinking is essential for crafting unique and compelling stories that stand out and capture audience's interest.

Character Development – the skill of creating well-rounded, believable characters with distinct personalities, motivations, and arcs.

Importance – strong characters drive the narrative and make the audience emotionally invested in the story.

Plot Structure – understanding the principles of effective storytelling structure, including exposition, rising action, climax, falling action, and resolution. A well-structured plot ensures a coherent and engaging narrative flow.

Conflict and Resolution – the ability to introduce and resolve conflicts within the story, creating tension and satisfying resolutions. Conflict is a driving force in storytelling, and resolving it in a satisfying way contributes to the overall impact of the narrative.

Dialogue Writing – crafting natural and engaging dialogue that reflects character personalities and advances the plot. Well-written dialogue enhances character development and makes interactions authentic and interesting.

Emotional Resonance – conveying emotions effectively through storytelling to evoke empathy and connect with the audience. Emotional resonance enhances the impact of the story and makes it memorable for the audience.

Pacing – controlling the speed at which the story unfolds to maintain the audience's interest and build suspense when needed. Proper pacing ensures that the story neither feels rushed nor becomes monotonous, through tools like comic relief, keeping the audience engaged.

Setting and Atmosphere – creating vivid and immersive settings that contribute to the overall atmosphere of the story. A well-defined setting enhances the reader's experience and helps establish the tone of the narrative.

Narrative Voice – developing a distinctive narrative voice that reflects the tone and style of the story. A strong narrative voice contributes to the story's identity and can make the storytelling more memorable.

Adaptability – the ability to adapt storytelling techniques to different genres, mediums, or audiences. Being adaptable allows storytellers to cater to diverse preferences and effectively convey their message.

2

Attention to Detail – noticing and incorporating small details that enrich the narrative and contribute to world-building. Attention to detail enhances the overall realism and depth of the story.

Audience Awareness – understanding the preferences, expectations, and emotional triggers of the target audience. Tailoring the storytelling to resonate with the audience increases the impact and reception of the story.

Opening, Middle and Resolution – ensuring you have an intriguing opening (the hook), maintaining interest in the middle, and closing all loops for the resolution.

Editing and Revision: Let's go back and refresh our memory to the below chapter to see how important the edit and revision process is.

Part Three – Genre

In this section:

- Self-Help.
- Romance.
- Sci-Fi.
- Christian novels.
- Literary.
- Coffee table books.
- Young adults.
- Historical fiction.
- Script writing.
- Suspense/thriller/et cetera.
- Short stories and novellas.
- Writing for children.
- Trends in writing genre.
- Poetry.
- Illustrations.
- Magazine and newspaper writing.
- Report writing.
- Other writing tips.

Genre is a categorisation tool used in literature, film, music, and other forms of artistic expression to classify works based on shared characteristics, themes, styles, or conventions. It helps audiences and creators navigate the vast array of creative works by providing a framework for understanding and organising them into distinct categories. Each genre has its own set of defining features that distinguish it from others, such as setting, tone, plot structure, character types, and narrative style. Genres can range from broad categories like fiction, non-fiction, drama, and poetry to more specific genres like romance, science fiction, fantasy, mystery, horror, historical fiction, and many others. While some works fit neatly into a single genre, others may blend elements from multiple genres, leading to hybrid or crossover works that defy easy classification. Ultimately, genres serve as a means of both categorising and communicating the essence of creative works, helping audiences find stories that align with their preferences and providing creators with frameworks for artistic expression and innovation.

The following is a brief overview of different genres that may help you decide what you want to write (the list is not exhaustive).

Adult Novels, as opposed to Children's or young adult novels

"Adult novels" typically refers to fiction books written for and marketed to adult readers, as opposed to children's or young adult novels. These novels are often characterised by their themes, content, and complexity, which are more suited to an adult audience. Adult novels may cover a wide range of genres, including literary fiction, romance, mystery, thriller, science fiction, fantasy, historical fiction, and more.

What distinguishes adult novels from those aimed at younger readers can vary, but generally, adult novels may contain more mature themes, complex characters, and nuanced storytelling. They may explore issues such as relationships, identity, societal issues, politics, and existential questions in greater depth and with more sophistication.

Adult novels are intended to engage adult readers and often tackle topics and experiences that resonate with the complexities of adult life. While there's no strict boundary between adult and young adult literature, adult novels typically target readers who are over the age of eighteen and are looking for more mature and thought-provoking content in their reading material.

Self-Help books

Do not write the book to be the guru. Be the guru who loves writing.

Many writers write their book thinking that by doing so the audience will think they are 'the Guru' – after all, if he has written a book he must know what he's talking about.

That is not the right attitude to produce good writing. If you learn to love the writing it will flow, and the message will be firmer – your audience will know you are the Guru – you will have shown them, and not told them.

What you will also find is that the publishers you approach will also see and know the difference.

People do not buy what you do, they buy to help themselves.

Then how do you tell the story of why you do it?

You tell it through being authentic. You tell it with empathy. You tell it from the heart, you use your experience, you tell it through creativity.

If you are to be the guru, then you want to be authentic.

3

 *The word authentic has its root in the word author. So be an authentic guru author!*

Writing self-help is probably one of the easiest forms to write in. But if you really want to help your readers, take your time, and research it well to support your arguments.

Romance novels

> *Romeo and Juliet* by William Shakespeare (1597): "But, soft! what light through yonder window breaks? It is the east, and Juliet is the sun. Arise, fair sun, and kill the envious moon, Who is already sick and pale with grief, That thou her maid art far more fair than she."

To enter the world of fluctuating emotion, hope, despair, the vicarious lives of others where the reader is affected but distant from the protagonists – all with the hope of a happy ever-after.
There are many formats in this genre: dramatic, comedy, erotic, as subplot, all for escapism.
Romances are perennial, popping up every year to a demanding audience. As I write this, there are pandemics, wars, an acceleration of family violence, and more, and so readers want touchy-feely stuff, they want to hide in soft books.

Part Three – Genre

In times past, publishers had specific requirements as to what they wanted to see in a romance novel. The *Mills and Boon* formula was famous for the supposed method of the perfect romance. Yet, Valerie Parve, member of the Order of Australia for her contribution to Art, has written seventy novels, and sold thirty-four million in twenty-nine languages. She said, "There is no one way to write a romance novel. Nor is there a secret that can be applied to any writer and any story."

Some have great pleasure in writing romance, but how do they take on and explore the extremes of emotions? How do they build the tension to be high stakes: *does Joe love me? Will Hilda leave her partner for me?* For compelling romance, there needs to be good character development.

Some of the emotive words that you may need to explore in your romance are: control, need, duty, passion, desire, guilt, crushes, passion, lust, baggage, sex, emotion, trust, break-ups, heartbreak, unconditional-love, conflict, marriage, cheating.

Will it be a first love, or second, third or fourth time around? First love has a unique quality, with a devil may care attitude, as it is all about discovery. A fourth time round love comes with baggage, experience, and excessive caution, fearing repeated patterns of lost love. A virgin's first love will be very different to that of a menopausal woman.
Will it be boy to girl, girl to girl, boy to boy, a bi-sexual boy in love with a girl and boy at the same time? How do they identify?
What about deep love of the wrong person, such as a thirty-two-year-old teacher falling for a sixteen-year-old student? Forbidden love. Love does not follow the rules and can strike at any time.
Does the sexual aspect show romantic development, or is it raunchy, or do you gloss over it?
Is it acceptable for a wife of many years to be unfaithful for a 'true love' that has recently emerged? The husband would feel that it's cheating.

• • •

3

The wife would justify it because in her mind it is true love. The 'other party', how does he see it – could be just a fling and has no intention of leaving his wife and family.

When do you reveal that the love is reciprocated or is it to be unrequited?

Then there are all the conversations, for me the best part of the writing. This is where you give depth to the characters and the relationship.

If the book is a romance, the love, certainly from one of the parties, must be intense. But if there is a mainstream plot and the love is a sub-plot, then it does not need to be as intense.

Does the love require a happy ending? No, it does not, but you are likely to have a lot of miffed readers. I experienced just that with one of my books (I will not tell you the book name as it would spoil the ending), where I had emails asking me to rewrite the ending.

How do you 'show' the love she has for him? If the protagonist thinks in the first person, *I love him* is telling, as is *I love you* in dialogue. Once again, as given in characterisation (and specifically Anton Chekhov), where the love is displayed through action as the below shows.

• • •

Part Three – Genre

> *The English Patient,* by Michael Ondaatje offered stories within a story. It is Beautifully written, and study of characterisation and subtle romance. Katharine; "The night of her insistence on parting. She sits, enclosed within herself, in the armour of her terrible conscience,
> He is unable to reach through it. Only his body is close to her.
>
> "'Never again. Whatever happens.'
> 'Yes.'
> 'Do you understand?'
> He says nothing, abandoning the attempt to pull her within him.
> An hour later they walk into the dry night. ... She sees one tear and leans forward and licks it, taking it into her mouth... He has not asked if her husband is home in that high square of light, across the street.
> Now there is no kiss. Just one embrace. He untugs himself from her and walks away, then turns. She is still there. He comes back within a few yards of her, one finger raised to make a point.
> 'I just want you to know. I don't miss you yet.' His face awful to her, trying to smile... But they have separated already into themselves now, the walls up at her insistence, 'You will she says'...
> 'From this point on in our lives,' she whispered to him earlier, 'we will either find or lose our souls.'"

Meg Mason, author of *Sorrow and Bliss*, was asked if she likes her male protagonist. She replied, "Usually yes… I have to."

Today's publishers are less pedantic than the Mills and Boon type of formula. But they are just as rigorous in their scrutiny. They want romance novels that are well-written, with a great plot and originality. It can be spicy, but it is the overall story and romance that they are looking for.

• • •

3

Today's readers are less likely to pursue mindless escapism. They want good stories, real characters, and scintillating dialogue that briskly moves the story along.

In an interview, author of *Shuggie Bain,* Douglass Stuart said when asked the question: "What does he get from writing romances."
His reply:
"Oh, definitely the tenderness of young love".

Categories of Romance

Romance novels have encompassed almost every genre. If you like to write history, you can write romance history. Historical novels with heady romance have massive appeal, as does comedy-romance. After all, a kiss is a kiss in the 2020s or 1800s.

Perhaps sci-fi is your thing, and there are many who would love to read romantic sci-fi.

> *Pride and Prejudice*" (is chock-full of juicy writing) by Jane Austen (1813): "In vain I have struggled. It will not do. My feelings will not be repressed. You must allow me to tell you how ardently I admire and love you."

Science Fiction (Sci-Fi)

What are you like at speculation? Do you like technology, gadgets, formulas? Does outer space fascinate you? Do you understand chemistry; what about mathematics? Are you up to date on current technology trends and scientific breakthroughs? If the answer to all the above is yes, then you have some of the credentials to write sci-fi.

> Part Three – Genre

The vast expanse of science fiction allows writers to push the boundaries of the known and explore the limitless possibilities of the future, providing an exciting and boundless canvas for storytelling.

I see science fiction now as a survival strategy generally — a metaphorical tool for thinking about the future flexibly and boldly. Ian Watson (science fiction writer) Trouble with Tall Ones, The Embedding, The Jonah Kit.

> "The star-filled blackness of space stretched out infinitely before him, a vast expanse of unknown mysteries waiting to be explored. As he gazed into the abyss, Hari Seldon felt a thrill of excitement coursing through him. This was the beginning of a new era, a time of great discovery and adventure for humanity as they ventured forth into the uncharted depths of the galaxy."
> "*Foundation*" by Isaac Asimov (1951).

Science fantasy, such as fairy stories or *Batman*, appeals to the child within.

Having the above credentials is only the start. As with all good fiction, your characterisation and story must be enticing, where you weave the science and invented technology into a tight and fascinating story. Introduce an improbability, then use logic and the feasibility to overcome it.

If you are to write Sci-Fi, and if you have not had several years in space,

then how do you do this? You invent experience (refer above).
Jules Verne wrote the ultimate Sci-Fi novels of his time. His most famous were *Journey to the Center of the Earth* (1864), and *Around the World in Eighty Days* (1873), both of which became movies.
In his day he wrote about inventions yet to appear, such as aeroplanes, listening to people on a box where the people are on the other side of the country (radio), where paper documents were sent through the air (fax machines), submarines, vehicles, massive tall buildings which became known as skyscrapers, electricity, and all whilst he put down his stories using a quill-ink pen in semi-dark candlelight!
Imagination and an interest in modern technology are prerequisites for the Sci-Fi writer. For those who want to write Sci-Fi, there are literally millions of topics you can explore, such as:

Space Exploration – dive into the possibilities of interstellar travel, colonisation of new planets, and the challenges and wonders of space exploration.
Artificial Intelligence (AI) – Explore the implications of advanced AI, from sentient robots to the ethical dilemmas surrounding their creation and integration into society. (Refer to the discussion on AI and writing in the appendix)
Time Travel – Unravel the mysteries and consequences of time travel, exploring the past, present, and future in a narrative that challenges the boundaries of temporal existence.
This has been done many times but there is better Tech to use now.
Alternative Realities and Parallel Universes – Delve into the concept of parallel universes and alternate realities, where different versions of reality coexist or diverge based on pivotal moments.

Part Three – Genre

Biotechnology and Genetic Engineering – (great field this one) Imagine a world where genetic manipulation and biotechnological advancements lead to new species, enhanced humans, and unforeseen consequences.

Cyberpunk – Explore dystopian futures where technology and societal issues intersect, often featuring high-tech, low-life settings with themes of corporate control and rebellion.

Virtual Reality (VR) – Create narratives set in immersive virtual worlds, exploring the blurred lines between reality and simulation, and the impact of VR on human experience.

Climate Change and Environmental Sci-Fi – Tackle the consequences of climate change, environmental degradation, and the struggle for survival in a world altered by ecological shifts.

Post-Apocalyptic Worlds – in these troubled times imagine societies rebuilding after global catastrophes, exploring themes of survival, adaptation, and the resilience of the human spirit.

Nanotechnology – Explore the microscopic world of nanotechnology, where tiny machines revolutionise medicine, construction, and various aspects of daily life.

Biopunk – Merge biology and technology in narratives that explore the consequences of biotechnological advancements gone awry, often within gritty, urban settings.

Space Colonisation – Envision the challenges and triumphs of establishing human colonies on distant planets, moons, or space habitats.

Speculate on the nature of extraterrestrial life, their civilisations, and the challenges and opportunities that arise from first contact. Craft epic tales set against the backdrop of vast interstellar civilisations, political intrigue, and grand space battles.

3 Mind Uploading and Consciousness Transfer – Investigate the ethical and existential implications of uploading human consciousness into digital realms or artificial bodies.

> (1965) *Dune* by Frank Herbert
> "The desert stretched out before him, an endless sea of sand dunes that seemed to ripple and shift like waves on an ocean. The harsh sun beat down mercilessly, casting long shadows that danced across the landscape. In the distance, the towering cliffs of rock formations rose like ancient sentinels, their jagged peaks reaching towards the sky. Paul Atreides felt a sense of awe and wonder at the alien beauty of this barren world, knowing that it held secrets and dangers beyond his wildest imagination."

Christian novels

All that was written above in romance (of course, except for the spicy bits), applies to Christian novels. That is, the professionalism must be there. And a Christian work is also a self-help work, so the advice in the self-help section applies.

Just knowing your Bible and sprouting thy and thou here and there will not cut it in this day and age.

I once received a manuscript from a 'born again' Christian who thought he was the new messiah. His book was jam-packed with enough fire and brimstone to energise all the power stations of the world. Most of it was directly out of the First Testament. But every so often to show his gentle demeanour, he would tell his 'sheep' (yes, he referred to his would-be readers as sheep – collectively his flock) that we all can make mistakes. This was directed in the most infuriating and patronising way, and if any believed him, then they were like blind sheep.

It was a most difficult job trying to persuade him to be less 'holier than thou' – I am not sure I succeeded – after all, why climb down from his self-elevated pulpit?

Continuing with my diatribe about this chap, he wrote the book for the wrong reasons. He wrote it, primarily to make money. He also wrote it from a position of ego, and the desire to be the 'cult Christian leader.' Remember the earlier topic, *Don't write the book to be the guru*? He was what I was referring to in as much as he thought he would be the instant guru (like, just add water) by producing a Christian book.

The Christian fiction readership market is large and growing all the time, and like all current readers, they are sophisticated and demand quality. Perhaps in this genre the author needs to be even more original than in most. Yes, they can refer to tracks in the Bible, but their writing must be expansive. Nor do readers want to be preached to. Like a mystery novel, your story must unfold where you ultimately show the reader why they should follow Christian ethics, as opposed to telling them. And certainly, do not use guilt as your weapon, because you will not attract people into the fold if you do.

For characterisation: if your protagonist has Christian ideals but a flawed and regressive character, the readers will love it.

Make sure your story has conflict set within a contemporary situation, and if you can finish with the proverbial thunderstorm, you are likely to have done well.

3

Literary writing

Charles Dickens, a literary giant of the 19th century, may have long departed from this world, but the enduring admiration for his literary style and that of his contemporaries persists and is poised to endure for generations to come. The charm and richness of the Victorian era's prose, with its elaborate descriptions, intricate characterisation, and nuanced social commentary, continue to captivate readers and convey a sense of timeless literary elegance.

However, navigating the terrain of this literary style, often filled by its ornate language and elaborate narrative structures, can be considered a venture fraught with risk. The lush, dense prose of Victorian literature, while beloved by many, demands a careful balance to resonate with modern readers and their evolving literary tastes.

Despite the potential challenges, there are instances where contemporary authors have successfully embraced and reinvigorated this classic style. One notable example is the bestselling novel *Cold Mountain*, penned by Charles Frazier in 2003. Frazier skillfully navigated the nuances of Victorian-style storytelling, infusing it with a modern sensibility that resonated with a wide audience.

As readers continue to seek the timeless allure of Dickensian prose, the legacy of this captivating literary style finds new life in the hands of adept storytellers willing to take on the challenge.

Coffee table books

A) a coffee table book is a large, visually appealing book typically displayed on a coffee table or similar surface, often featuring photography, artwork, or other engaging content intended for casual

> Part Three – Genre

browsing and aesthetic enjoyment.

Examples: street food from around the world, festivals and festivities, old cars, nature. The list is limitless.

B) If your book idea is a coffee table book, consider the following implications:

- Weight, when posted it will cost more. International shipping costs could kill international book sales.
- Glossy, costs more to produce and therefore cost more for the buyer, which could reduce sales.
- Fads, coffee table books lend themselves to trends. Is your book in sync with current trends? Could be outdated too soon.
- People limit the number of coffee table books because when they move residences their books weigh a ton. But they do buy them for loved ones and friends as presents (let them have the problem).

Coffee table books need a great layout. Images must be top quality as readers expect perfection.

> Imagine you could follow people and pick up all their wasted hours – what would you do with them?
> Spend at least forty-five minutes on this exercise and fifteen minutes to edit it. Be concise in your imagery and story telling.

Young Adults

Roald Dahl, author of *Charlie and the Chocolate Factory* and *James and the Giant Peach*, and many more, espoused that a good children's book must enthral. Dhal was not only interested in entertaining, he wanted to make the story so good that children became life-long readers of all literature (many did).

Young adults are just as discerning as any reader, just in different ways. They hate being spoken down to or being preached at – they want to be entertained. They love strong characters, coming of age, and good storylines. And, because you will be competing with their devices, you will not have long to grab of their attention.
Young adults like uplifting and humorous stories. They like graphic novels, non-fiction and fiction.

Graphic novels are book-length narratives presented in comic book style, combining illustrations and text to tell a story, often targeting older readers with more complex themes and storytelling techniques than traditional comic books.

As I write this, I am in my seventies, so I would not try and pretend I know what makes them tick. I have too much respect for them to try and 'fit' into that genre. The point being, how well do you know young adults?
But capturing the right idea would be great fun.

Historical Fiction

Historical novels have been less fashionable over the last thirty years or so. But things seem to be changing and interest is growing again.

What about historical accuracy?
Depends. Are you writing a history book with a story, or writing a story with history as a backdrop to garner interest?
If a history book, you may be imagining the characters as there is not

Part Three – Genre

enough detail available, so your history needs to be spot-on, and you need to tell the readers that you have had to 'ad-lib' to fill in the gaps.

If you are using a historical period and events as the backdrop, then your history may not need to be as accurate. Yet, it is always a good idea to make your historical representation as reliable as possible.

The phrase 'loosely based on history' gives the author a safer platform to sit on. If the author's synopsis or marketing material suggests that the story is a historical novel, it is a good idea to add a statement to show that you have deviated from historic fact. This saves the author from losing credibility.

Why write a book loosely based on history?
Many readers want 'the feel' of the period and are not fussy about accuracy. Sabrina Jefferies (author of fifty romantic novels) has tagged her novels as 'Historical Fantasies'. Quite clever, really.

Hanya Yanagihara (*A little life*), loves what she can do with history in the novel. 'History', she says, 'was written from the bias of the times'. She enjoys 'editing' the version of history (playing God) to invent another story. For instance, in her book *To Paradise*, she made the acceptance of homosexuality a perfectly natural thing within society – men knitted, and women spoke about running countries.

• • •

> One of my favourite authors James A. Michener (author of over twenty best-selling historical novels), after submitting one of his last books, *Legacy* (a novel about the forming of the American Constitution) to his publisher, received a call from his editor, who advised, "Upon reflection and consultation with his superiors, the idea no longer appeals. But if Michener would resubmit the work in factual form it would be considered."
>
> Later, Michener was known to say, "When I found out this was all on speculation, meaning I would be paid for my work only if the manuscript were accepted. Yes, at my age (in his eighties), with my track record, with my constant demonstration that my work doesn't require (their) editing, I found myself writing on speculation. This is a tough ball game I'm in, and don't you ever forget it."
>
> (Source The Washington Post)

Historical novelist, Kim Scott (*Deadman Done*), spoke in an interview about his determination to completely deconstruct the language of history to better understand and represent it.

Script Writing

Script writing is different to normal story writing. The difference is analogous to different runners. A marathon runner trains and strategises entirely differently to that of a 100m sprinter – yet, both run. Writing skills are required for all forms of writing, but the script writer has the understanding that it is the actors that will bring the words on the page alive. Actors will play with dialogue, and offer gestures to make them their own. Movies are a visual medium, whereas books are more introspective.

Part Three – Genre

A good actor cannot bring to life badly written dialogue. A bad actor can destroy well written dialogue. A good actor, coupled with good dialogue can be breath-taking.

Many of my authors bring their manuscript for publishing, and say, "While you are at it make a movie". Yeah, sure! They do not understand the implications; often, a story is just too difficult or complex to adapt for the screen.

It could be that your manuscript is good enough for a movie, but can the producer see it as you see it? Or is she the wrong producer, and is not faithful to the story? There are likely to be many elements of your story that are left out. And worse, the producer may think that the watchers of the movie would prefer a different end-resolution. When presented with a new script, a producer will ask, "Why would anyone want to watch this, and is it uniquely different from movies of the same genre?" Their subjectivity can be wrong (apparently both *E.T.* and *Star Wars* were predicted to be failures).

Of course, it is right a director consider the commercial potential as he or she will not be around for long if they make bad commercial decisions.

As I have tried to instil in you, writing as a creative form should never be done with a commercial imperative. This workbook espouses have fun when writing, and writing for a big pay-off should be far from the writer's mind. Writing for the buck often skews the writer's own feelings or morals on a subject.

You take influences from a successful book and multiply it with an unknown book, and unknown author, and many producers are wary.

3

> A script example from the screenplay of *The Apartment* written by Billy Wilder and I.A.L. Diamond (1960):
>
> INT. BAXTER'S *APARTMENT* - NIGHT
>
> C.C. "Bud" Baxter sits at his cluttered desk, surrounded by papers and office supplies. He sips a drink and stares out the window at the lights of New York City below.
>
> BUD: (Sighs) Another day, another dollar. Or in my case, another night, another key.
>
> He takes a drag from his cigarette and exhales slowly.
>
> BUD (cont'd): But who needs a dollar when you've got a view like this? A man could get lost in the city lights, forget all his troubles.
>
> He looks down at the telephone on his desk, hesitating.
>
> BUD (cont'd): Maybe I should call her. Tell her how I feel. But what if she laughs? What if she tells everyone at the office? Nah, better to keep it to myself.
>
> He stubs out his cigarette and gets up from his desk, heading towards the bedroom.
>
> BUD (cont'd): Tomorrow's another day. Maybe things will look different in the morning.
>
> With a resigned sigh, he disappears into the darkness of the bedroom, leaving the city lights twinkling outside the window.
>
> This excerpt from "The Apartment" showcases the sharp wit and introspective dialogue characteristic of Billy Wilder's screenplay writing. The scene effectively captures the protagonist's internal conflict and sets the tone for the narrative that follows.

Another consideration is the marketing, and if there is an adequate budget to tell the movie goers that it exists, while enticing them.

Not all movies derive from books as many are directly scripted.

Part Three – Genre

Film-maker Francis Ford Coppola, *Apocalypse* (based on *Heart of Darkness*), and *The Godfather* was awarded his first Academy Award for *Patton*. Coppola contacted polio as a nine-year-old and was bedridden throughout his childhood. He entertained himself by writing and staging puppet shows and, later, 8-millimeter home movies.

Filming *The Godfather* for Paramount was a frustrating experience, and he did not like some of the studio's ideas. "I had no power," he said, "and yet I had real opinions on how it should be done. And I was always just trying to bluff the studio to let me, you know, do it my way. And it was just the most frightening and depressing experience I think I've ever had." Paramount wanted to set the movie in the 1970s so they wouldn't have to pay additional expense for cars and clothes from the 1940s. They also disagreed with Coppola's casting of Al Pacino and Marlon Brando, but Coppola prevailed.

Many novels are 'adapted' for the screen. Note the word adapted, as the conversion is not straight forward – it's complex.
One such complexity is where the main character starts off as a child, becomes a teenager, then young adult, middle aged and then senior – five actors. Or, multiple countries, multiple eras. The cost of characters, country and research for the eras, clothing, period, all hellishly expensive.

If I was lucky enough to have one of my books selected for the screen, I am not sure that I would want to be involved in the scripting. It would be like spending years cultivating a garden, and then handing it over to a commercial gardener, who in his wisdom, hacks all and sundry with a chainsaw. I would not want to see my work treated as such.

There are many best-selling books that were box office failures as a movie. There are many reasons why this could be. Firstly, no producer can predict the fickle movie-watching public's behaviour. The actors may be top actors, but it still fails. Perhaps there have been a spate of movies with a similar theme or genre. Could also be the scripting from the original book failed to capture the glitter of the original work.

A script writer has conventions that are required to make a good script, such as foreshadowing, contrast, repetition and recurring motifs and the problems of unifying the script. Screenplay structure demands specific attention.

A great book to read on the subject is Making a good script great by Linda Seger.

Lastly, from manuscript to screen, there is usually a minimum of ten years of slog. If you can pull it off, fantastic.

Suspense/Thriller/ Mystery Novels/Crime Fiction

Depending on who you speak to, these categories are lumped in as a one category, or two or four.

Try selling your mainstream novel to a publisher, and unless it is exceptionally good, it is likely to be difficult. But if you offer them a well constructed mystery, you might have more luck. The demand for mysteries is great, but the number of (good) mysteries is few.

The most important rule for all novels is that there is CONFLICT.

Part Three – Genre

Try reading one of James Patterson's novels. Talk about active writing. The punch of the stories usually blasts through from the first line and continues to the last. I suggest that you read several of his books as an exercise on active writing skills.

'If' questions.
When writing a story, keep asking yourself "And if this happened, what then?" Or "and if that happened how would that end up?" Do a mystery mind-map and keep asking why, why? why?

James Lee Burk is a crime writer of distinction. Yet, in the middle of his career, for thirteen years, he had 111 rejections! He was fond of saying, "The gift is inside of the writer and that gift is usually developed over time."

I have never written a mystery, so be sceptical about what I'm about to offer: to write a mystery entails a certain kind of mindset and skill. It is one of intrigue, and analytical power, with a concise method of writing skill, with great storytelling ability. And do you like research? Because you would need to do a lot of it.
For this type of writing, I suggest you find yourself a mystery/thriller writing course.
The time to write a mystery would be considerably longer than it would take to write a mainstream novel of the same word length. Just the research alone could take months.

• • •

3

Psycho

"Norman Bates listened to the rain drumming against the windows of the Bates Motel office. He glanced up as the door opened, revealing a figure silhouetted against the darkness outside.

'My apologies, ma'am,' he said, his voice soft and polite. 'It's not often we get visitors on a night like this.'

Marion Crane stepped into the warmth of the office, raindrops glistening in her hair. She smiled nervously at Norman, feeling a flutter of unease in her chest.

'I hope you have a room available,' she said, her voice trembling slightly.

'Of course,' Norman replied, gesturing to the register book on the desk. 'We have a few vacancies. Let me get you checked in.'

As Marion handed him her driver's license and credit card, she couldn't shake the feeling that something was off about the young man before her. But she brushed aside her doubts, attributing them to the late hour and the storm raging outside.

'You're not from around here, are you?' Norman asked, making conversation as he typed her information into the register.

'No, I'm from Phoenix,' Marion replied. 'Just passing through.'

'Phoenix, huh? That's quite a drive,' Norman remarked. 'What brings you to our little town?'

Marion hesitated, her gaze flickering uncertainly. 'Just...needed to get away for a while,' she said, offering a weak smile.

Norman nodded sympathetically, handing her the room key. 'I understand,' he said. 'Sometimes we all need a break from our troubles.'

As Marion thanked him and hurried out of the office, Norman watched her go with a thoughtful expression. Rain continued to drum against the windows, casting eerie shadows in the dimly lit room."

This excerpt captures the atmosphere and tension of "*Psycho*" as depicted in Robert Bloch's novelisation, providing insight into the characters' thoughts and feelings.

Part Three – Genre

Do your research

L. A. Larkin, author of numerous successful thrillers says she does enough research to know she has a foundation of knowledge to support the premise. And, as the story grows, she spends time making it more credible.

But as an author she can make things up, so it is a cross-pollination of science and fiction to create the most realistic and exciting story. For instance, if your story is a psychologic thriller, you must study the psychology of those characters. You need to research police procedures using the latest technology. Do not write about horrifying coercive control and domestic violence unless you have had direct experience or conducted deep research into the subject as it is complex.

This is a great site to help with research, with over twenty-two million research papers: https://www.academia.edu/about

But what fun it would be... just imagine... having thousands, or even hundreds of thousands of people on the edge of their seats, sweating, hearts thumping... engrossed in your story. Of course, when you create a great character, one that your readers love, it paves the way for potential sequels.

Crime fiction has pace, intrigue, and asks questions. Questions about the consequences of violence, injustice, government action, and judicial systems. They help us question police procedures.

Real crime often reads like fiction, and crime fiction reads like true crime.

3

You need a good plausible story, with procedural, in an interesting setting, where often the crime (or crimes) is almost incidental to a larger story, which forms the backdrop. The story allows the author to sneak in what they want to say.

Does crime fiction or true crime need resolution? It is expected, but not obligatory. In normal life, there are many instances where there are no resolutions or happy ending, so why should it be so in a novel? A lack of resolution raises questions. Some readers derive more interest from no resolution. But most readers want everything all tidied up, and some form of justice given.

Do not have periods of suspense go on for too long. Readers can only hold their breath for so long.

Crime fiction is a good place to develop contemporary social issues.

I enjoy techno-thriller writer is Michael Crichton. He wrote *Jurassic Park* (the book is ten times better than the movie), *State of Fear*, *The Andromeda Strain*, and many more. Crichton's books are so good because of his masterly research, and his story-telling ability. He talks science and technology in a way that the pages seem to turn themselves.

Crichton espouses these two quotes:

"There is something fascinating about science. One gets such wholesale returns of conjecture out of such a trifling investment of fact." – Mark Twain.

"Within any important issue, there are always aspects no one wishes to discuss." – George Orwell.

This last quotation seems to be the determining factor of Crichton's work.

What are the requirements of a thriller writer? The following is praise for thriller writers.

• • •

Part Three – Genre

The first is Allan Folsom's *The Exile*: fast-past, exciting adventure... With a sturdy hero and a despicably clever villain, the novel grabs the readers from the opening scenes and rarely lets them loose. It does exactly what it set out to do: deliver breathless excitement – *Booklist*.

More twists and turns than a strand of DNA – William Blatty, author of *The Exorcist*.

A masterful epic, *The Exile* has the sweep and power of *The Da Vincie Code*, a global enigma of world-shattering proportions and a blistering pace that will singe your trembling fingers – Douglas Preston, *The New Your Times bestselling co-author of Relic and Cabinet of Curiosities*.

And for Stephen Leather's *Slow Burn*: Entertains and whisks the reader along at a breath-taking pace – *Shots Magazine*.
A writer at the top of his game... The sheer impetus of his storytelling is damned hard to resist – *Sunday Express*.

Summarising the above, you will notice such phrases as: breath-taking pace; sheer impetus; fast past; exciting adventure; the novel grabs the readers from the opening scenes and rarely lets them loose; breathless excitement; twists and turns; blistering pace.

Simple enough to do. Good luck!

> From crime fiction novelist Dashiell Hammett, *The Maltese Falcon*: "Samuel Spade's jaw was long and bony, his chin a jutting V under the more flexible V of his mouth. His nostrils curved back to make another, smaller, V. His yellow-grey eyes were horizontal. The V motif was picked up again by thickish brows rising outward from twin creases above a hooked nose, and his pale brown hair grew down—from high flat temples—in a point on his forehead. He looked rather pleasantly like a blond satan."

3

Short Stories and Novellas

Short stories offer economy, but still with waves of complexity, where the pace and framing of the story equal that of longer works. The challenge is what to leave out.

> It was not long before an ant found him, drawn by the smell of meat. It climbed up his left cheek and took a bite to assess the value of its find. Exploring further, it entered the moist cavity of a nostril, where it paused and drank before going higher up the passage.
> White Feather felt the ant climb his face. He shook his head to dislodge it but this did not work. The bite released a fresh wave of fear.
> He had two points of awareness, one that death was going to be long and painful. The other, that he felt every footfall of the ant as it scaled his cheek and entered his nose.
> The ant expressed pheromones – it was not long before a legion came, first in ones and twos, then by the dozens…

Short stories are my favourite writing genre. Invariably I fall in love with each one that I write – all my beloved children. I also enjoy reading short stories, especially when written from well-known authors, as I can see the difference from their longer form.

Short stories are often for those who may not have the time or desire to read a full novel. Conversely, readers of full novels want to ensconce themselves in an experience or journey. You need to keep this in mind when you write a short story. That is why it must have punch in a few pages or less – a quick fix.

Part Three – Genre

Things to consider when writing short stories:
   The difficulty is giving each story in a collection its own unique voice.

- Your opening must grab. The ending needs to be strong and thoughtful.
- Short stories are not big sellers, generally. They are starting to sell better than in the past, but if it is what you love, do them anyway.
- Do not have too many characters in each story, perhaps three. And keep in mind you do not have enough time to give details about the characters.
  Readers will know your characters through good dialogue, actions, and their thought process.
  Each new story will need new characters and a new setting.
- Short stories need to be works of perfection. Each word handpicked, so to speak. Certainly, over-writing kills the story.
  There is a balance between descriptions given and furthering the plot, with an eye on the reaching the end.
- The story should be fast paced with good dialogue. Above we spoke about tight writing. Short stories need to be tight.
- They need simple plots.
- Short stories of a contemporary nature can influence, which offers opportunity to write on politics, gender equality, business and morality, drugs, company monopolies. Short stories can be your platform.
- Writing stories of ancient times influence less. They are more about interest.
- Protagonists have less time for long introspection.

In John Steinbeck's novella *Of Mice and Men*, Steinbeck shows us on page three that Lennie is not all that smart, despite being a grown man. This showing is perfect for novellas and short stories, thereby saving words. But listen to who George is through George's dialogue: "George knelt beside the pool and drank from his hand with quick scoops.

'Tastes all right,' he admitted. 'Don't really seem to be running, though. You never oughta drink water when it ain't running, Lennie,' he said… 'You'd drink out of a gutter if you was thirsty.' He threw a scoop of water onto his face and rubbed it about with his hand, under his chin and around the back of his neck. Then he replaced his hat, pushed himself back from the river, drew up his knees, and embraced them. Lennie, who had been watching, imitated George exactly. He pushed himself back, drew up his knees, embraced them, looked over to George to see whether he had it just right. He pulled his hat down a little more over his eyes, the way George's hat was."

Novellas don't generally sell as well as full novels. I think buyers look at the cost and the number of pages and think the value is not there. Another reason may be that novellas are obviously small books with a small spine. When placed on a bookshelf in a shop, it is likely to be lost amongst books with bigger spines. Also, those small spines are difficult to read.

Those who like novellas often do so because they can read one in a single sitting.

Novellas can have a quicker turnaround, especially if the audience wants your next book.

They are usually anything from 17,000 to 60,000 words.

Celebrated author Jerry Jenkins suggests that new authors would do best to not start with a full novel. Rather learn the craft with short stories/novellas. He says, "That's akin to going for your PhD before finishing elementary school."

Part Three – Genre

> Pick a topic and write exactly 400 words on it. Then whittle it down to 300 words, then down to 200 words. You will see it can be done. This is wonderful practice for short stories and poetry, and indeed all writing.

There are many more genre that you could embrace. Here is a list of genre that was not discussed above. There are many sub-genre (not listed)

Writing for children – as this is such a large topic it has its own chapter further on in the book.

True Crime – involves real criminal cases and events, exploring the details of actual crimes, investigations, and legal proceedings.

Memoir – personal reflections and memories, often centered around specific themes or experiences.

Satire – uses humor, irony, or exaggeration to criticise or mock people, politics or society.

Fiction – imaginative storytelling that may include elements not based on real events.

Non-fiction – factual writing based on real events, people, and information.

Fantasy – genre involving magical elements, mythical creatures, and fantastical worlds.

Mystery – writing that revolves around solving a puzzle or uncovering hidden truths, typically in a crime or detective context.

Thriller – intense and suspenseful narratives that aim to keep readers on the edge of their seats.

Horror – writing designed to evoke fear, dread, or unease in the reader, often through supernatural or macabre elements.

Adventure – features exciting and daring journeys, often involving risk and exploration.

Biography – tells the life story of a real person, detailing events, experiences, and achievements.

Autobiography – A self-written account of one's own life.

Drama – focuses on realistic portrayals of characters and their emotional struggles.

Comedy – intended to amuse and entertain, often through humor, wit, and satire.

Poetry – expressive and rhythmic writing that often explores emotions, ideas, and imagery. There is a chapter on poetry below.

Essay – a short piece of non-fiction writing that presents an argument or explores a particular topic.

Science Writing – communicates scientific concepts and discoveries to a general audience.

Ghostwriting – Ghostwriting is the practice of writing material on behalf of someone else who is credited as the author. This can include books, articles, speeches, blog posts, and more. Ghostwriters typically work behind the scenes, often signing nondisclosure agreements to keep their involvement confidential, while the credited author takes ownership and receives recognition for the work.

Writing for children

This requires a special skill. You must read your work to different groups of children and have someone observe the children to see if their attention holds. If not, you need to make serious changes to the book.

Part Three – Genre

Popular children's author Robert Lawrence Stine recommends hanging out with kids so you can understand them better.

You are not only writing for the children, but also for their parents as they invariably purchase the book.

Write a plot and storyline, words, and phrases, that are relevant to the age group you are targeting. When we ask the author of a kid's book they have submitted to us, "What age group is the work aimed at?", they usually shrug their shoulders, and say between eight and fifteen. This is too broad – eight-year-olds and fifteen-year-olds have different tastes. You need to be in the mindset of the age group you are writing for.

Children like the protagonist to be a few years older than themselves; so, if the child is three, they want to read about five-year-olds. If they are eight, they want to read about ten-year-olds.
Keep the sentences short and clear, with no big words.
Children's laureate Cressida Cowell, author of best-selling *How to Train Your Dragon*, says, "Writing picture books for little ones is like writing haikus for aliens – harder than it looks".

I get asked, "Do illustrations or text come first?" Well, it depends. If the author is also the illustrator, it can be the illustrations first and the text later, or vice versa. But often the author needs to contract an illustrator, so the words come first. The process that I normally recommend for an author is as follows:

3

- You need to determine what each illustration is to depict, so it fits the story. If you do not know, the illustrator is working blind. It is like a movie director leaving the actor to determine each scene. You are the director of your book, so direct.
- It is imperative that the illustrator reads the book, understanding what you want to convey, and understands the age group.
- First let the illustrator offer you samples of his/her work. If you feel there is a connection, ask them to create one or two samples of illustrations that you require (they will have read the book).
- Your publisher may have their own illustrators who are likely to be good at their craft. But will they 'get' what you are trying to achieve? Try and find this out before you sign your publishing agreement.
- The author needs to insert instructional text into the body of the story, in the same place as the illustration is to be. The author could insert a box that says something like: *Image 3, show Mary sneaking along the passage, with her faithful dog Snowy close behind...*
- When the illustrator does the first draft, you must scrutinise the illustrations to ensure they are what you want. For instance, it is likely that the author has previously described Snowy the dog, perhaps a white-furred Maltese Poodle – it would not do to have a black German Shepard in the illustration.
- Often though, the canny illustrator intuits something in the story that is not in the text or instructions, which they reflect in the illustrations. The author, therefore, should give the text a final amendment to ensure the illustrations and the text are in sync. For instance, the text may say a low wall, the illustration may show the wall is at a grown man's height.
- Make sure to work with the illustrator reverts back and forth until the images are perfect.

Part Three – Genre

Another aspect that the author should understand is the book size, and which text and illustrations go on which page. By doing so, the illustrator can create the sketch relevant to the orientation (portrait or landscape), amount of text, and sizing. This can save a lot of reworking. The same with colour; is the book to be colour or black and white?

If you are self-publishing, be aware of the Health and Safety aspects of ink, paper, staples, hard corners, non-rip covers, etc. Do your research.

Of late, there have been many kid's books that have a strong moral or teaching component, such as showing the wrongs of racism or bullying. Many of these are very good and are certainly needed. The problem though, is over-saturation. Recently, I read an article that related bookstore managers complaining about the volume of these books, and as good as they are, children still need to be children, and laugh and have wonderment. But Roald Dahl advised, "Never shelter children from the world."

Age and sizes (as recognised by most publishers):
Two to five Y/O's, simple picture books, with up to 300 words.
Six to seven Y/O's are beginner readers, 500 to 3,500 words.
Eight to nine Y/O's are Young Fiction, short chapters up to 10,000 words.
Nine to Twelve Y/O's are Core or Middle Grade Fiction up to 30,000 words.
Above twelve (teens and young adults), 50,000 to 80,000 words.

3

Trends

For young children aged three to eleven, rhyme is important. The words must work together. It must make them laugh (if you're writing a funny story).

David Crystal, in his book *Spell It Out, The Singular Story of English Spelling*, has a suggestion he offers to the writers of children's stories. He referred to odd spelling of character names or words, "such as Thwerll or Wumbus – Clearly the author wants names which look or sound strange, and mature readers respond well to them. I delight in every one of the names I have just listed. But there is surely a problem for young children who love to hear these stories read aloud, and who want to read them themselves, while at the same time struggling to make sense of the English spelling system. It is an unnecessary barrier. How are they supposed to work out which is the basic pattern when 'Snuvs and Gloves' are before their eyes as equals? It is perfectly possible to have weird names which respect the basic patterns of English spelling, such as Dr Seuss's 'Grinch, Gootch, Flustard...'"

Poetry

Poetry, seems to beckons the soul's emotion, sometimes in rhyme, conjuring meaning woven in succinct verses.
The cadence, echoing from utero, Mother's heartbeat's embrace, vocalising from a primal depth, profound, cherished, often beyond comprehension.
Must understanding be a prerequisite?
Poetry – a messenger conveying the injustices of society, invoking nature's enigma to an audience less accustomed to such discourse.

Part Three – Genre

Poetry extends a sincerity that spoken words often overlook, eliciting genuine response. While spoken words may preach, poetry reaches, naked words revealing raw emotions, humor entwined with humility Powerful verses provoking powerful actions, educating, explaining, persuading, soothing, nurturing, painting imagery, inspiring.

Capturing a crowd, implanting ideas, instigating rebellion, consoling mourners after the loss of a loved one – not solely due to the words but the emotions they kindle.

A few meager sheets have been smuggled from detention centers, gulags, jails, and oppressive regimes, enlightening the world, etched on toilet paper, napkins, cigarette boxes, bark, perfumed paper, silk.

Today, typed and shared across the Internet, reaching thousands, poetry knows no boundaries or limitations, crafted skillfully by individuals from every corner of the globe, rich or poor, educated or uneducated, all possess the rhythm and words within, awaiting thoughtful arrangement, requiring only a pen, paper, time, contemplation, passion, and inspiration.

Or poetry is just for fun.

I started this workbook telling you that I cannot teach you how to write, but I can present the tools that allow you to acquire the skills for good writing.

The teaching of poetry is an even greater challenge and with the exception of a few introductory examples the subject is best left to dedicated books.

I offer these examples because I love words and poetry is fashioned with the extraordinary use of words. With this morsal I hope to inspire you to pen your own poems - for when you learn the discipline of good poetry, you will be a better writer.

You will improve:

● ● ●

- Metaphor.
- Tight writing.
- Flow.
- Brevity.
- Imagery.
- Having something to say.

Brendan Kennelly, professor at Trinity College in Dublin with twenty published works of poetry and literature, said, "Poetry is, above all, a singing art of natural and magical connection because, though it is born out of one's person's solitude, it has the ability to reach out and touch in a humane and warmly illuminating way, the solitude, even the loneliness, of others. That is why, to me, poetry is one of the most vital treasures that humanity possesses; it is a bridge between separated souls."

The great 17th century Japanese Haiku master Matsuo Basho wrote: "Go to the pine if you want to learn about the pine, or to the bamboo if you want to learn about the bamboo. And in doing so you must let go of your subjective preoccupation with yourself. Otherwise, you impose yourself on the object and you do not learn. Your poetry arises by itself when you and the object have become one, when you have plunged deep enough into the object to see something like a hidden light glimmering there. However well-phrased your poetry might be, if your feeling isn't natural – if you and the object are separate – then your poetry isn't true poetry but merely your subjective counterfeit."

Part Three – Genre

American poet Billy Collins advises, "While the novelist is banging on his typewriter, the poet is watching a fly in the windowpane. And Wordsworth said poetry is the spontaneous overflow of powerful feelings."

Poet May Swenson said: "When I talk about my work, I don't say, 'I wrote,' I say, 'I made,' or 'I am making.' I want my poems to be like three-dimensional objects instead of just words on the page. I want them to have that immediacy, as if you could walk around them, see them from several aspects, notice many facets." She also said, "The best poetry has its roots in the subconscious to a great degree. Youth, naivety, reliance on instinct more than learning and method, a sense of freedom and play, even trust in randomness, is necessary to the making of a poem."

The principles I share in this workbook regarding the editing process apply seamlessly to the art of crafting poetry. It commences with an uninhibited burst of creativity, akin to a poetic outpouring. Subsequently, the delicate dance of refining ensues, where metaphor and language pirouette gracefully from the recesses of the mind onto the awaiting page. It is in this meticulous refining process that the true craft of poetry emerges.

Finessing a poem is a task that refuses to yield to hastiness; it demands patience and the commitment to undergo numerous revisions until the verses resonate with perfection. Each rerun serves as a brushstroke, refining the nuances of the poem and sculpting it into a piece that not only captures emotions but does so with an eloquence that transcends words. This intricate dance of revisiting, reshaping, and honing is where the artistry of poetry flourishes, revealing the beauty that can only be unearthed through dedicated and mindful craftsmanship.

But, finessing a poem requires more than what the above editing suggests. The French phrase *'je ne sais quoi'* applies as an overrider of the master's stroke. 'Je ne sais quoi' is often used to describe an indescribable or elusive quality that makes something or someone unique, charming, or special. It is akin to the concept of the 'x factor or an intangible quality that is difficult to pinpoint but contributes to the overall appeal or attractiveness. Without *je ne sais quoi* your poem is likely to fall flat.

Good friend and poet Dorian Haarhoff, author of *Route 77* and some twenty poetry volumes says, "I'm interested in the way poetry enters, moves and transforms us rather than cold analysis. Sets us yearning. It's about unlearning the left-brained, rational way many of us were taught at school. Gets us out of the hole we have self-dug.

Poetry can be a hard sell. According to an Australian Publishing Association webinar (2022), a good poetry book will be lucky to sell 300 copies. 1,000 copies sold is good, but this will usually be over numerous years. The author will have to roll up their sleeves to really sell copies. Having said that, do not let that stop you, as there seems to be a poetry renaissance recently. If you love writing poetry, do so, and do the best you can to sell it.

French poet Stéphane Mallarmé said, "There is nothing but beauty — and beauty has only one perfect expression, Poetry. All the rest is a lie."

Emily Dickinson said of good poetry, "If I feel physically as if the top of my head were taken off, I know this is poetry." The following does that to me:

Part Three – Genre

> **Vincent** (written by Don McLean)
> Starry, starry night
> Paint your pallet blue and gray
> Look out on a summer's day
> With eyes that know the darkness in my soul
> Shadows on the hills...
> Colours changing hue
> Morning fields of amber grain
> Weathered faces lined in pain
> Are soothed beneath the artist's loving hand...

The above is part of a poem; it was also sung by McLean. It demonstrates how so few words – beautiful words – can convey so much about the brilliance and pain of Vincent van Gogh. Phrases such as *Sketch the trees and the daffodils, Catch the breeze and the winter chills*' paint wonderful pictures in our mind.

After experiencing the poem, I am sure that you now understand how poetic skill can improve your writing.

According to McLean's marketing material, he is the most widely read poet in the modern era.

Samuel Taylor Coleridge's definition of poetry is simple, "Use the best words in the best order".

3

Good poetry evokes powerful imagery

And again Dorian Haarhoff says in his *Route 77* introduction "…in which metaphors take us as far as language can go before it touches silence and enters the inexpressible."

In an interview with Poet Charles Simic, the question was posed, how does a poet prepare for a life in poetry. "There's no preparation for poetry. Four years of grave digging with a nice volume of poetry or a book of philosophy in one's pocket would serve as well as any university."

And Billy Collins, says about writing a poem, "The opening of a poem should not need breaking and entry, hacking though the forest to get to the princess, but a welcome mat for your reader."

Jane Kenyon, American poet advised poets, "Tell the whole truth. Don't be lazy, don't be afraid. Close the critic out when you are drafting something new. Take chances in the clarity of emotion."

The following by Thiele, B & Weiss, G. in 1967, was sung by Louis Armstrong:

"I see trees of green, red roses too, I see 'em bloom, for me and for you. And I think to myself, what a wonderful world.
I see skies of blue, clouds of white. Bright blessed days, dark sacred nights. And I think to myself, what a wonderful world.
The colors of a rainbow, so pretty in the sky, are also on the faces of people going by. I see friends shaking hands, sayin' 'how do you do'.
…They're really sayin', 'I love you'.
I hear babies cry. I watch them grow. They'll learn much more than I'll never know.
And I think to myself, what a wonderful world".

● ● ●

Part Three – Genre

How beautiful a string of words can be.
Consider the following aspects when writing or editing poems:

Poem Title – Keep the poem's title in mind as it provides direction and understanding for both the writer and the reader.

Word Organisation – Pay attention to the arrangement of words within each line and stanza, ensuring they contribute to the overall flow and impact of the poem.

Textual Pattern – Organise the pattern of text on the page thoughtfully, as visual presentation can enhance or alter the interpretation.

Readers Language Patterns – Examine language patterns, including rhyme, rhythm, and literary devices, to harness the full expressive potential of the poem.

Literal vs. Metaphorical – Determine whether the message is conveyed in a literal (direct) or metaphorical (suggestive) manner. Recognise that metaphorical expressions often introduce complexity.

Mood Reflection – Reflect on the mood of the poem, which is usually a reflection of the poet's emotions. Consider how this mood influences the reader's experience.

Message Clarity – Identify the central message or theme of the poem. Ensure clarity in conveying ideas to evoke the intended response from the reader.

Narrative Elements – Determine if the poem follows a narrative structure. Assess the use of storytelling elements, characters, and plot development if applicable.

By keeping these considerations in mind, poets can craft and refine their work, ensuring that each element contributes harmoniously to the overall artistic expression.

3

Kazuo Ishiguro, author of the novel *Klara and the sun*, is also a lyricist. In a radio interview he was asked, "Is there much of a difference in writing lyrics for songs or text for novels?"

"Indeed, there is... When writing a novel, you must be explicit. But when writing for a song you have to be less explicit, thereby leaving room for the performer to imbue emotion and their signature."

Poetry, said Robert Frost "begins as a lump in the throat, a sense of wrong, a homesickness, a loneliness." Frost won the Pulitzer Prize for poetry four times.

Illustrations

Weak illustrations have the potential to stifle the full potential of what could otherwise be a remarkable book. Whether it is a report, a children's book, or a 'how-to' guide, the inclusion of compelling and visually appealing illustrations is crucial.

Illustrations serve as a visual language that enhances the reader's understanding, engagement, and overall experience with the content. To ensure that the illustrations align seamlessly with your vision for the book, establishing clear communication and collaboration with the illustrator is essential. Both author and illustrator must be on the same page (pun intended), working in tandem to bring the narrative to life visually. This collaboration is particularly crucial for children's books, where the illustrations play a central role in capturing the young audience's imagination and conveying the story effectively.

In the context of children's books, it is advisable to employ a method that facilitates effective communication between the author and the illustrator.

One approach is to create a comprehensive illustration brief, outlining specific details such as character designs, color schemes, and the overall tone you envision. Providing visual references, whether through sketches, mood boards, or examples from other works, can be immensely helpful in conveying your expectations. (above, under Children's books, I outline a working method to show your illustrator what you want.)

By taking the time to establish a collaborative and communicative relationship with the illustrator, you increase the likelihood of achieving illustrations that not only complement but enhance the narrative. Remember, the synergy between text and visuals is a powerful combination that elevates the reading experience, making it more memorable and engaging for your audience.

Magazine and newspaper writing

This section on publication writing (writing for magazines or newspapers) is a brief overview that will give you a taste as to what is required for this type of work.

HELPFUL TIPS

From about 2005 magazines were said to be heading in the way of the dinosaur. But magazines sales are reviving. In Australia, magazine sales are up by around 5%, and trending upwards. This trend is reflected in other parts of the world. Research suggests that this is because of 'digital fatigue' – many want to get off their devices and just relax with a mag on their lap.

3

If you would like to write for publications, there is much research you need to do to prepare yourself.

Why write a column?

- To earn money.
- A good way to become known.
- By having a column, you become a perceived expert.
- The discipline will improve your writing.
- Change of career.
- Challenge.
- You write it once and sell it many times (to other publications), especially if you are organised.
- And the last, and most important reason, is to say what you want to say to a large audience – that is, if the publication will let you.

What to write?

- Tell people something they do not know, or something they do know, but in a different way – your way, from a new perspective.
- The work must be topical; last year's court case is old hat, unless you have a new angle.
- Write what you know and what you are passionate about. But think about this.
  However, when you write what you are passionate about you could be limiting yourself. Your growth as a person and as a writer is steeped in adventure, putting your toe in the other pond, learning new things, keeping it fresh, playing with the unknown – after all, if you are to be a good writer, it is almost irrespective what you write, and surely the variety will not only make your life more interesting, but give your writing the opportunity to explore itself.
- Editors can be tough, but they know their readers, so do your homework.

Part Three – Genre

 **HELPFUL TIPS** — *This may be a career change, so you need to do it properly.*

Sample topics:

- Interviews.
- Business.
- Social commentary.
- Feel-good stories.
- Self-help.
- Politics.
- Travel writing.
- Health.
- Animals.
- Hobbies.
- Hi-tech.
- Landscape/gardening.
- Sport.

How to find topics:

- Seminars or workshops are full of suggestions, just listen and they will present themselves.
- Newspapers are a great source of ideas. You read an article, and bingo, something the writer mentions switches your lights on.
- Television and radio.
- General conversation.
- Podcasts are in abundance and many have hidden gems.

Ideas are everywhere, be open to them.

3

> "She always looked swell when she sat reading the magazines on the terrace—attentive and lovely, her hair loose and shimmery, the light doing nice things to her face. She'd lose track of time that way, turn down invitations, not feel like talking. She'd just be looking at the pictures, reading the captions, not bothering with the articles—anything to keep from being alone."
> *Breakfast at Tiffany's* by Truman Capote

Which publication?

- Once you know what you want to write about, you need to select the publication and mould your writing accordingly.
- Do your research to make sure that your material matches that of the magazine.
- In-house or commercial publications?
- Browse news agencies conduct Internet searches and contact companies. Finding the right publication or publications can be time-consuming. Take your time, be patient and methodical.
- Keep a database of all the companies and contact details you accumulate. Make sure you have keyword tags attached to each. For example, if you are looking for an article to be placed for children, you can search your database (say for all publications with children) using this tag.
- Buy two or three issues of the magazine to ensure that you understand what they are looking for and who their target audience is.

The writing style of the publication

- Each publication has its own tempo and format depending on its

Part Three – Genre

- readership. You need to know what this is. For instance, they will have sentences of relatively consistent length, or roughly the same number of sentences in a paragraph. You may laugh at this, but it is true. They have a tried and tested formula, and you must know what it is.
- In newspaper writing, paragraphs usually contain only three or four sentences.
- If your submissions are not in their required format, you will be rejected by the editor.
- Is their work short and punchy with lots of slang for a young audience, or more languid aimed at a mature reader?
- Some publications put out a 'style sheet'. These help give you information on the format and style the publication requires, as well as the demographics about the readers.
  Ask for their style sheet.

Approaching the editor of the publication

- Only contact the editor when you are sure about what you want to offer and that this will fit the style of the publication.
- Before making contact, write some test work in the style of the magazine and share it with your friends to see if they think it fits the publication.
  Depending on the subject write enough for at least eight additions. You do not want to get caught with not enough material, and deadlines approach quickly.
- It is acceptable for you to phone an editor and ask for a few minutes to go over your suggested column. They are also normally receptive to an email submission. If you email, make sure it is well written. Although they may be open, they expect most to be duds, so invariably they display the attitude, "Yeah, I'll listen, you got two minutes so get on with it".
- Unless you are well known, do not tell them you have articles you would like to show them. Rather tell them you have an idea for a column that you would like to tell them about. If the editor accepts

- the idea in concept, finesse it and send it within the given time-frame. Do not be late, do not rush it.
- When making your submission, ensure your name and contact details are included and give them a word count. Make it as easy as possible for the editor. They will appreciate your consideration.
- After that initial contact, follow up at regular intervals. Persevere and be persistent in a courteous and friendly manner. Never show frustration – this is the way the industry works.
- Each editor has his or her own idiosyncrasies. The sooner you understand these, the easier it will be for you to work with them.
- If they are interested in using your work, obtain a written agreement before continuing. Amongst other things, this will cover the fee (usually per word), payment terms, deadlines, and the number of words.

  Editors are also business people who drive a hard bargain. Know what the industry offers but know your worth, and press for a fair deal. As a beginner, it is likely you will get paid at the lower end of the scale.
- You grant the publication permission to use the story once. Do not give them copyright, unless it is worth your while to sell it. Ensure that this is covered in your documentation.

Considerations when writing the piece:

- Be certain that the message is what you want to convey. If it is not clear to you, it will not be clear to the reader or the editor.
- Use your full arsenal of writing skills to make your work compelling, but some column types do not allow for too many metaphors.
- Each sentence must have relevance to the overall message, with no wasted words.
- Be methodical and logical in the organisation of the work.
- Stick to the agreed number of words.
- Use the structure as given earlier on in this workbook, that is, an interesting opening, sustained interest in the body, and a resolution or summary.

- Pay attention to detail, and make sure there are no grammatical errors.

Loving the piece

There are several quotations in this book from different authors who suggest, 'Walk around the work... look at it from different angles'. Good writing becomes good because you spend time on each piece. Much the same as a lovely garden becomes so because of the care and attention given – where the owner wanders around it, gently caressing the ferns, softly touching the pansies, snipping here, and trimming there. The gardener is in no hurry, and nor should you be. Yet, there are always deadlines.

The feature can be a story, or a descriptive piece, and is normally in the third person. Usually feature writing teaches or informs. The length of the work varies from article to article but typically would be between 600 and 2,500 words.

Use the AIDA approach for your articles: first gain Attention, then Interest. You need to invoke Desire to Action or response(such as getting readers to phone their local member of parliament).

Write a Sunday magazine article of 1,000 words called *The State of the World*. Make sure that you have an introduction, a body, and

> a summary. Maintain interest throughout the article, try to be fair and unbiased, showing all sides of the argument.

When you write a column for a newspaper or magazine, they will inform you of the number of words required. If they say around 1,500 words, then you have room to manoeuvre. But around 1,500 words means no more than 1,550 and no less than 1,450. Here the leeway is around 3%. If you submit your article and it has 1,600 words, it could be rejected or trimmed in ways that you do not like. You may not be asked to submit again.

If the editor says 1,500 words, it must be no more than 1,505 and no less than 1,495 words, to fit the space they have allocated for the feature.

Many writing competitions ask for the work to be a set number of words as this levels the playing field for all contestants.

It is for this reason that many of the exercises I have given you have a set number of words. The discipline to trim down or increase the word count will help you with your general writing skills.

Under the editing section you will learn that most people over-write. Writing to a set number of words teaches you how to replace three or four words with one word, kill duplication, eliminate superfluous words and avoid wandering.

> *Walden* by Henry David Thoreau:
> "We set out early, the morning sun already warm upon our backs. The trail wound through towering pines and leafy maples, their branches swaying gently in the breeze. As we walked, the scent of wildflowers and damp earth filled the air, a symphony of fragrances that invigorated the senses. Birds sang overhead, their melodies echoing through the forest, while squirrels chattered and scampered among the trees. Eventually, we came upon a tranquil meadow, bathed in sunlight and alive with the buzzing of bees and the fluttering of butterflies. We spread our blanket beneath the shade of an ancient oak, its branches stretching out like open arms, and unpacked our feast. There, surrounded by the beauty of nature, we enjoyed a leisurely picnic, savoring each bite and each moment of tranquility."

Database

At the beginning of this section I said money can be made through article writing. Yes, you can make money, but only if you are good at what you do, and organised.

Where the 'cream' comes from is writing it once but selling it many times (that is why earlier I suggested you retain copyright). Often though, you will need to amend a piece and perhaps give it a different name.

You need to set up a good database as to which articles you have pitched to which publication. Imagine, you have now written 100 articles. And perhaps there are 50 publications world-wide you can (over a time) pitch to. That is 5,000 different submissions. There's no way you will remember sending Article X to Publication A.

It is in this 'production' organisation that one article can be sold several times. Sure, you will update it with the latest events, and customise for it each publication, but essentially, the article is the same.

3

When doing this, you do have a moral responsibility to each publication that has previously published it, so the amendments and the time frame will allow you to do this. If they only pay for a usage, then you are entitled to resell it. If they do not want you to resell it, then they must pay extra for copyright.

How the time frame works is as follows: two years ago X-mag buys your story on *Child safety whilst riding their first bike*. There is no reason why Y-mag cannot publish it now. But check the fine print of the previous agreements.

For the database, a good spreadsheet will work, and they are easy enough to set up.

Last comment on writing for a magazine or newspaper

You could be doing this for a long time, so like any new business, be prepared to put a couple of years into it to get it off the ground.

> If any man wishes to write in a clear style, let him be first clear in his thoughts; and if any would write in a noble style, let him first possess a noble soul.
> Goethe.

Report Writing

A written report is a presentation of facts that are offered in a concise and direct way. There should be no unnecessary words and it should be tightly written. Each idea must be clear to the readers and so flow is important.

Part Three – Genre

Academic papers must be direct and concise and if they stray from a dry presentation of words then they are regarded as imperfect.

A well-researched project can be spoilt if it is not well-presented. The way you present it can make you look good or bad.

Although there is a greater use of technology than in the past, the basics of report writing have not changed all that much.

Know your deadline and have the work finished well before the due date, even if it means working late into the night. This gives you time to perfect it by laying it down for a while. When you go back to it, you will see errors and ways to improve it. Of all the advice on report writing, this is the most important.

Before starting the report:

- Do a mind map that covers all the topics.
- Make sure that you know what is expected.
- Work out a task timetable with completion dates.
- Understand your audience.
- Pinpoint the reason for the report.

There are usually five steps to creating a report:

- Investigation.
- Analysis.
- Consideration of the arguments.
- Writing the report.
- Editing, checking and double checking.
- And a sixth is to get a colleague to read it and discuss it with you before you present it.

Reports must be:

- Complete.
- Accurate.
- Linear in the presentation of the material.

Reports to include:

- Cover page.
- The author/s of the report.
- Table of contents.
- An introduction or overview.
- A heading for each topic
- Recommendations and conclusions.
- A summary of the main topics, arguments, and recommendations.
- Appendices.
- If a large report, an index.
- Bibliography.
- A cover-letter if the report is to be sent by post or email.
- Readers' distribution signing list, if read by many people.

The Tone

- Understand the tone that is required. Not all reports need to be serious. Choose your tone according to the readers and the material.
- The less serious the tone, the more colour/metaphors you can use.
- Be impersonal, let facts speak for themselves, express no emotion.
- Use the third person as it will separate you from the report.
- Are you expressing your own opinions or those of others? If they are the opinions of others, be impartial. If they are yours make it known.
- If you are asked for recommendations, be clear on why you recommend A over B. Understand the responsibility and implications of making those recommendations.

- Try to adopt positive words and phrases, as positive statements are more compelling than negative. For instance, change; *Please do not hesitate to call me*, to '*For further information...*'.
  Or, '*In this report I have endeavoured to get all the information*'; to '*I have packed this report with the latest findings*'.

Rules for report writing:

- Do not use four words if you can use one.
- Limit the use of contractions (abbreviations)
- Keep your sentences short, containing one subject.
- Where possible avoid jargon; use an English word if there is one. Do not use slang and stick to the rules of good grammar.
- What important facts have you left out? Do not set yourself up for embarrassment.
- Do not use a big word if a small word fits.
- Make sure that the arguments are balanced and impartial. Be careful not to malign people.
- Do not waffle or wander, stick to what is relevant.
- If the report is long, it is a good idea to have a summary of each chapter after the introduction. This allows readers to scan for key ideas/chapters.
- Check and double-check your facts. The same for calculations.
- Ensure that the contents page numbers and actual page numbers match.
- Make sure that every argument or thread is complete.

Enhancing the report

- Support the text with graphs, diagrams, and other visuals (remember some people are more visual than others).
- Set out the report with convenience to the reader.
- Take time to develop supporting material.
- Use colour.

- Use recognised authorities to substantiate the argument.
- Do not forget to acknowledge all sources and reference material.
- Use the editing checklist as given below.
- Have one copy of the report printed for checking before doing the group copies.
- When printing, use dark ink, as this gives power to the document.
- Use a digital printer and not a photocopier as the quality is better.
- Use well-defined headings and sub-headings.
- Too much information on a page frazzles the reader, whereas open space offers balance. Do not try and save on pages.
- Bind the printed copy with a harder cover. This is better than spiral binding and looks more professional and permanent.

Academic Writing

Academic writing refers to a formal style of writing used in educational settings and scholarly work. It encompasses various genres such as essays, research papers, theses, and dissertations, characterised by clear organisation, logical argumentation, and adherence to academic conventions and citation styles. Academic writing aims to convey complex ideas, theories, and research findings in a precise, unbiased manner while adhering to the standards of academic integrity and rigor.

Part Three – Genre

OTHER WRITING AND MISCELLANEOUS TIPS

> When you find yourself in that creative flow, you and the text become indistinguishable, seamlessly gliding along without a care in the world. It's a harmonious dance between you, the text, the page—the unfolding story.
> This state of seamless creation can only be achieved in the absence of pressure. It thrives when time is abundant, allowing thoughts to manifest organically. It blossoms when self-censorship is set aside, and the primary objective is to revel in the act of writing.
> In these moments, writing becomes a joyous exploration, unhindered by constraints. It is a journey of unbridled expression, where the narrative unfolds naturally, and the pleasure of the process becomes as significant as the story being told.

- Clichés: do not use them – be original (see the edit checklist below).
- Colloquial slang usually does not work and sounds corny, that is unless you are a very skilled writer. It can be fine for certain characters in dialogue. It also may limit the work to the country of the slang.
- Writing as you speak seldom works and comes out disjointed. The flow is hampered.
- Support your work with research – do not use false facts as there are readers out there who just love to prove you wrong, whilst belittling you over the entire Internet.
- No plagiarism.
- Enter writing competitions as they are good for skill development. Some competitions send back evaluations, which is valuable information.

****

Book size

It helps with the conceptualisation of the final product and page layout to write the book in the same size that the book will be printed. This could be A5 or A4 (landscape or portrait). Before you start writing, change the page size on your computer.

****

If your novel covers a topic that is close to your heart – perhaps on climate change or religion – do not moralise as the third person narrator. It is the character's job to tell that 'story' in their words, as part of the character's make up.

****

How much money do authors make?

It is a well-known that book authorship is not well remunerated for many members of the profession. The findings of this Macquarie University Business School survey (2014) bears this out:

"...nearly one fifth of authors earned $101,000 or more in the 2013-14 financial year. Once again, the highest proportion within each genre in this band of income constitutes scholarly (44.4%) and education (26.5%) authors, followed by literary fiction (15.7%), creative nonfiction (15.3%), other nonfiction (14.7%), poetry (14.3%) and genre fiction authors (12.8%). (These percentages are calculated as a proportion of authors in each genre who earn over $101,000.) The findings demonstrate that while the majority of authors earn modest incomes, some authors can earn a good living, especially if they can derive income from a range of sources.

Part Three – Genre

Although nearly 20% of authors work full-time on their creative practice, less than 5% of authors earn the average annual income from their creative practice alone. There are only two categories of authors represented in the highest band of income of $200,000+ derived from an author's creative practice alone. These are fiction and education authors."

Although the report is ten years old, it is indicative of author earnings. The following report from ASA (Australian Society of Authors) was written in 2021 about Australian authors:

Earnings of
$ 40 000+ at 9.2%
25 000+ at 5.0%
15 000+ at 5.8%
10 000+ at 6.8%
5 000+ at 9.5%
2 000+ at 14.0%
1 000+ at 14.7%

Excuse the pun, but pretty poor really.

****

Another snippet by Macquarie:

Authors spend on average 43% of their working time on their creative occupation as a writer, including writing, research, administration, promotion, networking, etc. This amount of time is matched, on average, by other paid work. Trade authors are particularly affected by changes in the promotion of books, with over half of trade authors spending more time promoting their work than five years ago.

****

3

Do not ever trash your work

Stephen King nearly tossed out his book *Christine*. It was his wife who retrieved it from the bin. Thank goodness she did, otherwise we would not have that work today.

Sometimes we get too close to our work and cannot see it objectively. Put it away for a time and let others, whose opinions you trust look at it for you.

****

When to use large or sophisticated words?

It is always good form to use the simplest word possible, that is, providing that a simple word can fit the meaning.

There are some who do not like to read large or sophisticated words. For instance, I could say "...and I took this course of action to *ameliorate* myself..." Or I could say "...and I took this course of action to improve myself..." But there are times when a longer or more sophisticated word is a better fit, because by using that one word may save two or more words that say the same thing, for example "his action was an *anomaly*..." instead of "his action was different to the normal". Using *anomaly* saved two words. Fewer words, better flow.

It also depends on your audience. If you are writing for people younger than twelve, you would not use the word *ameliorate*. Nor would you use it if you were giving dialogue to a peasant who existed two hundred years ago. However, if you were writing about someone with doctorate then it is likely that you will need more sophisticated words.

If you write for a more sophisticated audience of Sci-fi or history, then

> Part Three – Genre

that audience will expect expediency (I could have used *the most efficient wording,* which is four words replacing one).

To summarise, try and use shorter, simpler words where possible, but use longer words if your audience is more sophisticated, or when you are trying to write with brevity.

****

The word very is a very overused word.

Is being **very** astute better than being astute?
Is being **very** good-looking better than good-looking? Would Miss Britain be **very**, **very** good-looking and Miss World **very**, **very**, **very**, good looking?

Getting back to the first question, is being **very** astute better than being astute? The answer is no, as you are either astute or not astute, in which case the word 'very' is superfluous.

In manuscripts that I receive, the most commonly overly use word by new writers is **very**, which is used literally hundreds of times in the manuscript: it was a **very** hot day, we had **very** nice cake, we had a **very** good chat.

In most instances the word very can be eliminated, and so if you want your writing to be simple and direct be **very** sure that you use the word **very** wisely.

3

> This writing is from his *Klingsor's Last Summer* by Hermann Hesse (a recipient of the Nobel Prize for Literature (1946)
>
> "Alone and helpless, he sat with fevered brow and painful pressure around his head, gripped by a fear of fate which held him spellbound like a bird watching a snake. Fate, he now knew, did not come from anywhere; it grew within himself. If he found no remedy for it, it would consume him.
>
> Anxiety, this horrible anxiety, would pursue him, would dog his every step, would drive him farther and farther from rationality, until he reached the brink. Already he could feel how close the brink was."

YOUR WRITING GOALS

At the start of this workbook, you wrote down your writing aspirations. Go back to that section and review what you wrote.

You will finish this course off by writing down your new goals and aspirations. If I have worked this book correctly, you should be more motivated and confident, and so your aspirations should be much greater and clearer.

Part Three – Genre

> In 1869, Walter Pater wrote an essay on Leonardo da Vinci's Mona Lisa, and the interest the painting created;
> "She is older than the rocks among which she sits; like the vampire, she has been dead many times, and learned the secrets of the grave; and has been a diver in deep seas, and keeps their fallen day about her; and trafficked for strange webs with Eastern merchants; and, as Leda, was mother of Helen of Troy, and, as Saint Anne, the mother of Mary; and all this has been to her but as the sound of lyres and flutes, and lives only in the delicacy with which it has moulded the changing lineaments, and tinged the eyelids and hands.

Endword

You and I have travelled far. If you have done the exercises, what probably began as hesitant writing will now have emerged as powerful and competent writing. I am proud of you. I am proud to have been of assistance to you, a small influence that pointed the way. This was easy to do as the writing and creativity was already within you; all you needed was encouragement and direction.

It is possible that for a time life will take you in a different direction and your writing may languish. Do not be concerned as what you have learned has now become a part of you and will always be there, just like a faithful dog, quietly waiting for you to come home.

Writing can be a pilgrimage – it can be where you are one with the words and that it is the 'other' you who is writing and learning.

In our time together we covered much ground but the last advice is that you enjoy your writing. Do not be a slave to writing or hooked-up on the result. Writing is not about money, but you can earn money.

3

Write for fun, and if you do, you will write well, you will write with creativity, and you will earn money.

Part Four – Editing And Revision

In this section:

- Style manual
- American or UK English
- Clichés
- Editing checklist
- A book critique

4

Ever engaged a builder for renovations, only to find the aftermath resembling a chaotic construction site? Picture this: rubble and discarded paint cans scattered across the yard, cement bags flapping against the fence in the wind, whilst a fine layer of building dust settling on the new window glass.

Did the builder bother to tidy up, level the ground post-drainage, or wipe away paint drops from the pristine tiles? If not, the sense of incompleteness likely lingered.

Imagine a different scenario – a builder who not only completes the main tasks but goes the extra mile. The debris is cleared, windows are spotless, the ground is leveled and raked, and lush turf laid. This attention to detail transforms the experience, leaving you with a profound sense of completeness.

In the world of editing, a parallel truth unfolds. Much like a builder's job, the editing process is only truly complete when executed meticulously. Poorly edited work, on the other hand, is akin to the discomfort of scraping fingernails across a blackboard or the sudden jolt of hitting your funny bone – thoroughly unpleasant. The essence lies not just in the completion of the task but in the finesse with which it is executed.

For you to get a publisher's interest there must be no scraping fingernails across a blackboard. Otherwise, the publisher will not get past the first page. The onus is on you to edit and revise the work so that it is as clean as possible. Rarely is a book or document perfect the first time. There are many steps to take to make it perfect.

A well-prepared manuscript will improve the efficiency of the author and the publisher. It will reduce processing time for the publisher and limit proof-reading effort. The result for all involved will be a book that is produced with efficiency and speed.

Part Four – Editing And Revision

It is possible a publisher likes a book but will not publish it because there are too many errors. Consider the errors in a book of 100,000 words and 300 pages. If you think you did a good job of editing by getting it 95% clean, you still have 5,000 errors. Yes, 5,000, or about seventeen errors a page. Any publisher who sees seventeen errors on the first page of a manuscript will dump it into the bin.

When I edit a book, we aim to get it 99.5% accurate, but there are still 500 errors, with over three per page. Some are small, such as a missing comma, or too wordy, but still, they are errors.

Next, our proof-reader trawls through the manuscript to remove another 0.3% of errors (they get harder and harder to find). We must settle on thirty or so. But later, if we discover these, we rectify the manuscript once more.

I receive manuscripts from new authors that are only 80% clean. This means 20,000 errors need to be eliminated. If an editor takes thirty seconds to rectify each, that is 167 hours to edit – you should by now be gaining an understanding of the requirement.

Now you know why publishers will charge extra for editing, that is if they have not ditched you. You should do at least ten revisions before you submit the manuscript.

For budding authors, the editing and revision process holds an untapped richness often overlooked. Through the edit the narrative comes alive, the story flows giving clear direction. It is with the second, third, fourth, or eighth revision where the latent potential of the plot is fully realised.

Here, is where *Words are Transformed into Stories* becoming vibrant imagery that leap off the page. Characters evolve from mere sketches to intriguing personalities, each contributing to the narrative. The once elusive explanations are eloquently expressed to further the tale.

In essence, the editing and revision stages are not merely a chore but a creative requirement where every tweak, adjustment, and refinement brings the story closer to its zenith, unveiling layers of depth and complexity that may have remained dormant in the initial drafts.

Editing is not proof-reading. After you edit your first draft there should be considerably less words than when you started. This helps to keep the book 'active'.

Margaret Bechard, author of *Hanging on to Max*, voted Best young adult novel of the year by the *American Library Association*, says, "Revision is when I can use my whole writing self … all my talents—my creative risk-taking, experimental side, and my regimented, nit-picking analytical side as well." And Steven King jokes but with an element of veracity, when he says, "to write is human, to edit is divine."

Trust the revision process and know that even the best authors consider it a creative imperative. For instance, you may say, 'She arrived home drunk…' At the time of writing, 'drunk' was the word that fell out. When editing, the silent voice may whisper, 'Perhaps there is a better word'. Upon scanning your thesaurus, the words smashed, intoxicated, inebriated jump out at you. Based on the nuance that the context requires, the perfect word will jump up and shout, 'Me, me!' and so you amend the text to, 'She arrived home, smashed…'

If your work is a novel, look at how each character contributes to the story and plot and how each are different. Does their dialogue fit and further the story? Does it reveal the character? And is it obvious who the character is?

Part Four – Editing And Revision

The revision process does not have to be a 'roll up your sleeves and grind your teeth' sort of process. With the right attitude and mindset, it can be fun and just as stimulating as the first creative draft of the work.

I tend to get my authors to edit their work with different processes as this gets them to realise the many requirements of editing. First, I get them to check the flow and the grammar. If OK, they go onto the second check, which may be looking for 'showing and not telling'. The third run might be for brevity and duplication of words. Authors have favourite words that rush out of them like snow in a blizzard. In a manuscript they may use this word several hundred times.

Another edit is making descriptions colourful. Use names of things, for instance, do not just say flowers, say geraniums, or dove for a bird, as one is a generic nothing, and the other the reader can see.

Easy reading is damned hard writing"
Nathaniel Hawthorne (1804 -1864),
author of The Scarlet Letter.

4

> *Lonesome* Dove by Larry McMurtry, published in 1985 but set in the late 19th century:
>
> "The sun was hot on their backs as they rode across the vast expanse of the open prairie. Dust billowed up behind them, kicked up by the hooves of their horses. The sky stretched out endlessly above, a brilliant blue canopy dotted with fluffy white clouds. In the distance, they could see the silhouette of distant mountains, their peaks shimmering in the heat haze.
>
> Gus and Call rode side by side, their hats pulled low over their brows to shield their eyes from the glare of the sun. They rode in companionable silence, their thoughts turning to the long journey ahead. Behind them, the rest of the men followed, their cattle lowing softly as they plodded along.
>
> As they rode, the wind whispered through the tall grass, carrying with it the scent of sagebrush and wildflowers. The sound of the horses' hoofbeats echoed across the prairie, mingling with the mournful cry of a lone coyote in the distance.
>
> For Gus and Call, this was the life they had chosen—the life of a cowboy, riding the range under the endless western sky. And as they rode, they knew that there was nowhere else they'd rather be."

In many ways this chapter is one of the most important for without these skills, you will not have the success that you desire, no matter how creative you are. It is literally where *Words are transformed into stories*.

A student, Mary-Anne, only ever wanted to get her thoughts out and did not worry about presentation. She could not understand why her audience showed so little enthusiasm. This concerned her because she wanted her ideas to be read.

Part Four – Editing And Revision

She produced good work but it went no where because there was no structure. The difficulty for me as her writing coach was to encourage her creative flair whilst instilling discipline. This was like breaking in a wild colt, without killing its spirit.

Once she finally got it, her work flew off the page and into the appreciative mind of her readers. I was particularly pleased because Mary-Anne had lost confidence in teachers. As a student of fine art, she found that some of her professors were more concerned about the work than the student.

I also have new authors who are happy to pay us to fix those 5,000 to 20,000 errors I mentioned above. That signals to me that they do not really want to put in the time to become a skilled writer – but they do want the adulation that comes of having a published book.

When Stephen King said in his book *On Writing* that he normally works through his manuscripts about twelve times, he meant that is before it goes to his publisher's editor and proof-reader. And if that is not enough to convince you, Konstantin Paustovsky wrote that upon visiting the Russian writer Isaac Babel there was a meter high stack of pages on Babel's desk. Upon enquiring if Babel was perhaps writing a full novel, as opposed to his normal short story form, Babel replied, 'No, this heap is each of the twenty-two edits for my latest short story. There will be a few more'.

4

> William Golding – *The Spire*
>
> You tried to frighten me as you might frighten a child with a ghost story. You thought it out carefully, didn't you? And yet you know you can't go. Can't go.
>
> Can't get away. And all that time, your curious, valuable mind was finding a way round the impossible.
>
> You found it too because that's what you're for. You don't know if it's the right answer but it's the best one you've got. But you're frightened. The best part of you would like to try, but the rest snivels and whimpers.

A wonderful example of clear and concise writing, but did you notice the abbreviations he used to create the voice he wanted?

Quality, not quantity

We rush to do as much as possible in as short a time as possible. You cannot race editing. You must approach it with patience.

When you edit, do it with the mind-set of 'slow and steady' and not, 'I must get X amount done per day'. Editing is a slow and creative process and so your attitude must be one of 'chill and process'.

Thoughts on editing

- The way that a writer approaches editing separates the serious writer from the not-so-serious writer.
- Editing take up more than 60% of the overall writing time. So, at the onset of the book, be aware of the need to spend time editing.
- The writer must make it easy for the publisher to say YES.
- Skilled writing and editing is about getting the message across clearly and accurately, and to do that you need to know the rules.
- Editing impacts the writing.

Part Four – Editing And Revision

- In essence, having one's work edited by another can be seen as a constructive form of critique. Embracing this process as an opportunity for growth and learning is essential for honing one's writing skills and mastering the craft, as it offers valuable insights and perspectives that can enhance the clarity, coherence, and effectiveness of the written work.

> Dig out something around a page long that you previously wrote and edit it. You will see it improve as you go.

Contractions (abbreviations), when to use them and when not to use them?
Once again, I use these standards for my writing and that of my authors.

For direct speech I encourage contractions as it helps define the character speaking. It is also how we speak: and with the knife firmly planted into his back he whimpered, "I didn't think you'd be serious …won't you pull it out? …"

For virtually all other non-direct speech writing, contractions are considered an 'uncontrolled-form'. I have authors who send manuscripts and there is not one 'cannot' (can't), 'do not' (don't), 'have not' (haven't), it is as if they have forgotten how to correctly write the words. But I can guarantee that publishers have not.

If you are writing a novel and there is dialogue, then use the non-contraction when not in direct speech. By keeping to this rule, the use of contractions in direct speech will bring colour to the dialogue, e.g., "Wach ware ya goin, ya rotta".

Abbreviations depends on the audience, and or conversational writing. If the writing is in a business context, such as a letter of complaint, an agreement, a referral, or general business correspondence, it is not good form to use contractions.

And btw, did you notice my two contractions in this piece? They were; btw (just used) and e.g. as used above.

Blog writing and SMS's are less formal and it is more about letting the personality show in a relaxed conversational form.

In your cover letter to a publisher, do not use abbreviations.

Style Manual

How do you know you have the correct presentation of dates, salutations (credentials), or citations, or any of the other style issue?

When preparing a book for publication there are hundreds of details that must be adhered to, such as how to express numerals or typography in a recognised and standard format. Yes, they do vary from country to country, but for you to present your work as professionally as possible, you need to focus on them. If you are not interested in doing it yourself, you could pay someone to do it for you. But if you want to save the money then I suggest you buy a Style Manual.

Most countries put one out every few years. The one I use here in Australia, is called *Style Manual*, published by John Wiley & Sons Australia.

Reasons for manuscript rejection

Firstly, errors in the work will annoy a publisher. The fact that the concept may be brilliant will be of no concern.

Second, a lack of flow

Part Four – Editing And Revision

Third, overwriting kills a manuscript. About ninety-nine percent of manuscripts that I receive have surplus writing. Some are over cooked by fifty percent, that is, they have been reduced from 120,000 words to 60,000 and still tell the same story. Each sentence, each paragraph can normally be edited down – lean writing is good writing.

I have been shouted at by would-be authors when I informed them that the work is too 'wordy' and they must reduce it. "But it will change the meaning," they implore. When they finally strip out the wordage, invariably they return with a sheepish look and mumble, "Yes, I now see what you mean". They still may need to reduce it some more.

To reduce a manuscript's size:

- Remove duplication of words, passages and meaning.
- Keep It Short and Simple (KISS).
- Reduce sentence length.
- One word may replace several.
- Remove superfluous words (such as the 'maybe/very).
- Eliminate that which does not contribute to the meaning. There is often text in a piece of work that the author considers valuable, but may not further the story or meaning.
- Tautology, where the same thing is said, but in a different way. Sometimes repeated for or five times.
- The overuse of researched material.

Fewer words and simplified meaning:

- Short distance away – near or close.
- Situated close to – near.
- Suffered a broken leg – broke his leg.
- Take into consideration – consider.
- Came to an end – ended, finished, stopped.

4

- He submitted his resignation – he resigned, or, he quit.
- A flock of nineteen sheep – nineteen sheep.

An exception to the above could be when using dialogue.

Things to look out for:

- Does your story work? Get your friends to read it and realistically comment on the story. Ask if you have the basics in place, such as an attention grabbing introduction, a well-crafted and sustainable middle, and a good resolution (more on this later).
- To give colour to the story, do you give enough attention to detail, such as 'the place' where the action is happening? Detail is well-placed description – like curry in the stew, not too much, just a touch, and after a while you know how much to add. Remember, the detail must be 'shown', not told.
- Don't talk down to your reader. Assume that your reader is smart, they will know when you are talking down to them.
- Have your personality in the work. If you try to emulate another's style it will be mishmash. Be original in your voice. This also applies to the story. Do not copy the last best seller, make your work the new bestselling idea.
- Research can add interest to the story, providing it is done properly. Many new authors think their manuscript is a dumping ground for dozens of Googled pages. It is better to use less research than too much– knowing what to leave out is a skill. If the research slows the pace or moves the reader from the story, delete it.
- Correct editing.

If a potential publisher receives your manuscript, and if within the first few minutes of scanning you have duplicated ideas or rambled, you will have lost them.

Part Four – Editing And Revision

 In your notebook, pick an image from a magazine and write about that scene. Make it complete, but exactly 500 words.

Reading aloud is one of the best methods to identify mistakes and see what the flow is like. When you read silently, the brain does not read every word and so errors are missed. Reading aloud will help you identify if the work is clumsy and identifies 'clogged' text. When you read your work to an audience:

- *You gain exposure.*
- *You can gauge the interest in your work.*
- *You gain confidence.*
- *Let them tell you what they think of the work.*
- *It can function as an editing process.*
- *It elicits the power of storytelling in practice.*

I quote from two students who were encouraged to read their work aloud to the group:

- 'You've given me confidence to be able to express my work.'
- 'Reading aloud has helped me find my voice.'

Shorter sentences are easier to read than longer sentences. But there are times for longer, more languid sentences where description and imagery are meant flourish. If the sentences are too short, often the work becomes flat, choppy, and characterless. Sometimes sentences need padding.

4

Editing practice will improve the way you write, as the editing will identify regular mistakes you make.

There is a story that Ernest Hemingway edited one chapter in *For Whom the Bell Tolls*, thirty-seven times. When asked why so many times, Hemingway reportedly said, "To get the words right". And, the average Hollywood scripts is edited thirty-two times?

> *Two Years Before the Mast* by Richard Henry Dana Jr.,
> "The wind was fair, and the sun shone brightly overhead as we set sail from the harbor. The ship glided gracefully through the water, its sails billowing in the breeze. The crew worked together seamlessly, their voices raised in song as they hoisted the rigging and trimmed the sails. As we sailed farther from shore, the coastline faded into the distance, replaced by the vast expanse of the open sea. The sound of the waves against the hull was like music to my ears, a soothing rhythm that seemed to carry us forward on our journey.
> The sun began to sink lower in the sky, casting a golden glow over the water. The air was filled with the salty tang of the sea, and I felt a sense of freedom and exhilaration unlike anything I had ever experienced before.
> As we sailed into the night, the stars overhead twinkled brightly, guiding us on our way. And as I stood at the helm, the wind in my face and the sea stretching out before me, I knew that I was exactly where I was meant to be."
> This excerpt from "*Two Years Before the Mast*" captures the sense of adventure and wonder experienced while sailing the open sea, conveying the beauty and majesty of the maritime world.

Part Four – Editing And Revision

Reading the above makes me want to be on that boat with them. Good, easy writing.

American or UK English?

This question comes up all the time with my new authors. What usually happens is that the writing is a mix of American English and UK English. I advise clients that the decision is one of financial expediency. Who is the audience?

If you have high hopes for it to sell internationally, then use American English. If your book is only likely to sell in New Zealand because the content may not hold interest beyond New Zealand, I would suggest you use **New Zealand English** or **UK English**

The reason I say that it is financially expedient is because approximately seventy-five percent of all English print material uses American English. Countries like China and many European countries use American English.

Most Internet content is in American English. If you want to reach the largest target audience possible, it makes sense to produce the book in the form that is most comfortable to them. This book is written in UK English, except where I have used writings that were in USA spelling. Whichever you adopt, you need to remain consistent. Check what your default setting is on your word processor. But do not be caught out, as you may have it set for American English and someone sends you a document in UK English, and so when you work in this document it will override the default settings and offer UK English. Of course, the opposite happens as well, and so even if your spell checker defaults to one format you need to check it in different documents, especially if you got them off the net.

● ● ●

4

Obviously, UK spelling is where the tradition and originality emerged. However, as the Americans rebelled and gained independence from the Brits, they, to a degree, rebelled with their spelling, and to their mind simplified many of the words. Most of the great (older) English literature and teachings came from Britain with UK spelling. But as the Americans have been so prolific in writing, and with the production of movies and other media, it happens that American publications (books, scientific papers, manuals, and the like) are greater than the output of UK publications. Therefore, their influence is now larger. Many people have been influenced (swamped) by American publications and their spelling.

So, which spelling to use? It depends. Most countries that are, or were, part of the British Empire tend to use the tradition of UK spelling, with some local amendments. These are countries such as Australia, India, New Zealand, and South Africa. Many non-Commonwealth countries like Japan and China, were influenced by the masses of American publications and so drifted into American spelling.

Which you should use is influenced by who is to read your writing. If you were to publish a book in South Africa, you are likely to upset South African readers with American spelling as their schooling system teaches UK spelling. Conversely, if you were to write something for the USA market, it would be pragmatic to use USA spelling. If you are writing for internal use (within your own country) think about what your school taught you, UK or USA spelling? If you are in school or university, it is important (and pragmatic) to use their standard and use the appropriate one, as you do not want to annoy your teacher or professor.

The worst mistake though, is inconsistency. That is writing a document that may read: I realise (UK spelling), that the color (USA spelling, no u)

Part Four – Editing And Revision

you used is to be analyzed (USA spelling), so I apologise (UK spelling). This will annoy many readers.

Avoiding native speakerism entails not discriminating against individuals based on their native language or accent, recognising and valuing diverse linguistic backgrounds, and promoting inclusivity and fairness in language-related contexts such as hiring practices, education, and social interactions.

"The limits of my language, means the limits of my world" – Ludwig Wittgetstein.
I first learnt of this concept through Vygotsky (pioneering Russian psychologist) when he articulated, language as the primary vehicle of conscious thought.
I have always thought that when I write I clarify ideas. Writing, therefore, is thinking with the pen or keyboard. The limits of our world are extended or reduced through the limits of our language.

As writers it is imperative that we extend the limits of our reader's worlds through our expressive and vibrant minds, and clear skilled writing to help the readers grow. This is irrespective of the genre.

> *Of Mice and Men* (John Steinbeck)
> "George's voice became deeper. He repeated his words rhythmically as though he had said them many times before. 'Guys like us, that work on ranches, are the loneliest guys in the world. They got no family. They don't belong no place. They come to a ranch an' work up a stake and then they go into town and blow their stake, and the first thing you know they're poundin' their tail on some other ranch. They ain't got nothing to look ahead to.'"

4

> Go to the 500-word story that you wrote earlier. Edit it down to exactly 450 words.

Leave the work for a time

As you edit, you eventually become 'word blind'. To overcome this, put the work aside for a while. Get others to read it, so they can pick up what you missed.

HELPFUL TIPS

Print the book out and read it, as it is easier to spot mistakes than on a PC screen. But on the screen, increase the magnification to say 14CPI, as with bigger text is easier to spot mistakes than smaller text.

Sequence of events

It amazes me that I receive manuscripts where the sequence is about-face. One that I received had the prince sitting down, engaged in conversation, and several lines later had him arriving at the door. I wonder if these authors first puts on their shoes, then their socks? One minute she is in a green coat, then it morphs to yellow!

When you edit, you must be methodical when working on the sequence of events.

Part Four – Editing And Revision

Clichés

In the Edit Checklist below there is a list of about 100 clichés that you would do well to eliminate from your 'creative writing'.

I recently edited a new author's manuscript, where the third person narrator wrote, and when Jim sat down, he was comfortable, and it was *ever so nice* (which is a UK cliché). However, in dialogue, saying "it is ever so nice" helps to form character and period.

Editing checklist to use when you edit

Use this checklist for all your writing.

Flow Edit for flow Creativity Add metaphors to create interest in a story.

Brevity, the secret of good writing.

Repetition, There is nothing worse than reading the same words over and over again. Scan for these and use your thesaurus to replace with synonyms.

French poet Charles Baudelairesaid, "A book is a garden, an orchard, a storehouse, a party, a company by the way, a counsellor, a multitude of counterparts."

Tenses, Always do one edit on the tenses. Decide if it is past, present or future – **Lie**, **lay**, or **laid**. I lie on the bed (present), earlier I lay on the bed (past). I lay the book down (present), I laid the parcel down (past).

He enquires, I nodded (present and past tense mixed)

Singular and plural, Always check whether you need a singular or plural.

Few is plural.

You pick up one thing and gather several things.

Make sure that you know how to make a singular word a plural (baby – babies) – sheep for a flock (not sheeps), etc.

Structure, Ensure that the writing has structure.

Edit for the first or third person consistency.

Do not have this muddled.

The message Is this consistent throughout the work?

Look for deviations.

Do things tie up? Too often things do not tie up – one minute it is green, three pages later it is blue. In a well-known mystery I read, one page he was stabbed, just above the elbow. The next page, the cut was three inches long, and on the shoulder.

Correct words and usage (homonyms and homographs)

Check that you use the correct form for words such as; fore, for or four – to or too – no or know – meet or meat. It is your right to be able to write right, as a rite (of passage), alright, Mrs Wright?

Are you using the appropriate word for the context? **Accept** means to take or receive; **except** means not including ('He took the lot *except* for...')

Angel is the divine, but **angle** is a geometry term.

Bare as in exposed. **Bear** as in 'you bear the weight', or bear as in polar bear, bear with me.

Part Four – Editing And Revision

Believe means to regard something as true or **believable**; a **belief is an opinion or a conviction** as in 'I had no **belief** in astrology...')

Berry is the fruit and **bury** something in the ground.

Brought it along from home and **bought** it from the shop.

Born = birth, and **borne** = the load was borne by the slaves.

Censor means to cut and edit, whilst **censure** is to criticise harshly.

There are hundreds more.

And just for fun – single words that are spelled the same but usually pronounced differently and that have several meanings (author unknown, but on dozens of web sites).

1) The bandage was wound around the wound.
2) The farm was used to produce produce.
3) The dump was so full that it had to refuse more refuse.
4) We must polish the Polish furniture.
5) He could lead if he would get the lead out.
6) The soldier decided to desert his dessert in the desert.
7) Since there is no time like the present, he thought it time to present the birthday girl with the present.
8) A bass was painted on the head of the bass drum
9) When shot at, the dove dove into the bushes.
10) I did not object to the object.
11) The insurance was invalid for the invalid.
12) There was a row among the oarsmen about how to row.
13) They were too close to the door to close it.
14) The buck does funny things when the does are present.
15) A seamstress and a sewer fell down into a sewer line.
16) To help with planting, the farmer taught his sow to sow.
17) The wind was too strong to wind the sail.
18) Upon seeing the tear in the painting, I shed a tear.

19) I had to subject the subject to a series of tests.
20) How can I intimate this to my most intimate friend?

UK or USA spelling? Be consistent.

Say what you mean. Is your meaning clear? Recently I saw a newspaper placard that said, 'Actor left naked'. Does this mean that the actor was left naked after a break-in, or did the actor leave the house with no clothes on?
Some more:
Police begin campaign to run down jaywalkers.
Giraffe mating, veterinarian takes over.
Miners refuse to work after death.
Red tape holds up new bridge
Astronaut takes blame for gas in spacecraft.
Kids make nutritious snacks
Hospital sued by seven foot doctors.

Get the idea?

This type of confusion happens all the time, but it will not happen with attention to detail.

Tautology Saying the same thing more than once, in a different way, such as, 'I will see this afternoon at 17h00 today', *this afternoon* is not needed as 17h00 says it all. Or *today* is superfluous if saying *this afternoon*. Tautology is more common than you think, so guard against it.

Part Four – Editing And Revision

Is the grammar clean? Remember that grammar is an evolving form and changes from time to time.

Active or passive voice This is part of creative writing. Edit the passive voice to become active, unless it has deliberately been used for effect.

Capital letters Check that you use capital letters where required.
Punctuation Refer to your grammar book.

Clichés Be original. Savvy readers hate clichés. Here is a checklist:

a penny for your thoughts	black as coal
cold shoulder	all smoke and no fire
easier said than done	a feather in his cap
piece of cake	ahead of his time
fresh as a daisy	for a good cause
the plot thickens	what goes around comes around
live and let live	another way of saying it
beauty is in the eyes of the beholder	the eleventh hour
give and take	dare to be different
as white as snow	as pure as snow
stranger than fiction	straight as an arrow
tailor-made	making a mountain out of a mole hill hill
as clear as mud	lead from the front
hoping against hope	around the clock
better half	tomorrow is another day

4

bite the dust	as a matter of fact
at a snail's pace	by hook or by crook
fighting like cats and dogs	in a nutshell
time is money	out of the blue moon
as white as a sheet	count your blessings
hard to swallow	buckle down
last but not the least	first and foremost
the darkest hour is before dawn	every rose has its thorn
blood bath	as cool as cucumber
free as a bird	beating around the bush
do or die	no pain, no gain
as easy as pie	to err is human
like father, like son	sleep like a baby
bridge over troubled waters	down in the dumps
fall head over heels	burning the midnight oil
look before you leap	caught red-handed
dawned on me	society at large
cock and bull story	put to rest
keep your fingers crossed	change of heart
there's no place like home	raining cats and dogs
don't worry, be happy	beauty is a fading flower
eye to eye	curiosity killed the cat
following in his footsteps	practice makes perfect
through thick and thin	better safe than sorry
dressed to kill	crocodile tears
as fast as lightening	dead in the water
as good as gold	beggars can't be choosers

Part Four – Editing And Revision

practice what you preach	up for grabs
deep inside	picture perfect
out of this world	love is blind
blows hot and cold	open door policy
close shave	better late than never
no news is good news	long time no see
on top of the world	down and out
laughter is the best medicine	a cock and bull story
on cloud nine	eat, drink and be merry
never say never	every dog has its day
tough nut to crack	mind over matter
make hay while the sun shines	time heals all wounds
all's well that ends well	tried and tested
kiss of death	words of wisdom
knee deep in shit	no stone unturned
big brother is watching	lost for words
a stitch in time saves nine	the grass is greener on the other side
butterflies in the stomach	a bottomless pit
easy come, easy go	the first impression is the best impression
fit as a fiddle	birds of a feather flock together
against all odds	figure of speech
haste makes waste	a half-baked idea
sleeping like a log	a bitter pill
all is fair in love and war	above and beyond the call of duty
getting off on the wrong foot	put on your thinking cap
eager beaver	good riddance to bad luck
the writing is on the wall	glimmer of hope

4

all in good time	every cloud has a silver lining
ashes to ashes, dust to dust	taken for a ride
too hot to handle	as busy as a bee
no point in crying over spilt milk	time and tide waits for no man
no time like the present	using sledge hammer to crack a nut
a time and a place	all in a day's work
happy, like a pig in muck	good as it gets
happy chappy	the devil is in the detail

There are many more.

Many of the clichés contain good wisdom. If you present the wisdom but in your words, your readers will appreciate them.

Clichés are more permissible in dialogue as it helps define character.

Commas:

Avoid commas where possible as they can interrupt the flow of the reading.
Use commas between adjectives, such as: 'he ran, hopped, skipped and crawled all over the place'. Words such as moreover, however, therefore are usually followed by a comma.
The following is well known, I do not know who was the originator The panda eats shoots and leaves. Or the panda eats, shoots, and leaves. See the difference? Another example: lonely beach walk; as opposed to; lonely, beach walk. The comma gives completely different meanings, one that helps to clarify or confuse.
Generally, you should leave out commas after conjunctions (joining words): or, as, at, and, where, this, that, such, how, but, when. But you often include a comma before 'which' – The house,

● ● ●

Part Four – Editing And Revision

which was built of stone, stood on the cliff.

A comma may be used after a conjunction if the next phrase is a different subject.

Apostrophes are used for several purposes, i.e., omission of a letter or word, or as an indication of possession. To indicate the omission of a letter or letters from a word, for example: *it's hot* for *it is hot*, or *don't* for *do not*. To indicate possession, i.e., ownership. An apostrophe placed before the last letter if the word is singular, e.g. *'This is John's house'* and placed after the word if plural; *'This is the workers' house'*). *For Pete's sake* has a possessive apostrophe as it literally means *'for the sake of Pete'*. They are not used to indicate plurals, e.g., the runners finished the race (because the race does not 'belong' to the runners i.e., the sense is not possessive). Where the noun ends with an s (such as Jones), the plural may be placed after the word e.g., the Jones' house.

Quotation marks for direct speech (speech marks)
Speech marks help readers navigate the difference between normal writing and dialogue, when it starts, and when it stops. Of late, some authors/publishers have done away with them. But the general consensus is that readers get muddled, and often have to back track to where the dialogue may have started/ended. They serve an important function, and you need to be aware of their correct and consistent use. When I went to school a double quotation mark (") was used for direct speech and the single (') for indirect speech. But over the years there has been a swing, for instance, Canada and the USA reversed this convention. Whichever you select, be consistent.

Sentence structure Are your sentences easy to follow? The same with your paragraphs.

Conventions check all dates, formats, etc through your style manual.

One word instead of two (compound words) Somehow, not some how **Himself** and him self. **Subconscious** not sub conscious

Two book critiques

I thought you may find two actual critiques I did for two of my authors. Both were for novels. By giving you these I duplicate some of the work that I have already given in this book but practical examples will help in your identifying issues with your own writing. I have only retained the relevant aspects (all names have been changed).

Hi Dale

I have read and enjoyed the story. It has potential.

Here are my comments.

Readability

Dyslexic or not, your work is very easy to read. That is a great advantage that many need to acquire. When you add more skill, metaphor and colour, you could be a very good writer.

If I was to give a rating for the work (and story), at this stage it would be around 6 out of 10. This is excellent for a dyslexic, new writer, who has had no exposure to writing skill. But 6 out of 10 is not compelling enough for a published book. But if you spend time with Detail, and Metaphor, I think you could easily elevate to 8/10 and so would be in the right area. And, as you apply some of the skills that I will teach you, there is no reason why the book would not be a 9/10. A 9/10 does not guarantee you will sell a lot of copies, but you give it the best chance to do so, and gives you something to be proud of.

Apprenticeship

It is a good idea to consider this book as your writing apprenticeship. In

Part Four – Editing And Revision

an apprenticeship, the apprentice is shown and grows with the practicing of the skills. But in your case, consider you are a PhD candidate where your research, interest, and dedication will result in you being a skilled writer. Hope my metaphors make sense.

The Period

It would be good to tell the reader what year it is in. But in our quest of saving words you could have chapters dates as chapter names. The first one could be (for instance) August 15, 1874. That immediately puts the reader into the period. The period is a drawcard, you need to include more detail.

The novel is not a historical novel as such. But it is set in a historical period, and I think you can enrich the reading experience by describing more or 'the period'.

Have you read some of the classics for the same period? If not, do so. Try and get a better feel for the dialogue, the clothes, the saddlery, buildings. Look for museums to go to 'feel' the period. Then put all of this in the pages as most readers will love it.

Opening (the hooking of the reader)

Yours is good and compelling. Well done.

The middle (which is about 80% of the story)

Ongoing interest is often lost with new novelists but you do a pretty good job of keeping the story alive. I like the swapping back and forth between the characters.

The end (resolution)

I found it interesting and was not expecting that ending. So that is good.

You have left it open for a second book, that's smart and because the story has an open-ending, it may be pragmatic to keep it as a novella, and now do another novella, picking up and continuing the adventures. A series of quickly produced novellas can do well. What you do is to create a love for the characters and the story and story-setting and you gain a dedicated audience, wanting your next book.

Dialogue

You are doing it far better than most newbies. Try and use the dialogue to further the story as opposed to adding information.

Place and detail

There is story, that conveys happenings. Then there are stories that are so intriguing listeners lose track of time and all sense of where they are. This emerges from the detail and place (the setting). I'll not elaborate here but your story could be rich because of the period and the environment but you (mostly) miss that opportunity – it's like having fish n' chips without salt, or cornflakes without milk... if you know what I mean.

Humour

Readers absolutely love a humorous story. Not too much, just gems here and there.

A full novel or a novella

At the moment it is a novella. From a selling potential a full novel is likely to do better. If it is to remain a novella, then not much needs to be added, just a good edit, and a bit more colour.

If it is to become a full book, by the time you add the place and detail it will be adequate for a full book. I suggest you don't make that decision at the moment but read the below, try and attend to the edits. Only then make up your mind. That is, unless you are sick of it and want to leave it.

Where to from here?

The story is a good one and does not need much effort. It is colour and padding that you need (detail and place), and of course, editing. Try the editing and the samples I have given. Work through your manuscript

Part Four – Editing And Revision

much the same as a dedicated gardener converts a rough piece of ground into a place of beauty. Take your time, put on your creative hat, and enjoy the process. By doing do, I promise you the work will become better than 8/10.

Hi Jill,
The first thing you want to know is, what I do think of the work? In short, it has aspects of excellence. But there are some but's, which I shall go into later.

It really is a good story – there is too much in it to be ignored. The way that you describe the various governmental situations is eloquent. I will now get to the nitty-gritty.

Writing skill

It is a pleasure to receive writing that is well written and easy to read. Not much needs to be done, only a few mistakes that will be cleaned up in the final edit.

There are however a lot of the incorrect' (quotation marks) for the dialogue that need to be amended, where at times you use (') single and other times (") double.

I also think that it is (generally) easier reading to have new dialogue on a separate line.

And now for the but's... Too many words between the story
What I am about to tell you is common amongst new authors; and that is, it is too wordy. I believe the manuscript could be reduced by 20% (perhaps more) and without losing meaning.

It is too wordy from two points of view; the one is that there are times when the writing is long-winded (mainly in explanations), and

4

there are other times when there is material, that to my way of thinking is superfluous.

The following are two examples from your work, followed with a rework of mine.

You wrote: It took several seconds but the response came. To his relief Joe found himself addressed with something approaching trust rather than rejection.

"That's true, Joe", Margie replied quietly, then smiled and resumed walking. Relaxed now, and said loudly, with laughter bubbling through, 'We're a couple of very important people, aren't we?'

My suggestions...

Joe was pleased to be trusted.

"That's true Joe", Margie chuckled, "we're two important people, aren't we?"

Eighteen words replaced fifty-two, yet the essence of the conversation has not been altered. The dialogue showed the comradery that both felt at that time and so the explanation was irrelevant.

Another example, you wrote: He wanted nothing more than to be indoors, away from the mounting heat and glare. Normally he would have avoided walking on the beach this close to the middle of the day.

Or Usually, he tried to avoid the heat of the day, and so wanted to get indoors.

Thirty-two words replaced by sixteen.

To show you another use of superfluous words in your writing is where you use the words **would have** avoided... It reads better if you said; he **would** avoid ...

Part Four – Editing And Revision

Reducing word count through dialogue

A writing skill that you may want to look at is to use the dialogue to show action. This is **showing and not telling**, showing the reader what is happening through action and dialogue. An example: you wrote, **her beautiful body on the bed**... By using the word beautiful you are telling the reader, yet the reader does not see beauty the way you do. If you said something like; **her flat stomach and pair-shaped breasts**... You show the reader her beauty.

You can use the dialogue as a tool to show and not tell, whilst reducing explanation. As I said, your dialogue is generally good but you tend to rely more on explanation when the dialogue can show it better. You wrote, **this made him angry and so he retorted with...** But if you wrote it like, **he retorted, "Who the hell are you to..."** The words convey the emotion. It also indicates aspects of the character as being explosive. But if you wrote it like; **I... I... ...I'm not sure if I agree with you...** This would show a diffident or self-deprecating character. See what I mean?

Jill, if you can reduce the explanation, through amending the dialogue, and also 'show' the character through the dialogue then you have achieved writing skill. It does not mean that every single explanation or dialogue needs to be reworked, but it does require attention. I think that the distance between your good book and that of a terrific book is what I have just given you. The above can reduce that distance.

The structure (plot) of the story

To introduce this point I'm going to give you two explanations of structure. The first is for a movie, whereby there is always a distinct introduction, a middle-story, and then the end or resolution. It is the same with 98% of all novels. However, if you look at soaps on TV, they do not really have that structure, they kind of just 'roll' on as one long-winded saga with numerous innuendos.

As mentioned above, I think your story has potential. But for me it only really got going on about page 27. This is far too long. In many aspects those first 27 pages were written almost as if they were 'a soap'. Yes, you start off the story well but then for the next 27 odd pages it was soap-like. I do understand that many of those pages contained important material that supports the latter part of the book, but there is so much there that can be deleted.

Also, in your desire to get across as much researched information as possible – **where facts seem more important than story**. And once again, a lot of this information is good information, and interesting information, but the trick is to know what to leave out.

Before the wind is taken out of your sales, I do not believe that it would take much to adjust the feel of the story.

Characterisation

The main characters were fine, but with the above suggestions they would be made stronger.

To summarise

Aspects of excellence, great story, wonderful insight, but too wordy. Take heart Jill, you have done a wonderful job.

● ● ●

Part Four – Editing And Revision

> Again, go to the 450-word story that you edited earlier and reduce it to 400 words.
>
> Doing these exercises is great skill-building.

4

Part Five – To Have Published Or To Self-Publish, That Is The Question

In this section:

- Self publishing.
- Traditional publishing.
- Preparation of manuscript.
- Vanity publishing.

The aloof nature of traditional publishers forces many authors to self-publish. With advances in technology, this is not only possible but often a good option.
I was asked to write the following explanation for a magazine. It will give you an understanding as to what is required to publish or self-publish.

5

To self-publish?

Have you ever tried to find a publisher for your manuscript? I did with my first work. In doing so I learnt about slush piles, egotistical editors, and impersonal replies. In fact, I don't know which was worse, the impersonal replies or no replies.

At the time I did not understand why most publishers could not be straight and courteous in their dealings with authors. Authors just want to be treated with respect and dignity and if their ten years of midnight slog does not stand up to scrutiny, so be it.

I continued looking and finally found a small publisher. Minnetonka took the book on, and I was grateful. Mari Wessels the owner was a sweetie. Throughout my process from writer to published author, to publisher, I had literally dozens of writers tell me how their attempts to secure a publisher were as demoralising as mine. But it was worse for some, as they were never published.

I also met authors who, after getting tired of the 'run around', went the self-publishing route. For some this has worked out well, but sadly for most it has not.

There are several reasons for this. One is that book buyers from retail outlets look at self-published authors with scepticism – they know that often self-published authors lack the final quality that is required to bring a professional product to market.

Another reason for the non-movement of books from basement into the hands of the book buying public is because the author does not know how to sell or market a book. And then there are those who have the attitude of; "I am an author, surely you don't expect me to do that work?" And so, their books gather dust, turn mouldy and become rat food, whilst the author dreams of what might have been.

Either way, I urge you take that manuscript out of the cupboard or off your hard drive and get it out to the world. After all, you have nothing to lose.

> **PART FIVE – TO HAVE PUBLISHED OR TO SELF-PUBLISH, THAT IS THE QUESTION**

I have had two books published by two traditional publishers, and have self-published about eight books, and now I am a publisher myself. I have helped some sixty authors to publish, so I feel that I am in a good position to give you fair comment on whether to self-publish or go the traditional publishing route.

I want you to dream that you are a published author. This is a story about you being published. It must be at least half a page. Do not write this in your journal, but on a separate piece of paper. Write the story in the first person, and include:
An overview of the book.
Why you wanted to write the book?
Who is the market?
Your submission to a publisher.
The acceptance of the book by the publisher.
Successfully selling the book.
When you finish, edit and clean up your work, as you are to put it on your study wall or somewhere where you will see it and be motivated. Whenever you see it, stop for a moment, and keep the dream alive.

HELPFUL TIPS — *The above exercise is goal setting and visualising in action.*

5

Self publishing - the good and the bad

If you self-publish, you are effectively running a business. As a business, there are four aspects:

- Production.
- Marketing.
- Distribution.
- Administration.

The challenges

Believe me, there is so much work attached to getting your own book out and selling it that unless you have hundreds of hours to dedicate to it, you will not make it. There is a lot to learn, and the ongoing monitoring is constant.

Points to consider:

- All the promotion, as given in the next chapter.
- The entire production process can be arduous and full of pitfalls. The printing and cover design require a lot of work, and both can spoil the book if not done properly.
- The distribution process entails that you personally go to hundreds of bookstores. Most chain book stores (worldwide) have autonomy as to which books they purchase. You may drive across town to see a manager, who may take one copy from you. Three months later, he may email you requesting you collect the book because it did not sell. If you have been paid, you will have to return the money. The result is lots of wasted time and frustration.
- You must consider how to get your book to stores on the other side of the country, and also the world.
- The media are also difficult and will not always show interest if you are unknown. You need to create media kits, with good copy

> PART FIVE –TO HAVE PUBLISHED OR TO SELF-PUBLISH, THAT IS THE QUESTION

and be persistent in sending and resending. If you do not get to lots of media, then your book will not be known and will fail.

They are not interested because the media contact had probably fifty other requests in the last few months.

There are other challenges:

- Many retail outlets will not see you as they do not want to deal with individuals. They want to reduce their administration by reducing their number of suppliers.
- You must fund the book out of your own pocket.
- You will be on a learning curve, so quality can slip, which means that you will have paid for a book that may not sell.

You must decide if you have the time and desire to do all of the above or if you want to be a writer and focus on your core abilities.

HELPFUL TIPS — *You want to self-publish? Know what is required.*

The benefits of self-publishing

For those who have the time, knowledge, and energy, self-publishing may be a better option. The main benefit is that you earn 100% of the net profit.

As I said at the start of this chapter, to self-publish properly you need to work it as a business on a full-time basis. But what a great business as everything you do could lead to more sales or publicity.

5

Running your own self-publishing company could be gratifying and profitable for the right person with the right book.

Assume you self-publish, but after six months you realise the cover design does not work. As a self-publisher you can change it. You can update information. Perhaps you have great feedback for the book, you can add that in. Whereas a publisher is seldom likely to make amendments – you are stuck with it.

To run your own self-publishing company, you need to be methodical, and like to play with technology.

Another thing to take note of is that this aspect of the industry is changing so fast that information you get today could be out of date in eighteen months.

There has been a massive growth in the Indi (Independent book Publishers) publishing scene, and around that is a wealth of support.

Traditional publishing

Publishers' agreements are not always fair to the authors. Be aware before you sign.

Royalties can be a low percentage of the sales value and slow in coming.

You have no control over quality, performance, pricing, etc.

Although you will still own the copyright, it will not mean much for the duration of the agreement.

The average time-frame for most publishers to get a book out is around two years. It can even take up to a year for a publisher to give you an acceptance or rejection. If you self-publish and are organised you can get a book out in a few months.

A publishing house is a company that takes people's work and does with it what the author cannot.

Publishers have the reach to be able to distribute widely. They also have international contacts so they can sell international rights. They can be frustratingly cumbersome, or amazingly efficient. You get a good one and you could do well.

Another way of looking at this is – to self-publish successfully, you need to be more entrepreneurial (along with your creativity). For those who are creative but not entrepreneurial, a traditional publisher would be best.

Preparation of the manuscript

For your book to be ready to submit to a publisher with the best chance of success, the following is advisable:

- Your biography must be included, as a publisher will want to know about you.
- Paragraphs should be indented (usually five spaces).
- The final edit will have been done.

- You need a synopsis. This must be well written, so let the creativity that you possess flow.

In addition, it can be helpful to submit a written back cover text. The back cover of a book is a 'silent salesperson' and so needs to convey as much about the ethos of the work in the least number of words.

- It is preferable to have your testimonials in place, as remember you need to sell the publisher on how good the work is and how good you are.
- Lay the text out, Chapter one, Chapter two, contents, etc. and use double line spacing.
- Make sure you have a covering letter that includes your name and contact details.
- Who is likely to buy the book.

Each publisher has their own requirements when it comes to the submission of a manuscript. To find out what these are, ask for a submission form. We have a document called How to submit your manuscript which contains our requirements. Providing an author fills it out correctly and answers all the questions, we will get a good idea if we want to look at the full manuscript.

Typical submission forms will ask for:

- Information regarding the format the manuscript is to be in, such as double or single line spacing.
- A synopsis
- A list of the chapters
- Sample chapters, to assess the writing ability of the author.
- Marketing information – who is the book aimed at? Are there similar books on the market? The book categories, etc.

If you get a rejection:

- Use the opportunity to learn, try and find out from the publisher why they rejected the manuscript.
- A slush-pile is a pile of trashed books that have not had a fair reading. It is possible that your book is one such book. You will never know, so continue the hunt for 'your publisher'.
- It may be possible that the publisher has recently produced a similar book and may not want another on the same topic. Perhaps their production capacity is full, and they are only looking for the cream. Publishers also have a budget and it is possible that they have exceeded theirs before you submitted your manuscript. There are many reasons for rejections that may have nothing to do with your writing ability or the quality of the book.
- Remember that publishers are subjective and so their comments may not be accurate, but in most instances, there is likely to be truth in them.

Pre-Publishing

When preparing a book for publication there are many details that must be adhered to, such as how to express numerals or typography in a recognised formats (we spoke about a Style Manual).

The synopsis

The writing of a well composed synopsis separates the amateur from the professional. Your book may or may not be published because of your synopsis standard.

To sell your book, you must take enough time and become an expert in writing your synopsis (there are people who specialise in this, for a fee).

5

> Scarlett's voice was sharp. 'I can't think about the war today. I don't want to hear any more about it. It's all anyone talks about, and I'm sick of it.'
> Rhett's eyes narrowed. 'You can't bury your head in the sand forever, Scarlett. The war affects us all, whether you like it or not.'
> 'Well, I don't see why I have to listen to you lecture me on it,' Scarlett retorted. 'You're not my husband, and you're certainly not my father.'
> 'I may not be your husband, but I am a friend,' Rhett replied coolly. 'And as your friend, I'll tell you when you're being foolish.'
> 'Foolish?' Scarlett's voice rose. 'Me, foolish? Look who's talking! You're the one who's always been nothing but trouble.'"
>
> *Gone with the Wind* by Margaret Mitchell. In this excerpt, Scarlett and Rhett engage in a heated argument, exchanging sharp words and differing viewpoints. Their dialogue reflects their tumultuous relationship and the tensions of the time period in which the novel is set.

Vanity publishing

Vanity publishing is a cross between traditional publishing and self-publishing, where you pay to have the book produced. The vanity publisher acts as a facilitator.

Is vanity publishing a good way to go?

Be careful, for the following reasons:

- You take the risk. It is your money that is put on the line, not theirs. Even though you fund the project, you are (usually) still locked into an agreement.

PART FIVE – TO HAVE PUBLISHED OR TO SELF-PUBLISH, THAT IS THE QUESTION

- The following happened to me in my early days of my writing: The manuscript I submitted was not good enough for publishing (at the time I was not aware of this), yet they accepted it and even told me that the work was good (standard reply to suck me in). This was quickly followed up with their invoice and agreement. Being gullible I would have paid them if I had had the money.
- Many vanity publishers work the numbers game and do not seem to care how many books they produce as they operate hoping that one will be a seller. That is how they make their money (cover their operating costs with the fees they charge, and get 'the cream' from the odd book that sells).
- Once you pay your deposit, it's gone. If you have complaints, no matter how valid, you will never see your money again.
- Many tend not to be as meticulous as a normal publisher (as you are taking the financial risk), so you could end up with an inferior product.
- They also tend not to be too active with promotion and distribution as there are costs involved in doing so.
- Some charge exorbitant fees as they know that many new authors are so keen to be published they are gullible.

The vanity industry has a bad name, and many are in the business to receive money and not to pay it out.
This component of the industry has improved and although there are many sharks, there are good honest vanity publishers that do their best for an author, and at a fair price.

What is good about vanity publishing?

- For the first-time author it is a softer way to go than self-publishing.
- Some are sincere in their efforts to help the author.
- A major benefit of using a vanity publisher is that the royalty you receive will be higher than from traditional publishers.

- The good ones will include you in some of the decision making, such as cover design.

Be open to the fact that your book, for whatever reason, may not be good enough for publishing. Treat the book as a learning process and start again. A baker has a three-year apprenticeship to bake a loaf of bread. You also have an apprenticeship to learn to write. Don't give up.

HELPFUL TIPS

Although we have left the writing skills section of the book behind, your writing lessons continue.
Write exactly 750 words on a boy (describe him) who meets a girl (describe her). 'Show' the setting and express the emotion of the boy for the girl, and the girl for the boy. As you write about the emotions, try to access emotions that no doubt you have experienced in the past and transfer them to the text.
Remember, it is a story, and so there must be an introduction, body, and resolution. It can end in a happy or a sad way, but either way, it must have a strong ending. I want you to enjoy this writing.

How much can you sell your book for?

Looking at bookstores will confuse you, as there seems to be no governing factor on pricing. You may get a top-selling author with a low price. It could be that the book was printed in the Far East and they may have printed many thousands of copies to gain an economy of scale.

Another book could be from a local author, and you think, 'Ah, no *ad valerian* (tax), shipping fees, and not charged for in American Dollars'. Yet the price is high. Perhaps the author or publisher only printed 100 copies and so there is no economy of scale. It could also be the author was overly charged by the printer, or that the author wants to get rich in as short a time as possible, and so the mark-up is too high.

Nevertheless, you do need to get a feel for price as you will have to justify this to customers and retail outlet buyers. You do not want the book to cost too little, nor do you want to miss out on sales because it is too expensive.

Other factors to consider when setting the price:

- Different market sectors will pay different prices.
- Different types of books, such as coffee table books or novels, attract different buyers and therefore different price tags.
- The quality of the paper, the cover, the pictures, and the printing, will mean a higher or lower production cost – the better the quality, the greater the mark-up.
- A well-known author can command a better price.

Don't be like some panicked clients who come to us needing to make a fortune in a few weeks. Make sure that you have your normal monthly overheads covered from other sources of finance. Book sale profits are a bonus, not the be-all and end-all.

5

What about an agent?

The industry has changed over the last twenty years, and agents are not as widely used as they were. And, over the years, the profits in publishing have steadily diminished. As a result, agents' fees have been squeezed to the point that in most instances it is not viable for agents and authors to work together. Because of the squeeze of profits, some agents are now charging a fee for their services.

There are two exceptions to the above. The first is that agents are usually used for better known authors with big sales, as the book sales volumes allow for the agent's fee. If you are a new unknown author, and that is probable as you are the target audience of this book, then you may not be able to afford an agent.

The second exception is that some publishing houses will not receive submissions from individuals. This forces authors to share the royalties with agents.

Those publishers only work through agents, as:

- They want to reduce the number of submissions from literally thousands of individuals, to a more manageable number of 'pre-assessed manuscripts.'
- They believe an agent will have scrutinised the book for content quality and writing skill.
- They would prefer to do the legalities with a well-versed agent as opposed to an inexperienced author.

PART FIVE – TO HAVE PUBLISHED OR TO SELF-PUBLISH, THAT IS THE QUESTION

Your chosen publisher may demand that you go through an agent. If you do use an agent ensure that the royalties are reasonable. Agents' services are usually helpful, as they do their best to secure a good publisher, whilst ensuring that the terms are beneficial to all parties.

If you feel that you do want to use an agent, get hold of The Writers' and Artists' Yearbook as this list's agents throughout the English-speaking world.

Do not stop trying to find a publisher. You may have had ten rejections but pick yourself up for the eleventh as it may be the eleventh that comes back with a yes. Trust your ability; remain positive whilst continuing to improve the manuscript.

Remember – it is not the number of rejections that matter, but the one acceptance that does.

Make sure that you research the market the publisher operates in. For instance, some publishers only focus on war history.

5

> Look at your desk and imagine that you have X-ray vision, and you can see into the wood, metal, or plastic. As you look, you see a colony of microscopic creatures that have a life of their own and are totally oblivious to you or anything beyond the wood, metal, or plastic. This is a lovely theme that could explore the parallel between us in our world (or plane of existence), where there could be other far more intelligent creatures that are aware of us, whilst we remain oblivious to their presence. Or it could be about the millions of different life forms that make up all that there is in the woodwork.
> Take as long as you need and have fun with it.

Over the last fifteen years there have been a plethora of web-based 'self-help' publishers that have sprung up. Some of these include: Amazon, Smashwords, Creative Space, Lightening Source, Xlibrisl, etc. These are a cross between traditional publishers and vanity publishers. Some charge heavily, others just a few setup costs.

As their economy of scale is large, they can do well for your book.

In essence, their offering is to make the self-publisher's job as easy as possible. And what is also of benefit is that you can cancel the agreement with immediate effect if for some reason you are dissatisfied (but you will not get a refund).

A word of caution on these. As their systems are designed to receive as many books as possible (hundreds of thousands), the options for layout and design are limited, and therefore the book may be flat looking. I recommend that you pay a freelance layout artist to get the best job possible.

> **PART FIVE – TO HAVE PUBLISHED OR TO SELF-PUBLISH, THAT IS THE QUESTION**

The options are for both print and ePubs (electronic publications).

> *The Great Gatsby* by F. Scott Fitzgerald, published in 1925:
> "Daisy's voice was strained. 'You know I love you.'
> Gatsby's eyes flashed with anger. 'Love me? How can you say that when you're married to him?'
> 'Please, don't start this again,' Daisy pleaded. 'You know I can't leave Tom.'
> 'But you could leave him for me,' Gatsby insisted. 'We could be happy together.'
> 'Happy?' Daisy laughed bitterly. 'Do you really think that's possible?'
> 'I do,' Gatsby said firmly. 'I know we could make it work.'
> 'You're living in a dream world,' Daisy snapped. 'This can never be.'
> 'But it could,' Gatsby argued. 'If only you had the courage to leave him.'"

In this excerpt, Gatsby and Daisy engage in a passionate argument about their relationship and the possibility of being together. Their dialogue reflects the tensions and complexities of their romantic entanglement, as well as the societal constraints that prevent them from being together.

Summary on self-publishing versus traditional publishing

Both methods can be successful. For self-publishing, this book gives you all the tools for you to do it well. Self-publishing is time consuming. However, if you have the time to manage your new business you can do well.

If you do not have the time or the desire to self-publish, then traditional publishers are the way to go.

5

If you cannot secure a traditional publisher, then look for a vanity publisher, but heed the warnings given.

Part Six – Marketing And Promotion

In this section:

- Market research.
- Promoting your book.
- Building the brand.
- Your Website.
- Search Engine Optimisation (SEO).
- Keywords.
- Metadata.
- Nielsen bookdata.
- Backlinks.
- Domain and page authority.
- Blogs, Facebook, Twitter, et cetera.
- Newsletter.
- Amazon.
- Goodreads.
- Trade magazine advertising.
- Media kit.
- Book reviews.
- Retail outlets.
- Libraries.
- International book rights.

6

The trick is to write your book once and sell it in as many ways as possible – print; ePub; audio, and workshopping.

Now your book is ready, or soon to be ready, you need to 'get the word out there'. In many ways, this is harder than writing the book as many of the players within distribution and purchasing are beyond your control. But by following the below advice you will give yourself the best chance of success.

Market research

How do you segment the market and determine if your book is likely to create interest? You do market research.

As market research is a massive subject, I only include these few important guidelines:

Who is going to buy the book?

- How many other books have been written on the same topic? Probably many but that should not deter you. That is, providing you say it in a different way (in your voice), or extend what has been written. It must offer a different angle.
- How big is the market? If you were to write an interesting book on microbes inside your desk, there may not be that many who would want to buy it.

Part Six – Marketing And Promotion

We are increasingly moving towards specialisation. Readers want to hone in on specific subjects. You must identify those subjects and serve that market. Just a glance at all the magazines in a news agency will confirm the diversification of subjects. Then there are literally thousands on the net.

So many marketing options

Have you ever dropped a plate of mincemeat on the floor that splattered far and wide only to see your dog, delightedly bounce in to help you vacuum the floor with her tongue? Once the bulk of the meat is devoured, the nose scoots around the floor to ensure that not a single morsel escapes detection. To market your book, you must be like that dog and sniff every opportunity; none should go unnoticed. This takes time, but it is what is required. The effort can be worth it.

Know it will take in the region of two years to fully market your book.

Marketing and promotion

Authors need to have a strong brand. In fact, according to Dr Rachel Noorda, *"The author's brand is stronger than that of the Publisher's brand."* You can only create one by hard work, doing email lists, newsletters, lectures, workshops, posting on social media, SEO. Then, and only then, after continuous analysis of your customers can you make sure you fit what they require.

6

As an author, published by a traditional publisher or self-published, it is unlikely your book will sell if you are not a 'brand'.
The following sections will help you understand what is required to 'brand' yourself.

Promoting your book

Irrespective of whether you go through a publishing house or self-publish, you will have to promote and market your work. In the documents that I give prospective authors there is a section explaining that if the book is to be successful, the publisher and author must work as a team. We lose interest if an author is not prepared to help with the marketing. If a book, especially from an unknown author is not promoted it is unlikely to sell. We can see from book sales those authors who roll up their sleeves and do the work.

Building the brand

Authors who do it well start this process at least a year before the book is published. You need the audience as the book comes out, not two years afterwards.

So, who is the audience? That is your most important question – who is aligned with your writing and subject? What is your niche audience?

Where is your audience?

When you know who your audience is, you will easily find out how to reach them. You will be telling them what they long to hear.

The industry calls this 'Your platform'. Your platform is a powerful key to success. The other is a well-written and well-produced book.

Part Six – Marketing And Promotion

To create a platform will require you to put on a marketer's hat and one of a 'tech' specialist. These are more time consuming than difficult.

The marketing component is to know who your audience is through research. Know what makes your audience tick. Only then can you develop a strategy as to what message to offer them and how to offer it.

The tech component is expediting the message to that targeted audience; this can be through targeted advertising, social media, articles, blogs, guest blogs, podcasts, videos, interviews, speaking events, media appearances, and SEO.

As you connect to 'Your Tribe', you will get additional feedback from which to better understand and relate to them. But a solid platform could take years to develop. You do not need thousands of followers, but you do need followers who like your message. The time required is enormous, but think of it this way, it is not just your book you are promoting, you are a brand, that can last many years with many of your books.

A publishing house does not have the time to get to know you to the level required to offer that message. Nor do they have the time to make you a celebrity. Only you can do this if you have the desire. Your destiny is truly in your own hands.

Some Social Media stats (sourced from the Independent Book Publishers Association, based in the USA (IBPA) 2021, vol 39, 2).NB, these figures are likely to exclude China and much of ASIA.

As time passes the stats will change but you need a reasonable understanding of all these offerings, those that are losing and gaining ground.

6

Facebook; is used by 1.6 billion small businesses. 62% of people were more interested in a product after seeing it in a Facebook story.

X (previously Twitter); 82% of social media leads come from X.

Instagram: 69% of social marketers say they are planning to increase their use of Instagram.

300 million people use Printerest monthly, and they are projected to grow to 120 million monthly active users.

Tik Tok was the fastest growing social media app of 2020 (for the second year in a row).

YouTube advertising is massive.

41% of teenagers say Snapchat is their preferred channel.

The most obvious reason for using Social Media (SM) is to get to understand an audience, whilst they get to trust you – hopefully there is a fit. SM is not selling. People join SM platforms mainly for entertainment, they do not want to be sold to. But they will listen to good stories, and this can lead to a loyal following and then sales.

SM marketing is a slow process but with persistence there will be a steady growth of advocates for you and your book. The more people who respond to your blog, the more information you gain, analyse and utilise this information in understanding them better, so you are better able to give them what they want.

The different SM platforms offer different methods.

- X (Twitter) gives succinct information to potentially a large audience. But it helps if you become known and trusted on the platform as a 'person of influence'.
- Facebook gives you the chance to offer more information about the book and what you stand for. Whereby, you steadily build a

> Part Six – Marketing And Promotion

profile. This coupled with a FB marketing campaign is a good approach.
- Instagram is less likely to help as it is image and not text based. Good for promos of the book cover, images from within the book, and promo photos (book launches, etc.).
Instagram can be a good way to keep your name in front of the audience, once you have the audience.

The above are the three most used social media platforms used by professional marketers.

What you may have learnt over the last six months about social media marketing could all change tomorrow. The understanding of the metrics of social media marketing is the hardest component in promoting your book because of the constant industry changes.

Your own website

Coupled to your Facebook page (see below), can be a website that specifically promotes the book and your brand. The Facebook blog shows the readers that you are the guru and that you can be trusted. The website gives the nuts and bolts of the book and services you may offer, as well as a shopping cart and contact details. The Facebook page and website support each other. The website may only be one page, but that can be enough to start with. And of course, through an RSS feed, the blogposts are placed on the website.

On your website, make sure that you have sample pages of the book. This usually is set up by your webmaster as it can get complex.

6

A website will not be seen by Google, or the other search engines if it is not optimised. The main optimisation is SEO (Search Engine Optimisation, see below). As it is a changing game, this is best left to specialists.

The following are three processes that you can employ that will help increase interest and sales.

The first is an **offer for the browser to download a free chapter**. Pick one that is of interest and can be read without lead-up chapters. Never offer the last chapter.

Secondly, have a **sign up for my free newsletter**. Perhaps entice them with a free gift.

Finally, depending on the book, you could offer a free quiz. Look at the quiz ARE YOU READY TO BE AN AUTHOR? in the first chapter of this book as a sample.

Search Engine Optimisation (SEO)

I said a few lines back that SEO is best left to the experts. That is true. However, for those with the time and flair to do it themselves I offer the following.

(SEO) is a pivotal digital marketing strategy designed to enhance a website's visibility and ranking on search engine results pages (SERPs). The primary goal is to optimise various elements of a website to align with search engine algorithms, ultimately improving its chances of being discovered by users searching for relevant content.

Key Components of SEO:

Keyword Research – Identifying and targeting relevant keywords (see below) that potential visitors are likely to use in search queries.

Part Six – Marketing And Promotion

On-Page Optimisation – Optimising individual web pages to improve their content, structure, and HTML code. This includes title tags, meta descriptions, header tags, and URL structures.

Content Quality – Creating high-quality, informative, and engaging content that satisfies user intent. Regularly updating content keeps the website relevant.

Backlink Building – Acquiring high-quality backlinks from reputable websites to demonstrate authority and trustworthiness to search engines.

Technical SEO – Addressing technical aspects like website speed, mobile responsiveness, and crawlability to ensure search engines can easily access and index the site.

User Experience (UX) – Providing a seamless and positive user experience, including intuitive navigation, fast loading times, and mobile-friendliness.

How to Implement SEO

Keyword Research and Analysis – Use keyword research tools to identify relevant keywords related to your content or business. Consider the search volume, competition, and user intent associated with each keyword.

On-Page Optimisation – Implement targeted keywords naturally within your content, headers, and meta tags. Ensure that titles and descriptions accurately reflect the page's content.

Quality Content Creation – Develop informative and engaging content that addresses user queries. Regularly update and refresh content to stay current and maintain relevance.

Link Building – Build a diverse and high-quality backlink profile. Seek opportunities for guest posting, collaborate with influencers, and ensure your content is shareable to attract organic backlinks.

Technical SEO Audits – Regularly conduct technical SEO audits to identify and address issues affecting website performance. This includes checking for broken links, optimising images, and improving site speed.

Local SEO:

If applicable, optimise your website for local searches by claiming and optimising your *Google My Business* listing, obtaining local citations, and encouraging customer reviews.

Analytics and Monitoring – Utilise analytics tools such as Google Analytics and Google Search Console to track website performance. Monitor keyword rankings, traffic, and user behavior to make informed adjustments.

In summary, SEO is a multifaceted approach that requires ongoing effort. By understanding search engine algorithms, focusing on user experience, and staying informed about industry trends, you can sell more books through the digital landscape.

But if that is not enough, the above must be done for each of the major search engines, which typically include:

Google – As the dominant search engine globally, optimising for Google is paramount. Follow Google's guidelines for quality content, mobile-friendliness, and user experience.

Bing – Although Google is dominant, Bing is still a significant player, especially in certain regions. Ensure your website is also optimised for Bing's algorithm, including relevant keywords and high-quality content.

Yahoo – Yahoo search results are powered by Bing, so optimising for Bing often translates to improved performance on Yahoo as well.

Baidu (for China) and or Yandex for Russia – If your target audience includes China or Russia, they are crucial.

Part Six – Marketing And Promotion

DuckDuckGo – With a focus on user privacy, DuckDuckGo is gaining popularity. Although its market share is smaller, optimising DuckDuckGo can contribute to a more diverse search strategy.

While Google dominates the search engine landscape, diverse optimisation across these platforms ensures broader visibility and accessibility to a book buying audience. Adapting strategies to the specific algorithms and preferences of each search engine is crucial for a comprehensive and effective SEO approach.

Many writing sites recommend Tik Tok and Linkedin to grow readership.

And, if that is not enough… markets vary from country to country. So, a marketing strategy, or keyword analysis that works in the USA may not work in Germany (not to mention the language differences).

Keywords

Keywords are a component of metadata. On their own they are important, especially for all your marketing material that is on your website and as given above for the Book Metadata. Keywords bring visibility to the book, but the rest of the merchandising brings the sales.

When a browser inserts a longtail (a keyword phrase) search, say, *historical romance in Florence*, instead of just typing *Romance,* the browser is showing stronger intent. Try and use between 100 to 130 keywords and keyword phrases. Do not duplicate words in the book name. Think like a consumer.

The person who does the keywords and metadata needs a deep knowledge of the book, that is why *you* must do them.

There is more emphasis for keywords and keyword phrases embedded in content than keyword lists (which some sites will ask for).

That is why it is important for the back-cover page to have good content, embedded with keyword/phrases, without making it ridiculous.

When you have created your keywords, run them through some of the below listed sites to determine how good they are, play around with them, and watch the results improve or worsen. When you have inserted keywords or phrases, Google them, or search for them on Amazon to see if they are found.

When you Google them, look at other words Google offers and add the relevant to your list.

On an ongoing basis, try and improve poor performing keywords. As technology changes, the metadata must be amended accordingly, or it will be left behind.

For example, you may have written a book for dog lovers and want to embed keywords into the marketing material. You could come up with the words *dog enthusiasts*, or *canine lovers*. But these words or phrases may not attract as many hits as you thought. It is here that Google Analytics can help you determine the best keywords.

In this discussion I do not giving you specific instructions on how to do this, it is more about the concept. But if you research Google Analytics, you will see their options. If you insert say, *dog enthusiasts*, it will give you a list of words or phrases that have been searched on by the Internet searching population for anything to do with dogs over the past year. You might find your search criteria had only been searched on by 10,000 people. But the term dog lovers may have been searched on by 100,000. It makes sense to have words embedded that have been searched on by 100,000 people as opposed to those that have only been searched for by 10,000.

Part Six – Marketing And Promotion

Your book title must have a keyword or keyword phrase if possible. I also recommend that your book has a subtitle, which gives additional opportunity for a wider range of keyword or phrases. That way, if your book is called, *The dog book, a book for canine enthusiasts* and if they search on dog or canine enthusiasts it may come up with your actual book title.

To generate content info and keywords;

- Google Trends – compare search volume for search terms. To understand the intent of the audience.
- Answer the Public – top searches, prepositions, search volumes (a paid service).
- Google Analytics – (also a paid service) to determine where people are coming from and what their interest is.

Ubersuggest

- https://keywordtool.io/google-suggest or http://www.bing.com/toolbox/keywords for Bing's research tool.

If you have the time or funds, audience analysis is also important. From those that have purchased the book, see what words they use to describe it, to find and understand for consumer signals. These methods are mainly for the bigger players. It is a long and arduous process.

Keywords must be as specific as possible. Legitimate spelling variations of an important word (for example, "Hanukkah," "Chanukah," and "Chanukkah") or alternate spellings of words and names may be useful as keywords (UK and American spelling). While many search engines have dictionaries that will bring back spelling variations in search results, these dictionaries vary from search engine to search engine.

Use as many synonyms as are appropriate, like the book description and subject codes. A book about Christmas is a book about holidays, Santa Claus, presents, and December. Likewise, use varied spelling or misspellings of the title, themes, or your name: chrismas, xmas, Santa Clause, etc. Include awards, honours, and other notable achievements.

Try and use common phrases or words that came from the book.

Figure out who will want to read the book (demographics) and try and determine words that they would search for.

When a good keyword is found, you can use it multiple times as phrases, like Japanese cooking, Japanese gardening, or Japanese houses.

When a keyword is inserted into Google, a list of synonyms will appear. From these you may be able to select more words and use synonyms to get even more words.

Networking

Networking when marketing your book is a crucial step in gaining visibility and reaching your target audience. Building connections with fellow authors, industry professionals, and potential readers can lead to valuable opportunities for promotion, collaboration, and support. Effective marketing strategies, whether through social media, book events, or other channels, help generate buzz and interest in your book, ultimately contributing to its success and longevity in the competitive publishing landscape.

Metadata

Metadata is your content. This is also compiled by your specialist.

> Part Six – Marketing And Promotion

What are meta tags or Meta tagging?

Meta tagging is used in book marketing, as identifiers to help identify your book over the thousands like yours. Metadata, and its use, is one of the biggest changes in the book industry over the last twenty years – it is essential.

According to the Cambridge Dictionary: "Metadata is used by bookstores and book sites, digital marketers, search engines."

Metadata/tagging do not drive sales, they drive visibility and that I grow sales. That visibility will support your branding growth.
Metadata must be constant. Research shows that updated metadata increases sales. If the author gave a speech, writes new books, updates the book, or wins a prize, then update your metadata.

Nielsen Bookdata or Bookscan

When done properly, the book-trade discoverability of the book is much better. The figures show that with the correct metadata improvement across the industry is an 178% by improving SEO (2020).

Metadata, and good content is imperative for online digital resellers as a potential web-browser cannot pick up the book and look at it.

Most internet sales are gained because potential customers search a category. For them to find the correct book for their needs is not easy. The more metadata you have the better.

Gaining the skill of metadata is like sitting at the end of a large wedge; the further along you go, the thicker it is. To give you an idea, most publishing houses employ a Metadata specialist, and so should you, as you will have enough to do with all the other functions. Yet, because of its importance in promoting your book, you do need to understand the basics. I suggest you spend some time on YouTube or get books on the subject.

Make sure your book is registered with Nielsen Bookdata as they are the most important book search facility (using the ISBN) for the international book trade.

Before we continue with the next area of optimisation, the following will help maximise sales by having:

- A cover image.
- Author Bio.
- Citations.
- A Table of Contents, especially for non-fiction.
- First chapter exert.
- Keywords (see below).
- ISBNs (one each for print and ePub versions).
- Publisher.
- Date published.
- Where published.
- Categories (on the back page).
- Codes; THELMA and BISAG (see below).
- An index (dependent on the book).

Although I said use a specialist, they can never know the book or your audience like you do. They would just not have the correct feel to write your metadata. You need to be involved.

Then on any site you may place the book on:

- Have all the above Book Metadata, plus.
- Size of the book, eg, 148mm X 210mm.
- Number of pages.
- Price.
- Have the first Chapter (exert).
- Book descriptions (a short and long description). Short description (one or two sentences, about 350 characters. And include keywords.)

Part Six – Marketing And Promotion

Long description (two or three paragraphs, usually under 4000 characters. Use keywords and phrases. Do not use quotations or endorsements as some sites cut them out leaving holes in the work. Must be descriptive of the book.

In Australia, bookstores only stock about 2% of newly released thrillers per year. Also, in Australia there are over 100 000 new books a year that are not included in bookstores. Therefore, to have any sort of success, Metatagging has become one of the major marketing tools for book publishers and individual authors.

Backlinks

A backlink is a website link from another website to your website. The more of these you have, the more people will see your site, as qualified backlinks are a kind of 'stamp of approval'. However, backlinks must be 'high quality' and relevant to your website. Search Engines will blacklist your site if you dump hundreds of backlinks on your site that are inauthentic and irrelevant – they know that if your site is a book site, (promoting a doggy book), but you have a backlink from a pizza shop, then it is crookery.

The best way to build quality backlinks that appease the conditions as set by Google is to write quality blogs or newsletters, where relevant sites want to recommend you to their audience, and so they will put up a link to one of those articles.

Domain Authority (DA) and Page Authority (PA)

DA is a score developed by Moz that predicts how well a website will rank on search engine result pages (SERP). Domain Authority scores range from one to one hundred, with higher scores corresponding to a greater ability to rank.

However, the need is to not try and get to one hundred, but to test your site/book against your competitors. Besides, only companies like Amazon, Wikipedia or Facebook can afford to spend millions a month to keep their ratings as close to one hundred percent as possible. If your site/book gets more quality Backlinks than your competitor, you will do better relative to them.

You must keep in mind that technology constantly changes, and many changes will affect the ranking (up or down), so your score will fluctuate, usually downwards. DA is not a one-off event. Those changes just mentioned, along with changes in the way the Internet processes, the way Google works, and of course, the backlinks your competitors apply will mean it is an ongoing process. You need to work hard and build up a good level of quality backlinks, you can slow it down a bit and maintain momentum. Take into consideration though, that all your hard work, and cost, should give you a higher payback in sales or site visits. However, the income will always lag behind the hard work and costs so there could be a cashflow problem.

DA and PA are not Google metrics, but metrics that will measure Google's likely results.

Domain Authority is calculated by evaluating multiple factors, including linking root domains and total number of links into a single DA score. This score can then be used when comparing websites or tracking the 'ranking strength' of a website over time.

Page Authority (PA) is a score developed by Moz that predicts how well a specific page will rank on search engine result pages (SERP). PA works in much the same way as DA.

> **Part Six – Marketing And Promotion**

For either DA or PA links you add, it can take up to a month to affect a ranking.

You can confirm the above from https://moz.com/learn/seo/domain-authority.

Blogs, Facebook, Twitter and the like

The following is the most important component of the 'rolling up your sleeves' to create your brand and for people to know about your book. If you have the time, setting up profiles on social commentary sites can enhance your profile (your brand), and therefore sales. How effective this is, is a function of how well you do it and how much time you put into it.

This is not something you are likely to outsource, as it would be too expensive. Besides, you need to embed your personality in your brand building. As mentioned, those who do this are more likely to sell their book than those that do not.

There are literally dozens of ways to promote your site, your book, and your brand. Here is a list of some formats and comments below:

- Google Ads.
- Amazon.
- Email lists (but people are fed-up with email SPAM), gain them from a sign-up contact form from your newsletter. Nevertheless, see below.
- Banner advertising.
- Promos or advertising on Linked-In.
- More direct advertising on magazines (relevant to your book genre).
- Social media.
  # Facebook (see below)
  # X (Twitter)
  # blogging (content writing)

\# be on forums or as a Guest Blogger
\# Snapchat

X (Twitter) Blasts

They sound great when you think that the name of your book is going to be seen by a quarter of a million people. But sadly, the reality for many is that they have not had the return they had hoped and paid for. Many of the tweets go to 'dead' accounts, and browsers have a certain immunity to ads and hardly see them. Unless your Twitter blaster can prove the validity of their numbers be careful – there are better ways to promo your work.

Also be careful with banner advertising. Sounds great, pay X dollars and your banner ad will be seen by 30 000, 60 000 or 100 000 relevant people. You pay for each person that clicks on it. You would be surprised on what browsers click on when meandering around the Internet. They may be curious but have no intention of reading or buying your book (they may not even read books). You can pay a lot for 'dead-ends' for little result.

Your Newsletter

If you want to grow and reach clients, your website must offer a subscription for your newsletter. It is important to get subscribers, as from these you grow a database. From the database you learn more about your audience.
If done correctly, email marketing will surpass the cost and time to set up, especially to your subscribers.

Part Six – Marketing And Promotion

Do not buy lists as many of the names are stolen (you will reach people who already hate you). Many of the names are duds, where it was Joe Bloggs' email fifteen years ago.

What follows are a few pointers:

- be vulnerable, be real, from the heart. People want stories not products. Believe in your message.
- Have a formula that each newsletter follows; have content that is going to be of interest to recipients; offer something for free; try and have a real-life example; remind the reader that they have a problem or need and that it can be solved.
- Most people skim, so it must be skim friendly. Have clear headings. Simple and clean, one page, lots of white space.
- One photo, gains interest. Images increases engagement but do not clutter.
- Have only one main topic per newsletter
- Do not blitz your audience.
- No selling, build trust; just a call to action (CTA).
- Once you have the numbers, you can offer a free book to one of those who replies with information, questions, statements, as with this information is how you get to know your audience, and as stated earlier, knowing your audience is key to marketing.
- Use action words, be categorical, no jargon, and simple language.
- Have smart subject lines; compelling, concise, of interest to them. Let them know the email is from you.
- Make no grandiose claims.
- Send a test email to yourself and someone else to check. Check all the links work. Look at it on a phone.
- Repurpose past content.
- Be spam conscious, when you use the words like; prizes, free, or win as spam filters pounce and block these.
- Personalise, use their name. Most mail-tools allow this.

Template, design, and mailing?

- Must cater for the vision impaired.
- You need analytics to see who opened them, read them, or split testing work.
- Must be device (phone and tablet) friendly.
- Include logo.
- With a good tool you can start split testing.
- Be creative and courageous.
- Use a look and brand design that looks like your branding.
- As well as good layout design.

I recommend for new authors that they grow their list to 100 authentic names. Thereafter, they utalise a newsletter application and service offering such as MailChimp or Mailite as these have built in facilities that you can only dream about if you do it manually. It pays to pay for the right tools.

Amazon Marketing

Amazon is so dominant, it cannot be avoided or ignored.

In their description fields, Amazon seems to use at least 1,000 characters which could be around 140 separate words. So there are a lot of keyword options with Amazon.

Keywords, as a list, are more important on some sites than others, such as Amazon. Amazon (and many websites) makes less use of lists of keywords, but greater use of content. Make sure that your content is populated with keywords and keyword phrases.

Within Amazon, the more people who click on a book, the more resources Amazon will point towards the book. Conversely, no or few clicks on the book will reduce credibility by Amazon. This is what is

Part Six – Marketing And Promotion

known as the 'Virtuous Cycle', where a popular book gets better Amazon rankings, and where a low-ranking book is literally pushed to the mud at the bottom.

Amazon have tools to track previews. Play around with these and get to know them. Amazon is more structured and drills down to more separate detail, using the metadata and keywords that we place in our content, therefore giving the user a better chance of finding the correct book. Use as many categories as possible.

Amazon has a new book window time period that they work to. If at least twenty (new) hits do not reach the book within a month, the rankings diminish. Therefore, it is imperative that a campaign is deployed before loading the book, so momentum happens from the start.

Book Reviews are an imperative. Get as many as possible. This means books will need to be given away. Visibility and conversion are an ongoing function.

Know though, that Amazon has divisions (Amazon.co.uk; Amazon.de; Amazon.fr; Amazon.it; Amazon.es; Amazon.co.jp) and when you put your book on one it does not mean it will automatically appear on all of them.

How many Amazon sites to place the book on, and whether any of the sites transfer data from one to another is something you will have to determine at the time.

KDP (Kindle Direct Publishing) is owned by Amazon for small publishers and authors to grow their ePub sales.

Createspace is owned by Amazon and has been absorbed into KDS (but Createspace does still have its own login and interface).

Look at YouTube to learn as much about the Amazon process.

• • •

6

Goodreads

Goodreads is another company owned by Amazon and is a platform to allow you to gain reviewers, and then displays the reviews. This is a good idea, when it works! But it does not always work.

If you get even one bad review from a series of reviews it could kill your book. You cannot delete a bad review.

The way it is supposed to work is that you load your book cover, synopsis, etc, and allocate the number of reviewers you would like (you may want twenty). Goodreads' browsers apply to give a review, based on their interest in your book. Therefore, you will send each reviewer a copy (twenty books go out). However, there is no onus on the reviewer to actually do a review. This has happened to us several times. On the second occasion I emailed the Goodreads support and told them that many of their reviewers seem to have no intention of giving a review and just want a free book. The reply stated that they are sorry but have no control over their reviewers. So be careful.
Read their information and set your book up for reviews. The cost to you will be the number of free books you give out (plus shipping costs) to the reviewers.

Facebook

Amazon is a good place for people find and read about your book, and hopefully purchase it. Facebook is more about taking your book to an online audience. An audience that you create, if you have the time and funds, do both.

There are two aspects to FB, your platform (profile), and paid advertising. Along with your page and profile, you will make posts a couple of times a week.

Part Six – Marketing And Promotion

You set your Facebook page up depending on the genre of your book. It can be the perfect platform to promote yourself if you are a motivational speaker.

I suggest you plan at least twenty posts in advance so that they are well-conceived instead of rushed. Once again, I will not tell you how to do this as there are thousands of books and websites that will. Do not forget to search YouTube as it has much information on it.

FB will tell you the best way to go about growing your audience, but it will be a long learning curve. Posts can be boosted (a euphemism for paying) in Facebook but they are not nearly as effective as an ad campaign, and so the money does not go as far. Once again, play and learn for improvements.

Facebook Ad Campaigns

There is a free version but it is about as good as warm butter for concrete. It is not much use other than using it to learn before going onto the paid platform.

Without a doubt FB is the cheapest form of advertising. For as little at $20 a campaign, you can conduct a test. Much cheaper than Google's PPC (Pay Per Click). It is about the lowest cost per engagement. It is also time consuming but could be worthwhile as by doing so, you are likely to have some influence in the sale of your book. This form of marketing is advertising directly to the consumer, therefore it should give greater control and understanding of costs. But with seven million advertisers (2020) it needs to be done properly, as most browsers go to Facebook for leisure, not for products.

You must be patient because it could take up to a year to work. Patience and repeat campaigns = success – must test, change, keep testing, literally fifty or more times. Gradually there will be growth.
Great ads + the wrong audience.

or

the right audience + bad ads, are both losers.

You need; Great Ads + the right audience.

For your ads:

- Try and use the language of the audience.
- Research shows that videos improve sales by three to one and increase audience engagement and improve conversion rates.
  To make videos, most phones do a good enough job.
  Do not sell on the video. Tell a compelling story and they may buy. Be authentic, and natural.
  There is much information on the Internet on video making. Do your research.
- Start off with a low amount per day, say $20 and check the results, daily.
- FB changes all the time so to keep up to date and play around with it at least a couple of times a week.

Google Ads (previously known as Google AdWords)

Google Ads will place your ad in front of the audience you request, in the geographical location of your choice, for the budget you feel comfortable with. When you do this, Google will estimate how many leads you are likely to gain. At any time, you can place the ad on hold, increase or decrease amounts. At low costs, it is a cheap way to see if it will work. Google says it usually takes about a month for ads to have traction.

They offer metrics such as impressions, clicks, cost per clicks (CPC), and conversions. You will have to know what these represent, so study them.

Part Six – Marketing And Promotion

Working Google Ads is not complex once you make a start. Nor is it particularly time consuming. The problem though is that the tech changes on a regular basis. Learning and keeping up is the issue. Yes, you can do it yourself but it will take hours of fiddling. If you can afford it, pay a company to do it for you. And if you chose the correct company, for every $1.0 you pay them (and Google for the actual ad), you should get at least $1.5 back. You may get $6.00 back. Therefore, it is an investment, but like all investments, you pay now, you may only get a return in a month or so.

Another thing to consider. If you are an artist and selling your art online at a sales price of say $500 per piece, the cost of sales, relative to the selling price is doable. But when the cost of sales is the same but for a $25.00 book you have to be careful.

Irrespective of where your paid advertising is placed, it helps to differentiate whether the traffic is from organic or paid source. Organic, comes from the SEO, DA, PA, and Metadata as mentioned above. You need to be able to understand these metrics.

The difference between Google search and Amazon search is that Google is designed to collect data (information) from all over the Internet. It is not so much interested in individual Keywords, but chunks of metadata information that it finds from millions of sites.

Amazon is more structured and drills down to individual details, but directly for books, using the metadata and keywords that we place in our content.

Ethics – Facebook and Google?

I do not know anyone who enjoys being bombarded every time they turn on their phone or computer with ads from Google or Facebook. Last week you may have wondered what nutrition is in salmon, so out of curiosity you Googled it. Today, you are besieged by companies flogging fish supplements. It is annoying. Perhaps worse is where these platforms (openly) collect our data and use it for all sorts of nefarious purposes. Our information is exploited, sold, and hacked.

When you create and pay for a FB or Google ad, that is what you are subjecting thousands of people to. FB target those in their database that seem to be prospects because of the data they have collected on you.

I am not keen on FB or Google advertising for that reason as it perpetuates the scheme.

My proofreader asked me the question; "If I so disapprove of the Google/Facebook and other monopolies, why did I spend so much time above telling you about it."

I did so you would know and be able you make your own well-informed conclusions.

Trade Magazine Advertising

In most countries there are magazines dedicated to the book industry. Advertising or Advertorials in these can get your book in front of the industry book buyers.

For other magazine adverts, make sure that the readership is relevant to your book. You would not put a book on science in a kid's magazine.

Media Kit

A media kit is a valuable tool that every author must have if they are serious about pursuing media coverage for their new book. It can be used to solicit the media in the hopes that it will spark a story or interview.

Part Six – Marketing And Promotion

A media kit, at the very least, must consist of the following:

One page (try and keep it to one page).

The name of the book at the top and the 'Book Metadata' as given earlier.

The font cover image.

A synopsis of the book.

A short biography of yourself, containing why you are a guru on the subject. In your bio, put down credibility statements, such as other books you have written, TV, radio appearances and interviews.

More advanced media kits typically add in seven to ten questions (as well as the answers) that the media are likely to ask. These pre-empted questions can help secure interest.

One or two excerpts from the book.

Testimonials.

At the bottom, provide less interesting but necessary information, such as the book category, number of words and the projected selling price, and most important the ISBNs for print and ePub.

Sales selling points and keywords.

The above is a lot of information, so skill is required to include as much on one page without clutter.

There should be various versions of the media kit:

When a book is about to go into production you first send out an Advanced Information (AI) media kit.

Send an updated version when the book is released.

Send variations of the kit, based on the person or market that you are to send it to. For instance, if you are sending it to a retail outlet, it may include reviews or interview information that may encourage them to stock the book as opposed to ignoring it.

Set out the content in a catchy style that is likely to gain immediate interest.

For media, radio, TV, and print you will need to send a physical kit. This should be a high-quality, glossy colour document with professional artwork, as well as a copy of the book. Include a signed cover-letter that gets to the point of why you are sending them the book, which is to ask them for a review or interview.

Remember, your media kit must go onto your website as soon as possible.

You can create the kit using MS Word and convert to a PDF. This makes it easy to email.

Book reviews

Despite what I said about the Goodreads reviewing platform, book reviews are a must as they inform the public about your book. We have a database of newspapers, magazines, radio, and TV people who we ask for reviews. Without their message, no one will know about the book and therefore will not look for it in shops or on the Net.

This means that you will have to give them a free copy. But a word of warning – make sure you send the book to the right reviewer. It is pointless going to a newspaper and send a book on animal training to the lady who writes the fashion column.

Another option to consider is The Independent Book Publishing Association's (IBPA) 'Net Gallery Program', which is an excellent way to garner international reviews for a book or audiobook (already published or soon-to-be) from a network of over 550,000 avid readers,

Part Six – Marketing And Promotion

made up of book lovers, librarians, booksellers, media, and more. If you do use this option, try and get it going before your launch.

For radio or TV interviews, make sure you get the podcast or a copy. Place these interviews on your web site. If an interview is good, you send it (or the link) to other prospective interviewers. When seeing how well you perform, they may want to use you, as you can make them look good.

Practice. Take as long as you need and write a media release. This can be on a book that you are writing or an imaginary book.

Videos for your website and marketing

With the emergence of simple video production apps, such as Loom, it is smart to make several two-minute videos. Once you have them all up on your site, you can include the links in all your marketing material – after all, seeing is believing.

Book Readings

Do as many as possible as this is another way to become known and promote the book. Do these at:
- Bookshops (make sure that they send out an invite to their database).

- Companies (depending on the book).
- Informal groups.
- Book clubs.
- Associations.
- Cafes that host this type of event.

Once you have your venue, put an advertisement in the local paper that has the name of the book in bold, a small picture of the book, and words something like: 'You are cordially invited to the book launch of ...'

Before the reading, try and gauge the audience who are likely to attend. With this perspective, select sections of the book that are likely to appeal to this audience.

Retail outlets

It is not too difficult to get your book onto the bookshelves – it is harder to get them to sell, and for that reason bookstore managers will be reluctant. Often, if you visit a bookstore, the manager scrutinises your book for quality, and will ask, "How you are promoting your book, so customers will know that it's here?"

If you are well-known and have a following of loyal supporters, it will be easier. But you will still have to spend time marketing the work. Otherwise, the book is unlikely to sell, or sell in reasonable quantities to make it worth the effort.

If you have a strong budget, you can advertise the book with the intention of driving buyers into shops.

As a small publishing house, I have found segmentation helps, which is placing the book only in those outlets where there would be interest.

Part Six – Marketing And Promotion

In large bookstores, books can get lost in the clutter of thousands of books, so better to only try a few of the big stores and see how the book goes. Ferret out the stores that are more likely to have your type of audience. For instance, we have a doggy book, and we did not worry about the big stores, but went to pet shops, vets, and animal lovers web sites. For the physical spaces at vets we supplied the book with a holder that displayed the book at the counter near the till, so that when customers paid for their pet food, they saw the doggy book. Another book, on Tissue Salts, went into health food stores and to holistic health practitioners. A business book that we published went into business bookshops. We did a large email campaign to businesses as well as liaising with a tertiary institution book distributor.

The key to sales is the variety of options.

Be patient, Jim Alkon of Book Tribe reminds us, "Think of book marketing as a marathon, not as a sprint."

• • •

6

Jack London - *The Call of the Wild*

The wolf swung in behind, yelping in chorus. And buck ran with them, side by side with the wild brother, yelping as he ran.

And here may well end the story of Buck. The years were not many when the Yeehats noted a change in the breed of timber wolves; for some were seen with splashes of brown on head and muzzle, and with a rift of white centering down the chest. But more remarkable than this, the Yeehats tell of a Ghost Dog that runs at the head of the pack.

They are afraid of this Ghost Dog, for it has cunning greater than they, stealing from their camps in fierce winters, robbing their traps, slaying their dogs and defying their bravest hunters.

Nay, the tail grows worse. Hunters there are who fail to return to the camp, and hunters found with throats slashed cruelly open and with wolf prints about them in snow greater than the prints of any wolf. Each fall: when the Yeehats follow the movement of the moose, there is a certain valley which they never enter. And women there are who become sad when the word goes over the fire of how the evil spirit came to select that valley for an abiding-place.

In the summers there is one visitor, however, to that valley, of which the Yeehats do not know. It is a great, gloriously coated wolf, like, and yet unlike, all other wolves. He crosses alone from the smiling timberland and comes down into an open space among the trees. Here a yellow stream flows from rotted moose-hide sacks and sinks into the ground, with long grasses growing through it and vegetable mold overrunning it and hiding its yellow from the sun; and here he muses for a time, howling once, long and mournfully, ere he departs.

But he is not always alone. When the long winter nights come on and the wolves follow their meat into the lower valleys, he may be seen running at the head of the pack through the pale moonlight or glimmering borealis, leaping above his fellows, his great throat a-bellow as he sings a song of the younger world, which is the song of the pack.

Part Six – Marketing And Promotion

Jack London was an amazing storyteller and closed *Call of the Wild* beautifully.

Libraries

There are hundreds of libraries throughout the country that could use your book. Find the buying department for each and approach them. Yes, as with all government departments, there is a lot of paperwork, but once you work through it, you may get one big order to supply many libraries.

But libraries can be difficult in as much as their buying departments often work through specific library service suppliers, meaning that they may not want to deal with you directly. When that is the case, you have two options, the first is to approach a dedicated library supplier to take your book on. The second option is to market to the libraries, to bring your book to the attention of the buyers, but you tell them they can get the book through that specific library supplier.

There is another good reason to sell books to libraries, and that is for the 'Public Lending Rights' income that may accrue. PLRs mean that every time your book is borrowed from a library the government will pay you a small amount of money (cents). But if your book is in many libraries and borrowed often, that income can accumulate.

We use a company called EBSCO, who market our ePubs to thousands of libraries worldwide. Every time a library patron opens one of our books, a few cents drop into our till. Not a lot of money, but with all the books we have, and the thousands of libraries, it adds up.

Private libraries

Many corporate companies have a library. If your book is of a business, statistical or demographics nature then it could be worthwhile approaching company libraries.

The same applies to school or tertiary libraries. There could be an interest if the book is relevant. If you Google 'schools', 'universities', etc. in your area, you will find lists of schools.

Free web sites

There are many sites that will allow you to advertise your book. Some are free, such as *Hot Frog* and *Gum Tree*. Some sites will sell the book for you for a monthly fee or commission.

Certainly, you need to get the book on as many sites as possible. Of course, there must be a synergy with the site and the message of the book.

Book clubs

There are book clubs in just about every suburb in every city or town whose members want the latest books. And once again, there are websites and suppliers that specifically deal with book clubs.

Affiliate marketing

Simply put, affiliate marketing is getting people or other websites to market your book. Although we have not dabbled in this I will give you some information on it. They promote your book on their site and sell it for a commission. They also send emails to their database.

Part Six – Marketing And Promotion

International book rights

If self-published, find a company that sells 'Rights', as they will offer a platform for authors to register their book. At the same time, they have publishers and distributors from most countries who are looking for books to produce for their country.
It is a wonderful feeling to sell the rights for one or several countries.

Based on the information that you have just read, write a marketing plan. Write it as if you were to send it to a publisher.

Lastly, a fluid and ever-emerging book market

Amazon's dominance, ePubs, audiobooks, the closure of many bookstores, Self-publishing, and social media have all sent shockwaves throughout the book market. I cannot predict what will occur over the next twenty years, other than there will be more change. Some predict that the way Amazon is growing it will have 80% of the book market by 2030. Or another way of putting it is that most of the bookstores will be closed – a disturbing thought. This will have implications for your publisher, or if you self-publish.

Change represents disruption and opportunity. Change also represents hours of research to keep up and on top of it in a way that enhances opportunity.

(Four minutes)
To lighten up the mood after all the technical information, look out of your window and describe what you see.

• • •

6

PART SEVEN – Appendices

Part Seven – Appendices

In this section:
   Appendix One – The Rise Of Artificial Intelligence In Writing
   Appendix Two – Miscellaneous
   Appendix Three – Book Production
   Appendix Four – Resources
   Appendix Five – Index.

Appendix One – The Rise Of Artificial Intelligence In Writing.

The Rise of AI in Writing: A Writer's Guide to Embracing Technology
In an era where technology continues to reshape the landscape of creativity, artificial intelligence (AI) stands at the forefront, offering writers new tools and possibilities. This section explores the intersection of AI and writing, providing insights on how authors can leverage these advancements to enhance their craft and navigate the evolving literary landscape, whilst understanding the pitfalls.

Understanding AI writing tools, to help refine your work.
From grammar and style suggestions to content improvements, these tools offer valuable insights without replacing the human touch.

The inevitable merging of human creativity and artificial intelligence prompts a crucial question: where does the writer's voice emerge in the collaborative process with a machine?
You, the writer, must remain the driving force behind creative intent. AI tools can assist, generate ideas, or suggest improvements but the initial spark, and narrative direction must be yours.
After all, it requires emotional experience, that, at this stage come only come from human experiences to infuse a unique quality into writing. AI lacks personal experiences, and while it can simulate emotions based on data, it does not possess genuine feelings. The emotional resonance in a piece often stems from the writer's authentic voice.

• • •

Part Seven – Appendices

Subjectivity and Interpretation – Writers bring their subjective viewpoints and interpretive skills to the table. The nuances, personal biases, and individual interpretations that shape a narrative are distinctly human elements that AI, driven by algorithms and data cannot fully capture.

Collaboration, Not Replacement – AI as a Creative Partner
Rather than replacing the writer, AI can be viewed as a collaborative partner. It can augment the writing process, offering suggestions, providing inspiration, and assisting in technical aspects. The writer retains control and makes informed decisions about incorporating or rejecting AI-generated content.

The writer's voice is a unique signature that must persist through collaboration with AI. It is the stylistic choices, narrative nuances, and personal flair that distinguish one writer from another, regardless of the tools employed.

In the dynamic relationship between humans and AI, the writer remains the orchestrator, infusing the work with their creativity, emotions, and individuality. Collaboration with AI becomes a tool for empowerment, efficiency, research, and exploration, allowing writers to navigate the evolving landscape while preserving the essence of their voice. If there is a lack of creativity, it is the result of the writer's input.

Manuscript Analysis – Some AI can analyse manuscripts to provide insights into writing patterns, pacing, and overall structure. But dependent on the AI used, often you cannot feed it large chunks of writing. So, to analyse an entire book is beyond most AI capacity.

However, when you do get feedback it can be valuable for authors and editors during the revision process.

Enhancing Efficiency – AI streamlines certain aspects of the writing process, such as grammar and punctuation checking, and idea generation. However, as the long chapter on editing expresses, determined editing separates the serious writer from the not so serious writer, and by delegating all of the edit to AI will reduce much of the creative element.

Data Research – When doing research with AI, discernment is required.
Assume you want to write an article on 'Right Wing Activism'. You insert the query and press enter. Your AI will search many thousands of sites in milli-seconds. The problem though is that there are probably more sites propagating the need for 'Right Wing' activities than those that don't. Those that do are likely to have much biased information about their cause. The query output could also be skewed to that of the 'Right Wing' belief system. Your article may not be balanced.

Transparency with Readers – In cases where AI is used in the creation process, transparency with readers is essential. Clearly communicating the role of AI ensures that readers understand the collaborative nature of the work.

Generating Ideas with AI – Earlier on in the book we spoke of plot development. AI tools can assist in brainstorming and idea generation. Discover how to use machine learning algorithms to spark creativity and overcome writer's block.
Explore the concept of using AI as a creative collaborator. For instance, look at this AI generated answer to a question I posed;
Question: I believe the story of *Little Red Riding Hood* has been used.

Part Seven – Appendices

Can you give me another option to write?
Answer: Certainly! Here's a new and different story idea:

Title: "The Enchanted Lighthouse"

Once upon a time, in a quaint coastal village, there stood a mysterious lighthouse that held a magical secret. Every night, as the sun dipped below the horizon, the lighthouse would come to life, emitting a soft, ethereal glow that enchanted the entire village.
One day, a curious young girl named Lily discovered the secret of the lighthouse. Intrigued by its magic, she decided to embark on a daring adventure to unravel the mysteries hidden within its walls. Guided by the gentle whispers of the wind and the mystical light that danced across the waves, Lily set out on a journey that would change her life forever.
As she delved deeper into the secrets of the lighthouse, Lily encountered mystical creatures, ancient spells, and a forgotten world that existed beyond the ordinary. Along the way, she learned valuable lessons about courage, friendship, and the importance of embracing the unknown.

You can see that the story plot has merit. But it could not be used in its current format, as the text needs a good edit, mainly for flow, and there are superfluous words. Most important though, is the finessing, the nuance, that must come from your creative input.

AI-Generated Content and Plagiarism – Do not be caught with AI-generated plagiarism. Learn how to use AI responsibly and maintain the integrity of your work. Reflect on the ethical implications of using AI in the creative process. Consider issues such as intellectual property, authorship, and the responsible use of AI tools.

Another example. For this section I asked ChatGPT:

Question: When using bullet points in a report, are full stops used at the end of each point? How should they be finished?

Answer: The use of punctuation at the end of bullet points in a report can depend on the style guide you are following or the specific preferences of the organisation or individual for whom you are writing (refer to the discussion on Style Guide below). Different style guides may have different conventions regarding punctuation in bullet points. Here are two common approaches:

No punctuation at the end of each bullet point

This is a simple and common style. Each bullet point is treated as a fragment or incomplete sentence, and therefore, no punctuation (such as a period or comma) is used at the end of each point.

Example:
- Point one.
- Point two.
- Point three.

Punctuation at the end of each bullet point:

Some style guides recommend using a full stop (period) at the end of each bullet point, especially if each point forms a complete sentence. This can make each bullet point read like a standalone sentence.

Example:
- Point one.
- Point two.
- Point three.

When in doubt, it's a good idea to check the style guide specified for the document or to follow the conventions used consistently throughout the document or organisation. Consistency is key for a

Part Seven – Appendices

professional and polished appearance in your writing.

What follows is another use I put AI to. I received a thesis that was written in a non-English language. This had been translated by a translator, who clearly lacked English – the result was horrible. I was contracted to render it acceptable to English for an academic audience. The work was so clumsy I had difficulty following it and found my rate of edit abysmally slow. Nor was I sure if I was presenting the work as it was intended.

As a last resort I fed sections of the theses into ChatGPT, which in seconds translated the translation very well. Yes, I had to continue reworking the text but the end result was one that satisfied the academics.

In summary, AI is profoundly influencing the publishing industry across various facets, from personalised reader experiences to data-driven decision-making. As technology advances, the symbiotic relationship between human creativity and AI innovation is likely to reshape how literature is created, consumed, and shared in the future.

The rise of AI-generated content has triggered valid concerns among existing writers and authors who fear being lost in a sea of material produced by automated systems. The ease and speed at which AI can generate content might lead to a flood of material, saturating the market. This volume-centric approach could potentially overshadow the quality and craftsmanship traditionally associated with human-authored works.

With an influx of AI-generated content, there is concern that the unique voices and perspectives of individual human authors may be diluted or overshadowed. It will become a challenge for writers to stand out amidst a vast sea of content generated by algorithms.

● ● ●

Existing writers worry that increased competition, including AI-generated content, may make it harder for their work to be discovered. Algorithms and platforms may prioritise content that aligns with popular trends or patterns, potentially leaving out more nuanced or unconventional human-authored pieces.

Questions about intellectual property and authorship arise, especially when AI is involved in content creation. Determining rightful ownership and attribution could become a complex issue.

Yet, to remain relevant, writers may need to adapt their skill sets to coexist with AI. This may involve embracing technology, learning to collaborate with AI tools, and finding ways to leverage automation without compromising their unique creative contributions.

Appendix Two – Miscellaneous

Voice Recognition

Voice recognition is software that makes writing easy, that is once it is trained. You dictate into a microphone attached to your PC and as you do, the equivalent text appears on the screen.

There are two main tricks to these programmes:

Do not to trust them, as *rain,* stuff that makes you damp when you are late for an appointment, could become *rein,* a strap for a horse's bridle. Now unless you want bridle straps falling out of the sky, check the text, especially when you encounter homonyms.

Take the time to train it, as it will not work properly until at least thirty hours of teaching.

There tends to be less editing, especially if you have clumsy fingers like I do.

Part Seven – Appendices

You can produce work at speaking speed, which, unless you are a qualified typist, will be much faster than you can type.

You develop less shoulder aches and pains as you can sprawl in a more relaxed position.

If you are serious about doing a lot of writing, voice recognition is well worth the investment in time and money.

I use Dragon – Naturally Speaking. To find out more go to www.nuance.com. Microsoft Vista has a voice recognition program, but it needs a lot more development to be of use.

Voice Recorders

These can be of assistance when you want to put thoughts down whilst driving. A great time-saving method is to use a recorder in conjunction with voice recognition, as what you record whilst driving can be downloaded and converted into text.

Voice recorders are good for those great ideas that come when you are supposed to be sleeping. All you do is to pick up the recorder, press the button and speak. You do not even need to switch on the light, and once done you resume sleeping. However, do this too often a night and your partner may get a bit annoyed with the constant chatter.

Handwriting

There are many reasons to handwrite your book as opposed to typing it out on a PC:

- I tend to be more creative whilst lounging on a chair, sitting out in nature, in a coffee shop, or almost anywhere where a PC is not.
- Writing longhand can be enjoyable.
- You may not always be with your computer.
- Being dyslexic, I must edit more than most and so capturing from a notebook to PC offers the first edit clean-up.

A book is a path of words, which takes the heart in new directions – John O'Donohue (writer, poet)

Books (e-Publications, ePubs)

From the edited and final manuscript, you can produce an ePub, and by doing so you double your market range. ePubs comprise a massive part of the market and must be addressed.

Self-publishing and the ability to easily create an ePub has opened options for authors. But as there are now so many options it can be confronting to select the best. We have our own designers, but you could use Smashwords, Book Baby or Creative Space to produce and promote your ePub. By doing so the books go to all the major reading devices, such as Amazon's Kindle (Direct) and Apple itunes.

This raises a point within their agreement you will need to know. The Smashwords agreement says you cannot use other options whilst you are using theirs.

A further suggestion is that once the ePub is live, check it on the different reading devices, just to ensure that it looks good, because if not, then not many will buy it for that reading device.

Part Seven – Appendices

To ensure we get a good looking end product, we use a layout artist. This does cost more but our print book, cover, and ePub will look great.

When you prepare an ePub for many of the large ePub sites, the book needs to be converted to their required format. You will need to do your research.

How much to sell an ePub for?

As there is no physical book or ongoing cost associated with the ePub, it should sell for about a third to half of that of the price of the physical book.

ePub virtual reality

There are many tools that can be applied to ePubs to give the reader a more sensory experience. As this is highly technical and a book of its own, I will not go into detail other than providing this short list:

- Auditory input can be inserted to enhance a passage. For instance, if you read, "The noise of the bombs as they landed was deafening…" you could hear bombs going off… Kaaabooooom!!!!
- Visual links can be inserted directly into the text or through links that can take you to either still or animated images. This type of stimulus is good for instruction books.
- For textbooks, links can be inserted that will take the reader to other pages that may have supporting data or research. The good thing with these links is that the reader has the choice whether to follow them or not.

All the above add to the cost.

With technology as it is, the only limitation is what your mind doesn't conceive.

Orientation for an ePub

The orientation of the book is a process of giving the reader the best possible reading experience. The more effort put into this, the better for the reader. Once again, there are many skills involved in ePub orientation so, for your first ePub it would be better to leave it to the experts.

Our process is thus: we first create the print book. The original manuscript will be in an MS Word doc. Our layout team converts this using Adobe InDesign. When we are happy with the print book, we convert this to the ePub format, which looks great on all platforms. Many companies though, just convert the Word doc to that of a PDF, which looks 'clunky'. They also use this for the ePub. The end result is unprofessional, and you want your book to look better than that.

Creating a book cover for e-Pubs

An ePub cover is a virtual cover. This is a non-physical cover that you do not print. It is only the front cover, not the spine or back cover. It is used to help identify and sell e-Pubs from a web site.

There are free products, such as: www.ezinefire.com/ecoverbrand.html to help you design and set out the cover. However, these may be too simplistic for your professional requirements – we have never used them.

Part Seven – Appendices

E-Pro is a software programme that allows the creation of the various elements, such as text, virtual covers of E-books, as well as PDF files. To get a free copy of E-Pro E-Book software go to www.ebook-publishing-tools.com/about This is a good site to look at as it contains many hints about writing.

Categorising your book

BISAG and Thema are global book (print, ePubs, and audio) classification systems which excel at describing a book's subject, aimed at the book retail trade.

They support many languages, with over 3,100 subject codes (each) and 5,100 sub-qualifiers. These sub-qualifiers can be used across subject categories to give deeper meaning and build a more complex look at a book's subject matter, ultimately increasing discoverability.

BISAG (American market) and Thema (UK & European market) codes should be included on your book, your website, and all marketing material for your book (look on the back page of this print book and you will see the categories we have used). Book buyers in all aspects of the book industry (bookstores, Libraries, etc.) use one or both when trying to locate a book by subject.

For instance; BISAG (http://bisg.org/page/bisacedition) here is a screen dump from their site;

7

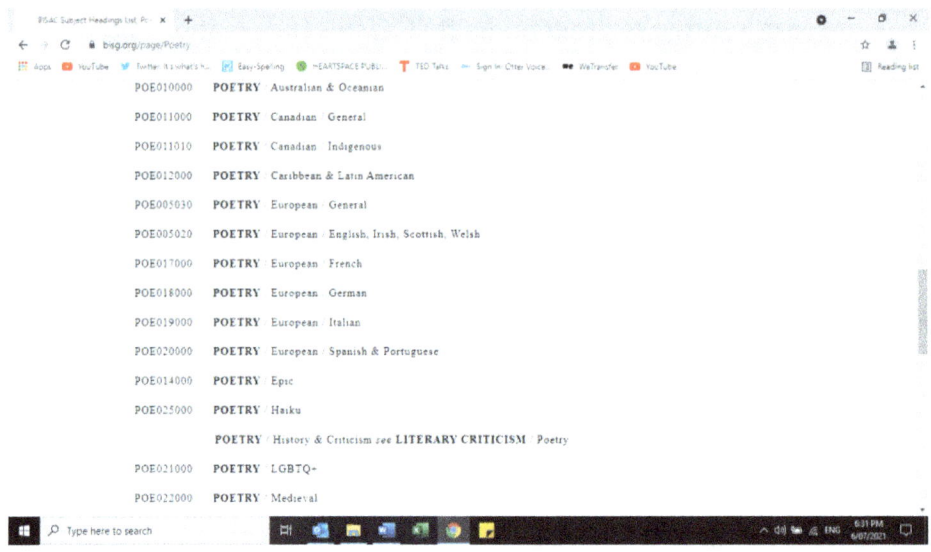

Thema (https://ns.editeur.org/thema/en)

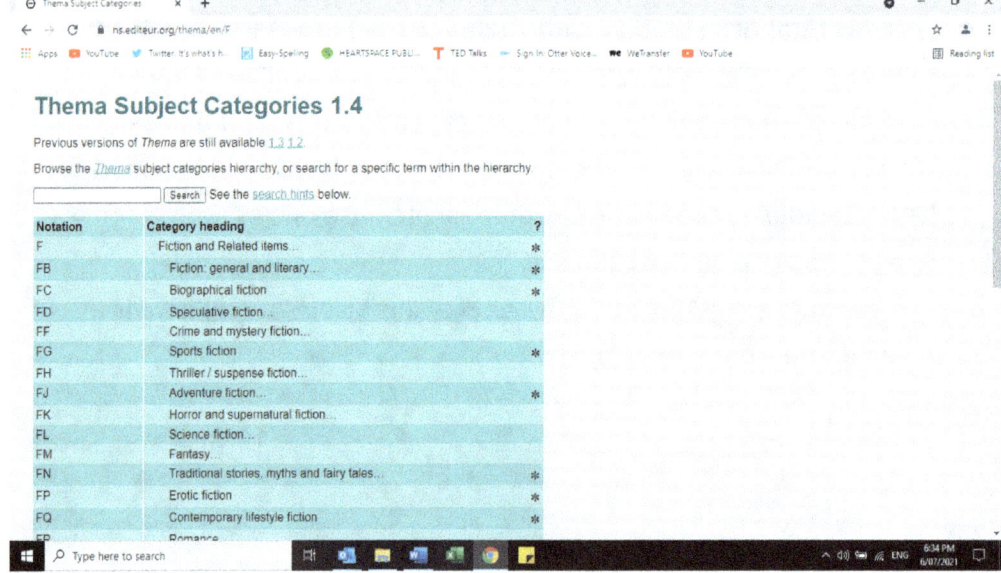

Part Seven – Appendices

Selecting the best categories (two or three of each) can make the difference if a bookshop attendant (who is searching for a book on behalf of a customer) to order your book.

What is written without effort is in general read without pleasure – Samuel Johnson

Audio

Once you have created your book, you can extend the selling options by creating an audiobook (or web link) of the work.

The audio market is not as big as the print or ePub markets but large enough to address, providing you have the funds, as it is expensive.

In most instances you would not want to use your own voice and you need to hire a professional. 'Voices' can be expensive, and the reading of an entire book can take time. But if you believe in your work then take the plunge.

You cannot just get a recorder and record, as there are likely to be background noises, such as your neighbour's dog barking. There are programmes that allow you to edit and 'mix' as required.

As with all programmes, there is a learning curve, and it is likely your first audio book will lack quality.

There are companies who, for a price, will create the audio and distribute it, the biggest being Audacity.

An Index – Unlocking Knowledge with Precision

If your book is one of information, such as this one, or an academic treatise, as opposed to a novel, then the inclusion of an index is a good idea.

A book index is structured in alphabetical terms, topics, and concepts found within a book, accompanied by corresponding page numbers. Serving as a navigational guide, it allows readers to swiftly locate specific information, enhancing the overall usability of the book – an indispensable resource for scholars, students, and curious minds alike.

Have a look at the index at the back of this book.

The fact that a book of this nature has an index can mean the difference of a buyer (for a library, educational facility, industry, etc.) purchasing the book. An index gives credibility to a book that those buyers place much value in.

Indexing takes hours, first for the author, then for the layout person. For instance, in this book we have used the word "creativity" some seventy times. Each incidence needs to be identified, referenced and on which page it is found.

Appendix Three – Book Production

As an author there are many things that you should know when it comes to the production of your book. What follows is not exhaustive, but perhaps the main considerations.

Part Seven – Appendices

A pre-print version (a proof)

This topic would normally be one of the last in a chapter on putting your book together; it is placed here because the pre-print (test) book is referred to throughout this section and so you need to read about it up front.

Once the book is finished and before you approach a publisher with the manuscript, it is a good idea to go to a print-on-demand printer (see below) and have one copy printed.

The reasons for this prototype are:

- Seeing it in the physical means that you will see design or orientation errors.
- You get a feel for the book – should it have more text; are there enough illustrations; and do the illustrations look as you would like them to? Not squashed.
- Doing your last proofread is much easier in a real-life format than in any other format.
- This prototype is more acceptable to your reading panel (friends who evaluate the book) than the PC screen or printed A4 pages.

Orientation

Orientation used to be called typesetting. The term typesetting is falling away as digital processes gain prominence. Orientation is the process of designing the page layouts (hence we use a designer).

Orientation is important, as the 'feel' of the book is governed by the orientation (as well as the cover, which is discussed below). There is less need for rigorous orientation in a novel than say in a textbook or coffee table book.

Orienting the work is a slow and tedious process, but it must be done with absolute care and attention to detail. It is a skill that needs to be learnt before attempting your own orientation. Until you learn these skills it would be best to hire a layout artist.

Certainly, a novel is easier to layout than of book like this one.

Typically, a book of 200 pages could take about twelve hours to orientate. This time could triple if you add your learning time.

What is to be oriented?

- Page numbers.
- Chapter headings.
- Indices (these take time, so add to the cost of orientation).
- Contents and links.
- Pictures, graphs, and tables.
- Opening copyright pages.
- Margins, headers, and footers.
- Finishing pages.
- Bibliography and appendices.
- And, the general paragraph indents, line size and spaces, and the general feel.

Do not think you will be able to do a layout in MS Word. The end product will look horrible, and you will go insane doing it.

There are many desktop publishing programmes that you can buy, but the good ones are expensive, and the learning curve is steep. Unless you are going to do several books, buying one of these may not justify the cost and learning time.

There are free software programmes that you can download for orientation, but to my mind, they are not for serious use.

Part Seven – Appendices

Font

For most books, do not use a harsh Times New Roman font, rather use a font that is gentler on the eye, such as Calibri. However, Times New Roman is good for report writing.

Professional Editing

Although you may have followed the editing checklist, I suggest you use and pay for the services of a professional editor, as it is unlikely that you will see all the errors. Professional editors should miss nothing. Your 'word blindness' is reason enough for a professional editor. Having said that, many so called editors miss a lot too.

Copyright statement

At the front of this book is our copyright statement. You can use this as your sample, and amend accordingly. You can pay your lawyer for a new one, or use a standard statement like ours.

Publication dates are important. If your book is due towards the end of a year, advance the date in the copyright statement to that of the next year. This is because it is always easier to get reviews and interviews on newer, rather than older books. Industry also prefers this year's books.

Copyright periods: usually seventy years after the death of the author. Titles or concepts are not copyrighted.

If you are concerned that a potential agent or publisher may take your work as their own, before sending do the following: have a copy made and acknowledged by several people. Then seal it, and hand it over to a lawyer with a date stamp. Get a receipt for it. If you find that your work has been plagiarised, then you have the copy and testimonials from your friends and lawyer as proof. But this seldom happens with publishers. However, some web-based publishers need watching.

There are software programs you can use where you cut and paste some of your text and let it search the net. If your work has been used, you will find it.

How to make the Copyright symbol ©

As you write your work it is advisable to include the copyright symbol. It is easy enough to make: Move and click the mouse pointer to where you want the ©

Type an open bracket (

Type a lower-case c

Type a close bracket) and as you do you will see it convert to ©

Photos

If many photos are placed throughout the book, the cost is higher for the orientation and also the printing, as in both cases there is more work involved. The cheapest way is to cluster the photos in the middle of the book, and many publishers use this method. We do not. We think it is easier for the reader to see the photos where the text discusses them, so we have them placed in relevant positions.

Colour photos add to the cost of the printing as they must be printed separately and inserted later. Black and white photos cost nothing extra for the printing.

Part Seven – Appendices

Foreword (this is the correct spelling)

Have the authority's name on the front cover, but only if they are well known.

A good foreword by an authority can help your sales.

There is no reason why you cannot have a foreword and several testimonials. These should be placed on the first page as browsers often look for a foreword and testimonials. They must be easy to find.

Create a business name

If you are to self-publish, it is a good idea to create a name (imprint) for your publishing company, with an accompanying logo. These will improve your credibility than if you produce the book in your name.

Another reason for creating a name is so that when applying for an ISBN number (refer below) you can get a business code as they are less readily available to individuals.

Covers

The cover needs to be designed by someone who does this professionally as there is much to know about cover design. For instance:

- There are calculations that determine the spine thickness. One way to calculate this is to divide the number of pages by two and multiply that by 0.117. This means that a book of 400 pages would have a spine of (approximately) 23.4mm. This is based on 80-gram bond and a normal cover thickness. It can get tricky though.
- Printers need to know things like the bleed, trim size and other specifications. If you do not understand these, then let the pros do it.

7

If the paper for the pages is too thin, it will feel cheap and you can see text from the back of the page. The only exception for using thin paper is for a big book, as the thin paper keeps the size, weight, and cost down.

It is not wise to make the paper too thick as it will add to production and shipping cost and will also feel odd. Some publishers will use a thicker paper as a ploy to make a small book feel bigger.

The paper weight is likely to be between 80 and 200 grams. The quality of the paper will also affect the print quality. For instance, if you print on normal photocopy paper, the print crispness of the print will not be there as the page absorbs the ink in a detrimental way.

Glossy pages give a professional appearance. Novels, non-fiction and most *How To* books do not need gloss.

Glossy pages are good for coffee-table books and books with lots of pictures. They do add to the cost of the book.

The above covered some of the technical aspects of cover design. Then there is the appearance, the look, the feel. This is where the creativity comes into it. Cover designs are so important there are cover design categories in literary awards. It would be a good idea for you to browse bookstores to look at the range of covers. The cover of this book was created by a professional cover content designer but with lots of input by me.

Cover Colour

- White covers tent to be bland.
- Black covers can get tracks across them as they are handled.
- I have seen the back cover text hidden because of the background colour. More so when there is a mixed background, such as bush.

Part Seven – Appendices

- Different topics lend themselves to specific types of covers. Novel covers are less flamboyant than creative books. Garden books do best with flower images.

Above I suggested having a pre-print run sample of the book done. This is important for many reasons, but as we are talking about the cover, the pre-print is imperative as it is the only way to see if the cover works:

- Does it impress?
- Is the colour as envisioned?
- It is insipid or garish?
- Does the writing stand out, and use the correct character size?
- Is there balance in the cover?
- Does the cover mark or smudge easily? Is it hardy?

Back Cover Text

Typically, browsers in bookstores will give the front cover an average of four seconds, and the back seven. If your book is to sell you need to keep them reading longer. This means that the copy (words) must be punchy and benefit and interest laden.

The back cover should also have a great headline, but not the title or subtitle. You have already told the reader what the name is and so the duplication will not enhance interest. This catchy headline should be in bold or a different colour.

Under this headline, have some sales copy, (two to four sentences), stating what the book is about and what the reader will gain from reading it.

Writ it and then do a précis:
A précis is a concise summary or abstract of a text or speech. It condenses the main ideas, arguments, and key points of the original

work into a shorter form while maintaining its essence and meaning. Typically, a précis is much shorter than the original piece, but it effectively communicates the main ideas and structure of the original work. Précis writing requires careful attention to detail and the ability to distil complex information into clear and succinct language. It is a valuable skill for summarising and analysing texts in academic, professional, and literary contexts.

Underneath that, have a testimonial or two (one or two sentences).

If the book is a tutorial, such as a *How to do XYZ,* have a sub-heading, such as, 'This book will teach you…' This should be followed by a list of some seven to twelve bullet pointed benefits.

> **HELPFUL TIPS**
> *The back cover must show that the author is the ultimate authority.*

At the bottom have the:

- ISBN (refer below).
- Barcode.
- Publisher logo. The logo does not have to be large as long as the text is readable.
- Book categories Thema and BISAG.

Spend a few minutes and write the text for the back cover of an imaginary novel. Above we spoke of the cover being a silent salesperson, so write from that perspective.

Part Seven – Appendices

Title

Select a working title and subtitle (except for novels). Keep the title short and make the subtitle descriptive. I like a subtitle as it provides added description and option for keywords. The following three books have been published by Heartspace Publications:

- Guided! How to communicate with your spirit guides.
- Paws & Listen – to the voices of animals.
- The Halo and the Noose – The power of storytelling and story listening in business life.

The title should be designed to attract attention and the subtitle to retain interest.

Publisher Dan Poytner tells the story of a company called 'Garden Way' in the USA, that sold 300,000 more books simply by changing the word 'squash' to 'zucchini' in the subtitle (I do not know the name of the book). That is how important the name and words on a cover can be.

You can brainstorm to find a name for the book, but here are some tips:

- Do not make it long, as a long name confuses, unless descriptive like this book.
- It should be punchy and different.
- The subtitle must be descriptive.
- Obtuse words or meanings will leave browsers flat.
- Be unique.

What to have on the front cover:

- Not much, it must be simple.

- The title and subtitle.
- The author's name.
- Perhaps a sentence, as a selling point, such as 'Foreword by …'
- The name of the book in large characters, to attract attention.
- If you are a known author your name can be in large text as your name will help promote the book. If you are unknown, make it smaller than the title.
- Background image that suits.

Other thoughts:

- If you have a logo (as the publisher) this should be on the spine and the back cover. You also insert the logo on an opening page and on one of the back pages.
- When designing the cover, play around with colour.

Your photo

- Do not have your photo on the front or back cover, because if you are unknown, it is a waste of good (convincing) text space. However, potential readers will want to know who they are doing this journey with so you must have a picture on an inside page. This is also where you give your biography.
- The photo can be colour or black and white (some believe that black and white is more powerful), preferably from the shoulders up with you looking at the camera. For ladies, if desired, have a small amount of make-up on. Cleavage is not a good look, but it could also depend on the book.

The spine

The spine must display the book name and author. Insert the publisher's logo at the bottom. Make the book name prominent.

The spine must be easy to read; use bold font.

Looking at paperbacks, you will notice a groove or score-mark on the front and back covers, a few millimetres from the spine. This acts as a hinge and has two purposes: it takes the pressure off the binding, so it is less likely to separate from the pages within; and it makes the opening of the cover and the pages within easier.

There are many sites that you can go to download cover layout software. However, many of these are too simplistic.

Hard Covers

In most instances you will not need a hard cover. Hard covers look good, whilst giving a solid feel to the book. However, they add considerable cost as the pages must be stitched and not perfect bound.

Upmarket books, such as coffee-table books, should have a thicker or hard cover of at least 410gms. The same applies to young children's books, otherwise they may tear and eat them.

Cover Material

Normal Cover thickness should be from 250 to 350 grams, depending on the feel you want. If it is too thin it will bend easily and have a magazine feel about it. It will also tear and crease.

The thicker the cover, the greater the cost, so it is a balance between quality and price.

Always laminate the cover (UV Varnish) otherwise scuff marks can spoil it. Use a matt varnish as gloss can be glitzy. Gloss not correctly applied can peel off.

Photos and clip art

Use photos or clip art to add interest to books. Use good high-resolution images.

There are many sites that offer free clip art or photos, or low-cost royalty payment methods. Try:

- http://office.microsoft.com/en-gb/clipart/download.aspx
- www.clipart.com
- www.openphoto.net
- I like www.pixabay.com

Check if you can use them for commercial use.

Printing

There are two main printing types: one is the older, tried and tested lithographic ('litho'), and the other is the more modern digital.

Litho printing involves a printer that transfers inks from a solid surface, like a metal plate, onto paper.

Digital is a computer-to-printer-based operation.

Pros and cons:

Litho needs larger print runs (1,000 copies plus) to bring down the costs to below that of digital. 800 is about break-even cost, below 500 it is expensive. Whereas digital can-do small runs at a reasonable price and quality.

The lead time for litho is longer than digital.

Litho usually gives top quality. With digital the quality is not as good, but is usually acceptable. Some digital is terrible.

Part Seven – Appendices

Print quality

The print typeface must be solid (or almost solid) black. I recommend you select a 90-point darkness. The print must look crisp with no ragged edges. When you get your test book, you can check for this. If the quality is not as it should be, demand better.

Print on demand (POD)

POD is where, without too much of a price premium, you can print a few books at a time. This is great for when you want to check quality control for the first print run.

POD is digital-based printing and has two main benefits, the first being that you can print small runs, so you do not have to tie up large amounts of capital printing lots of books. Obviously, the cost per book is a bit higher, but with less stock, if the book does not sell, then you can re-plan.

The second benefit is if you do a tie-up with a good POD printer in (say London), you can supply in London at a fraction of the cost and time of shipping a book across.

You also enter into an agreement with the POD printer where costs and commissions are established. Once set up, to issue the POD printer with an order (for a buyer of your book) all you do is send an email. In this you include the buyer's name and address. The POD printer will print and ship off within a few days.

Another benefit to good POD companies is that they have connections with all the big international sellers, such as Amazon and e-Bay.

Is POD a good or a bad thing?

If you can find a book publisher or printer who uses POD as well as larger quantities, then you get the best of both worlds.

We use a POD company that has a print facility in the USA, the UK and Australia. This means that if we get an order from the UK, then we print one copy locally in the UK, which is posted directly to the customer. This saves on shipping time and postage costs.

Binding

In the past all books were stitched, but because of improved adhesives and methods they can be glued. This is called 'perfect bound'. This book is perfect bound.

Stitch binding is the best but more expensive. A word of warning; bad binding is common in the industry, so check your test book by bending it backwards and try to dislodge pages.

Other things to look for in your test book:

- Are the page numbers in sequence?
- Are the header and footer depths consistent throughout the book?
- You may laugh at this one, but are the pages square? I have seen pages upside down, or running at forty-five degrees to the page.
- What are the margins like; are they large enough and consistent?
- Ensure that illustrations and graphs are clear.

In short, you need to scrutinise every page of your proof, as from the file you give the printer funny things can happen, such as: gaps appear or disappear, tables shrink or become rhombus like, margins are amended, and other issues.

Part Seven – Appendices

Publisher's Page

If self-publishing, you need to insert a Publisher's page. Go and look at the one at the start of this book.

Depositories

In most countries it is legislated that each published book be lodged with the depository in the country in which the book is published. The purpose is so the government has a Depository of every book published in the country. Google your National Library to ascertain the depositories required.

Your publisher will do this for you, but if you self-publish you will have to do it yourself. It is a legal requirement.

> Let's lighten it up with you spending twenty minutes on a story of your favourite cartoon character. Pretend that you have taken over the writing of the cartoon. To do this, you need to try and put yourself into the mind of the previous writer. What excited them about the cartoon characters and the situations they find themselves in?

What is an ISBN?

The International Standard Book Number (ISBN) is a thirteen-digit number that uniquely identifies books and other forms of publications published internationally.

The ISBN must appear on the back cover and on the Publisher's page.

The purpose of the ISBN is to establish and identify one title or edition of a title from one specific publisher and is unique to that edition, allowing for more efficient marketing of products by booksellers, libraries, universities, wholesalers, and distributors.

Barcode scanning supports retailers with sales transaction and stock management. They use the ISBN to create the barcode.

What is the format of the ISBN?

Every ISBN is preceded by the letters ISBN. The thirteen-digit number is divided into four categories of variable length, each separated by a hyphen.

The four parts are as follows:

- Group or country identifier which identifies a national or geographic grouping of publishers.
- Publisher identifier identifies a particular publisher within a group.
- Title identifier identifies a particular title or edition of a title.
- Check digit is the single digit at the end of the ISBN which validates the ISBN.

Who can assign ISBNs to a publisher?

There are over 160 ISBN Agencies worldwide, and each ISBN Agency is appointed as an exclusive agent responsible for assigning ISBNs to publishers residing in their country or geographic territory. The United States ISBN Agency is the only source authorised to assign ISBNs to publishers supplying an address in the United States, U.S. Virgin Islands, Guam and Puerto Rico and its database establishes the publisher of record associated with each prefix.

NB: there is a different type of number for self-published authors to that of publishers and so you need to make it clear if the book is being published by a publishing house or self-published.

Once you have your ISBN you must have it translated into a worldwide compatible bar code format.

Lastly, you will require a unique ISBN for each of your book versions, i.e., one for the print book, another for the ePub, and a third for the audio.

Appendix Four – Resources

Many resources are already given throughout the workbook. The following are other resources that may be of use.

The Public and Educational Lending Right schemes make annual payments to publishers in recognition of their loss of income from their books being available in public and educational libraries. (from http://www.copyrightservice.co.uk/copyright/)
While this varies from country to country they tend to be long and complex. I have included some more relevant aspects.

If the work exists in the public domain, then a translation automatically retains copyright as an original work. Generally, the copyright for a work of literature expires seventy years after the author dies. You can find a useful guide to searching for public domain works here http://publicdomainreview.org/guide-to-finding-interesting-public-domain-works-online/

There will be a Public Lending Rights in your country.

The IBPA (https://www.ibpa-online.org/) is a USA based organisation with the sole purpose of helping self-publishers and small independent publishers. They can better tell you about their offerings.

Although USA centric, they are still worth joining irrespective of where you operate. For what you get for the membership fee is well worth it.

Ingrams Spark (https://www.ingramspark.com/) is a good resource for small operators and self-publishers. When used they will:

- Produce and market your print and ePubs at a cheap rate.
- They will receive orders for you of books you have sold and do POD and ship directly (worldwide) on your behalf. This saves you having to stock books, packing books, and going to the courier or post office.
- You can use their Advertising Boosters, however, we have not found this to increase sales. When we bought this to their attention they did not reply to our email.
- They also have, for a small annual cost, a catalogue, which goes out to book sellers worldwide, including Amazon, Barnes and Nobel, and all the big book sellers. In theory, this sounds great, but the reality is not as good as it sounds, as your book is one of millions in their catalogue. They do sell on your behalf, but not in the volumes they suggest.
  The same applies for your ePub.
- A negative is that there have been times when their service fell short, and when brought to their attention they ignored it – they do have the attitude fit in or push off.
- All in all, Spark is worth investigating but you must make sure you do great metadata for it to make inroads.

Outsourcing

As a small outfit, it makes sense to outsource many of your functions, such as book design, video, SEO skill, illustrations, logo design, translators, virtual assistants, editors/proof-readers, branding experts, etc. There are many good outsourcing sites such as https://www.upwork.com and on these there are good consultants. But for each skilled person there are three chancers, so you must be

Part Seven – Appendices

careful. It took us several years to work through the rubbish to get a good team.

Virtual Assistance

As a small publisher, you get so busy there will be too much for you to do. This is where VA's come in handy. You can outsource some time-consuming tasks to them at low cost. Such as admin, bookkeeping, invoicing, client follow up, and everything that you need. But the warning as given in the above outsourcing section applies to VA's.
If you find yourself a good one, they are worth their weight in gold. Twice in the past they started off well, but the quality soon deteriorated. The VA we are currently using is great.

7

About Pat Grayson

Pat is a writer, writing coach, and publisher – he loves writing and books, which is just as well as he has written ten of his own, ghost-written five, and helped over sixty authors get their manuscripts ready for publishing.

Pat is a recipient of the prestigious literary *Award Independent Press Awards* in the category of Self-help general.

He recently ran a volunteer program teaching storytelling and writing to an indigenous community in South Australia.

Additionally, Pat is the CEO of the not-for-profit www.EasySpelling.org, which was created to help spelling in disadvantaged communities world-wide.

He lives in Australia, runs writing workshops, and often travels internationally.

To contact Pat Grayson for writing support, mentorship or writing workshops: pat@heartspacepublications.com or tel +61 450260348 Australia.

Other works by Pat Grayson

(all available on www.heartspacepublications.com)
- *Know ThySelf (Vol 1 and 2)*
- *The Intelligence*
- *Seeds of Potential*
- *Life, Does It Have to Be Fair? (for young adults)*
- *Yogi, the Tails and Teachings of a Suburban Alpha Doggy*
- *Oh Hell, of War, Dementia, Love, and a Glass or Two of Red Wine (Dementia)*

Part Seven – Appendices

- *Chinese Downunder (rights sold in China)*
- *Gruffian's Bare Teddy Bear (children's book)*
- *Easy spelling Sound Dictionary*

Workshops

Pat conducts writing workshops and public speaking, where he addresses both individuals and groups in private or corporate settings.

Appendix Five – Indexes

A book critique 261
A pre-print version 369
A Writer's Guide to Embracing Technology 354
abbreviations 268, 270
Abbreviations 269
ABC (Australia) 174
Active or passive voice 283
Advanced Information (AI) 344
Adventure 226
Affiliate marketing 350
Age 229
AI and writing
    AI-Generated Content and Plagiarism 357
    Generating Ideas with AI 356
AIDA 245
Alternate Realities 204
Amazon 312, 315, 326, 332, 333, 336, 337, 338, 341, 351, 362, 381, 386
American or UK English? 275
An Index 367
Analytics and Monitoring 324
Answer the Public 327
Apostrophes 287
Appendix .... x, 353, 354
    Book production x
    Resources x
    Writing and Technology x
Approaching the editor of the publication 243
Are you ready to be an author? 15, 17, 37
Attention to Detail 194
Attitude 77
Audio 367
Autobiographical Fiction 79
Autobiography 226

Part Seven – Appendices

Automatic Writing 46
Back cover 58
Back Cover Text 375
Backlink Building 323
Baidu 325
Balzac 67
Banner advertising 333
Barcode 376, 384
Bing 324, 327
Biography 226
Biopunk 205
Biotechnology 205
Blog 270
Book categories 376
Book clubs 346, 350
book production x
   AI tools 354, 356, 357, 360
   Binding 382
   cover design 300, 302, 308, 373, 374
   ISBN 373
   Print quality 381
Book Readings 346
Book Reviews 337
Book size 254
Building the brand 315
Carry Fisher 181
Categories of Romance 202
Categorising your book 365
Cathartic 25, 29
Character Development 192
Character sketch 58
Character Types 182
Characterisation 58, 93, 144, 295
Christian novels 195, 206
Clichés 134, 253, 261, 279, 284, 287
Coffee table books 195, 208, 209

Collaboration, Not Replacement	355
Colour	372, 374
Comedy	226
Comic Relief	181
Commas	287
Conflict	193
Contractions	269
Copyright statement	371
Copyright symbol ©	372
Cover Material	379
Covers	373, 379
Create a business name	373
Creative visualisation	93, 110
Creative writing	39, 94, 95, 100
Creativity	ix, 15, 42, 97, 98, 100, 102, 103, 109, 111, 192, 280
Cultural and Historical Context	182
Cyberpunk	205
Data Research	356
Database	247
Depositories	383
Detail	93, 176, 272, 289
Dialogue	93, 151, 167, 171, 193, 290
Different styles of writing	86
Do not ever trash your work	256
Domain Authority (DA) and Page Authority (PA)	332
Dorian Haarhoff	30, 44, 186, 234, 236
Dragon – Naturally Speaking	361
Drama	226
DuckDuckGo	325
Edit for the first or third person consistency	281
Editing	x, 128, 249, 264, 268, 274, 371
editing and revision	263
Editing checklist	261, 280
Elements of Style	125, 128
Email lists	333

Part Seven – Appendices

Emotional Resonance 193
Endword 259
ePubs .... ix, 313, 349, 351, 362, 363, 365, 386
Escapism 63
Essay 226
Ethics – Facebook and Google? 342
Exclamations and emotion 137
Facebook 315, 320, 321, 332, 333, 334, 338, 339, 342
Facebook Ad Campaigns 339
Fantasy 225
Feng Ping 148
Fiction 163, 202, 210, 225, 229
Finessing 233
First person 166
Flow 93, 123, 125, 126, 232, 280
Flow-stoppers 125
Font 371
Foreword 373, 378
Free web sites 350
Front cover 58
Genetic Engineering 205
Genre .... x, 195
   fiction ......xi, 34, 44, 48, 79, 95, 98, 110, 164, 183, 188, 190, 192, 195,
     196, 203, 207, 210, 219, 220, 226, 254, 255, 284, 330, 374
Goodreads 315, 338, 344
Google . 322, 324, 325, 326, 327, 328, 331, 332, 333, 339, 340, 341, 342,
   350, 383
   Google Ads 340
   Google Analytics 324, 340
   Google Search Console 324
   Google Trends 327
Google Ads 333, 340, 341
Google Analytics 326, 327
Graham Williams 186
Grammarly 24
haiku 227

Haiku	232
Handwriting	361
Historical novels	202, 210
Home and Away	188
Hooking the reader	15, 69
Horror	225
How do different writers generate their ideas?	50
How do I start?	53
How do you know if your book idea is the right one?	50
How much can you sell your book for?	308
How much money do authors make?	254
How to Implement SEO	323
How to submit your manuscript	304
If you get a rejection	305
Illustrations	195, 238
Imagery	232
Ingrams Spark	386
Instagram	320, 321
Intangibles	121
International book rights	315, 351
Introduction	ix, 58
Inventing experience	93, 141
ISBN	iii, 330, 376, 383, 384, 385
KDP (Kindle Direct Publishing)	337
Keyword Research	323
Keywords	315, 325, 327, 330, 336, 341
Language Patterns	237
Lastly, a fluid and ever-emerging book market	351
LGBTQ	61
Libraries	315, 349, 365
Link Building	324
Literal vs. Metaphorical	237
Literary Realism	157
Literary writing	208
Magazine and newspaper writing	195, 239

Part Seven – Appendices

MailChimp	336
Male – Female Energy	109
Manuscript Analysis	355
Market research	315, 316
Marketing and Promotion	x, 317
Book Reviews	337
Building brand	318
Media Kit	343
Your Newsletter	334
Memoir	225
Message Clarity	237
Metadata	315, 325, 329, 330, 341, 343
Metaphor	93, 121, 122, 232, 289
Metatagging	331
Mind Maps	64
Mind Uploading and Consciousness Transfer	206
Mood Reflection	237
Must a character be endeared by the reader?	155
Mystery	225
Nanotechnology	205
Narration	93, 163
Narration for Fiction Writing	163
Narrative Elements	237
Narrative Voice	193
Narrator	187
National Library	383
Newsletter	315
Nielsen Bookdata or Bookscan	329
No plagiarism	253
Non-fiction	225
Novel	97, 151, 375
Novelist	122
On-Page Optimisation	323
Opening, Middle and Resolution	194
Orientation	364, 369
Orientation for an ePub	364

Outsourcing	386
Over-writing	143
Pacing	193
Parallel Universes	204
Passive words	127
Pat Grayson	iii, xi, 388
Photos	372, 380
Photos and clip art	380
Place	58, 93, 139, 172, 173, 176, 290, 345
Plot	58, 60, 62, 154
Poet	101, 233, 236
Poetry	195, 226, 230, 231, 232, 234, 238
Post-Apocalyptic Worlds	205
Preparation of the manuscript	303
Pre-Publishing	305
Printerest	320
Printing	380
Production methods for your book	57
Promoting your book	315, 318
Publisher logo	376
Publisher's Page	383
Publishers' agreements	302
publishing	x, xiii, 234, 337, 345
Print on demand	381
Self publishing	297, 300
Self-publishing	xi, 229, 301, 302, 306, 307, 313, 351, 383
Traditional publishing	297, 302
Punctuation	284, 358
Quality Content Creation	323
Quality, not quantity	268
Quotation marks for direct speech	288
Radio National	45
Reading	19, 41, 163, 167, 273, 275
Reasons for manuscript rejection	270
Reducing word count through dialogue	293

Character Development	192
Plot Structure	193
Show don't tell	115
Yahoo	324
Yandex	325
Young Adults	209
Your first book	36, 54
Your own website	321
Your photo	378
Your platform	318
YouTube	320, 330, 338, 339

Part Seven – Appendices

Too many words between the story 292
Trade Magazine Advertising 342
Travel writing 241
Trends... 195, 230
True Crime.. 225
Trust yourself to write compelling stories 190
TV dramas 174, 182
Ubersuggest 327
User Experience (UX) 323
Vanity publishing.. 297, 306
Videos for your website and marketing... 345
Virtual Assistance 387
Virtual Reality (VR) 205
Voice Recognition 360
Voice Recorders 361
What about an agent? 310
What is an ISBN? 383
What is creativity? 93, 94
What makes a good writer?.. 32
What to write? 36, 240
When to use large or sophisticated words? 256
When to write creatively?... 104
Which publication? 242
Who is going to buy the book? 316
Why do we write? 22
Why do you need to acquire good writing skills?............................. 89
Why write a column? 240
Word Organisation... 237
Writer's block 15, 75
Writing and planning.. 15, 57
Writing and Technology x
writing drills... x, 15, 21, 107
Writing emotion 135
Writing for children.. 195, 225, 226
Writing skill.. 292
Writing Techniques

Stories	ix, x, xi, 95, 144, 186, 222, 263
Storytelling	39, 93, 142, 183, 188, 189
Structure	188, 281
Structuring your work	15, 72
Style Manual	270, 305
Suspense/Thriller/ Mystery Novels/Crime Fiction	216
Tautology	271, 283
Tenses	280
Tension	93, 142
Testimonials or credits	58
Textual Pattern	237
The benefits of Self-publishing	301
The body	74
The Brontë sisters	145
The Halo and the Noose, the power of storytelling	186
The Independent Book Publishing Association's (IBPA)	345
The Intelligence	51, 388
The International Standard Book Number	383
The introduction	67, 73
The Newsreader	174
The opening pages	15, 67
The Public and Educational Lending Right	385
The Rise of AI in Writing	354
The secret under the mahogany tree	148
The spine	378, 379
The word very is a very overused word.	257
The Writers' and Artists' Yearbook	311
The writing style of the publication	243
Thinking	31
Thoughts on editing	268
Thriller	225
Tight Writing	112
Tik Tok	320, 325
Title	237, 357, 377, 384
To reduce a manuscript's size	271

Part Seven – Appendices

Report writing 195
Representational systems 132
Research 58, 141, 152, 239, 272, 329, 340
Resolution 74, 193
Resources x
Retail outlets 315, 346
Revision 264
Romance novels 198, 202
RSS feed 321
Satire 225
Say what you mean 282
Science Writing 226
Sci-Fi 195, 202, 203, 205
Script 195, 212
Script Writing 212
Search Engine Optimisation 315, 322
Self-Help books 197
Self-publishing 313, 362
Sensory writing 93, 132
Sentence structure 288
Sentences 123, 125
SEO 315, 317, 319, 322, 323, 324, 325, 329, 341, 386
Setting and Atmosphere 193
Shakespeare 62, 67, 122, 156, 182
Short Stories and Novellas 222
Show, don't tell 93, 115
Singular and plural 280
Snapchat 320, 334
Social Media 319, 320
   Facebook 320
   Linkedin 325
   Twitter 315, 320, 333, 334
Social Media stats 319
Space Colonisation 205
Spontaneous writing 21, 90
Stanislavsky System 135

www.ingramcontent.com/pod-product-compliance
Lightning Source LLC
Chambersburg PA
CBHW080321080526
44585CB00021B/2429